The Way of the Archetypes
Volume I

Universal Principles and Individuation

The Way of the Archetypes
Volume I

Universal Principles
and Individuation

KEIRON LE GRICE

ITAS Publications

I T A S
2016

First published in 2024 by ITAS Publications

Cover image artwork "Symbols in the Snow" © 2021 Kathryn Le Grice. www.kathrynlegrice.com.

Astrological charts created using AstroGold software.

ISBN: 978-1-7355436-9-7

Jungian Psychology – Astrology – Spirituality – Philosophy – Mythology – Cultural History

To Kathryn and Lukas

CONTENTS

Introduction   1

Sources of Life Meaning   1
Spirituality and Cosmology   5
Synthesis and Application   7
Organization and Aims   9

PART ONE: Universal Principles

1   **Encountering Archetypes**   15

2   **A Brief History of Archetypes**   21

Origins and Evolutions: From the Ancient World to the   21
Modern
Science and the Disenchanted Universe   26
The Psychology of the Unconscious   27
Freud and Jung: Psychoanalysis and Analytical Psychology   29
Archetypal Psychology   34
Archetypal Astrology   36

PART TWO: The Way of Individuation

3   **Metaphors of the Way**   49

4   **Archetypes and the Individuation Process**   53

Self-knowledge   54
The Realization of the Self   56
Plurality and Unity   59
The Opposites and the Evolution of Consciousness   67

5   **Perspectives on Transformation**   72

The Hero's Journey   72
Alchemical Transformation   75
Perinatal Psychology and the Death-Rebirth Process   78

6   **Soul-Making and the Symbolic Life**   84

    Seeking the Symbolic Life   84
    Synchronicity and the Symbolic Attitude   88
    Soul-making and the Archetypal Eye   90

PART THREE: An Assemblage of Archetypes

7   **Spirit and Soul, Sun and Moon**   97

    Spirit, Consciousness, and Being   98
    The Ego and Solar Myths   100
    Logos and Nous: The Archetypal Mercury   103
    The Hero   105
    The Moon and the Great Mother   106

8   **Shadow, Super-ego, and Senex**   111

    The Shadow and the Ego Structure   113
    The Super-ego and the Weight of Tradition   116
    The Wise Old Man and Senex Consciousness   119

9   **Uranus and the Trickster**   125

    Functions of the Trickster: Disruption, Awakening,   125
    Liberation
    Freedom and Rebellion   127
    Creative Genius, Individualism, and Revolution   128

10 **Dionysus, the Will-to-Power, and Rebirth**   132

    The Id and the Underworld   133
    Dionysus and Instinctual Possession   133
    Descent and Rebirth   137
    The Daimon and the Evolutionary Power in Nature   139
    Mercurius and Alchemical Transformation   141

11 **Animus and Anima, Masculine and Feminine**   144

The Animus: Opinions and Critiques   145
Animus Personifications and the Inner Masculine Ideal   148
The Anima and Astrological Principles   149
Irrational Feeling and the Wellsprings of Life   151
The Mother and Feminine Being   153
The Differentiation of the Anima   154

12 **Fantasy, Enchantment, and the Spirit**   159

The Mana-Personality   159
The Archetype of the Spirit   161
Neptune in Depth Psychology   162
Participation Mystique and the Porous Self   164
Mystical and Psychedelic Experiences   166
Ideals and Illusions   168

13 **Growth, Inflation, and the Journey to Wholeness**   170

Growth and Improvement   170
The Archetypal Wanderer and the Journey Motif   172
Inflation and Excess   173

14 **The Self: The Archetype of Center and Totality**   176

PART FOUR: Principles of Archetypal Astrology

15 **The Geometry of the Gods**   185

The Planets and the Zodiac   185
Aspects or Alignments   187
Number Archetypes and the Meaning of Aspects   191
From the Universal to the Particular   202
Causality, Participation, and Fatalism   204
Sources of Data and Interpretation   207

Looking Ahead   213

Bibliography   219

Index   227

About the Author   249

TABLE OF FIGURES

1   Astrological Planetary Archetypes Mapped to Principles of Depth Psychology and Jungian Archetypes   179

2   Jungian Archetypes Mapped to Astrological Planetary Archetypes   181

3   The Orbital Periods of the Planets   186

4   The Movement of the Planets through the Zodiac—Sample Astrological Charts   188

5   Illustrations of the Major Aspects   193

6   Illustration of the Quincunx   198

7   Birth Chart, World Transits, and Personal Transits—Sample Charts   200

INTRODUCTION

Tere is a way, open to us all, by which we can discover profound truths about ourselves and our relationship to the inner depths of the universe. It is a way informed and impelled by *archetypes*—universal principles and powers existing in the background of our experience that shape what we are and all we do. Archetypes were known to the ancients as the gods and goddesses of myth, to philosophers as metaphysical forms and as universal categories of cognition, and to depth psychologists as primordial images and instincts. Archetypes are all of these and more, and their various forms—such as beauty, power, the hero, the child, the spirit, and rebirth—impact us immediately, intimately, and sometimes with dramatic effect.

This book sets forth an approach, based on the symbolic system of astrology and the psychology of Carl Gustav Jung, to help us recognize the presence of archetypes in our lives. By exploring their manifold qualities and themes as they find expression in human personality traits, biographical events, and cultural phenomena, it presents an engagement with archetypes as a way of being in the world, offering a source of orientation and meaning based on our unique position, in space and time, within the cosmos. With a broad understanding of the different archetypes at play in human experience, we can learn how to relate to them with greater awareness and insight, tracking their changing patterns as we move through life. Engaging with the archetypes constitutes a way or path by which we might participate on a daily basis with the great powers and structuring principles of the universe.

*   *   *   *   *

Sources of Life Meaning

We live in an age of debilitating fragmentation, polarization, and eclecticism in most every respect—from lifestyles and fashions to forms of religious practice, political ideologies, and personal identities.

In this climate, it can often seem that simplicity and certainty are forever gone. In seeking an authentic path through life, or contemplating pressing questions of our life aims and purposes, we encounter a plethora of fluctuating choices and possibilities. All is in flux; everything is doubtful. Where today might we turn for a source of reassuring orientation and sustaining life meaning?

By any standards, our era is also one of social tumult and upheaval, born of the seismic technological, socio-cultural, political, and ecological shifts defining our moment in history. We are living at a time of crisis and transition of our civilization and of our planet. How, amidst the chaos of this change, might we find some measure of order and perspective?

For millennia, a civilization's reigning myths, philosophies, and religions have provided meaning and moral prescriptions for determining how best to live. In the West, in the deeds recounted in the epic myths of ancient Greece and Rome, a warrior morality of heroism and nobility was the paragon of a life well lived; in Greek philosophical speculation, rational inquiry into the nature of things was the path to wisdom and the means to illuminate the eternal truths and principles by which we might order our lives; in Christian scripture, faith in God and the redeeming love of Christ was the means to salvation, if not in this world then in a life beyond the grave.

Today, however, the stories and symbols of myth appear, on the face of it, to be the relic of an age of long ago, with little or no relevance to modern life and now consigned to the vault of history. Philosophy, as an academic discipline now predominantly focused on logic and language, has often become far removed from our fundamental existential concerns. In the Anglo-American tradition of analytic philosophy, the contemplation of the meaning of life has become nothing more than the analysis of the meaning of words. In religion, similarly, the age of the great orthodox religious traditions, as Joseph Campbell observed, has for centuries been disintegrating, and for many people religious perspectives, like ancient myths and ancient philosophies, do not immediately speak to us in the language of our time or seem to address the problems of our time.[1] In the West, the former certainties afforded by the Christian view of the world have been eroded by science and critical reason, delivering us from an age of faith into a secular age. Many people no longer rest secure in the conviction that we are watched over by an all-powerful wholly benevolent God of love, for scientific discoveries have shattered the Christian world picture, with man, placed formerly at the center of creation by his maker, now dethroned and jettisoned into cosmic anonymity and meaninglessness. Moral values, once rooted in a religious framework, are radically open to question and the aims of life appear now as ours to choose rather than decreed from above. Those of us in need of connection to a life meaning beyond scientific materialism, personal psychology, societal improvement, and the consumerist values of our time might therefore find ourselves in a situation of existential disorientation and uncertainty, seeing only the stern face of material necessity without and the inexorable demands of desires and fears within.

This is not to say that the canon of myths, philosophies, and religions is no longer of value—quite the contrary, in my view. But to retain and apply the wisdom of these traditions for the global postmodern age, we may be obliged to look to the underlying principles shaping them—a strategy we will pursue in what follows. Indeed, people have always found within their life experience sources of transcendent meaning beyond the sphere of personal concerns and interests, and have understood their lives in connection to a greater frame of reference—whether this be a deity, a pantheon of gods, an ultimate reality, a cosmic order, eternal ideals, or a metaphysical system of thought. The quest for such meaning arises from an innate urge, a religious instinct, one that urgently impresses itself on us today, even as many of these established sources of meaning have lost their persuasive power. We are moved to reflect on the purposes and passions that stir us and work through us. We strive to make sense of our experience, to try to find a semblance of order within the flux of events, and to come to some degree of understanding as to why we think, feel, and act as we do. But many of us do so today on our own, outside of the well-trodden paths of the established religions.

It is in this context that I would like to present one perspective that I have found to be especially helpful in providing existential orientation and meaning to help us navigate the course of our lives. This approach is rooted in astrology, which to many people might seem an altogether improbable choice given astrology's current questionable status in the modern Western world. However, if one looks beyond the prevailing assumptions about astrology and seriously explores its application to human experience, one might, I believe, become persuaded of its value and its validity.

Astrology returns us to our basic existential orientation to the earth and the sky. It is centered on the individual person or event in relation to the actual positions and movements of the planets, relative to our experience of night and day, above and below, the horizon line, the cardinal directions, the orbit of the Earth around the sun, the equinoxes, and our planet's daily rotation on its axis. The key astrological insight, however, is that such orientation is not just a physical fact of our existence, but also possesses a psychological meaning, manifest in the qualities, themes, motivations, and archetypal categories of human experience. Our outer, physical orientation towards the cosmos corresponds to our inner, psychological orientation to the fundamental organizing powers of life.

Perhaps because of the acute need in the modern world for this kind of orientation, and in response to the diminishing appeal of organized religion, the ancient astrological study of the relationship between human experience and the planetary order of the solar system has enjoyed something of a renaissance over the course of the last century or so, and it has become today a growing and vital field, with a vast range of different forms of practice, evidenced in recent years by the emergence of a multitude of astrological websites and publications. Most people, one would imagine, tend to be exposed primarily to the forms of astrology catering to a popular audience, which can naturally be quite superficial, but at a deeper level it represents a serious, long-standing mode of engagement with the cosmos that over the centuries has received the attention of some of the finest thinkers in philosophy and science.

The specific approach I am setting forth in this book is called *archetypal astrology*, which is part of the larger academic field of archetypal cosmology. As the name suggests, this approach employs astrology as a symbolic system for exploring the expression of archetypes, or universal principles, in our lives. It follows the long-established astrological practice of studying the positions and the changing configurations of the planets in the solar system, and makes use of astrology's methods of calculation and principles of interpretation, yet it is a practice transformed by its encounter with depth psychology and supported by an emerging body of scholarship and empirical research into correlations between the movements of the planets in the sky and the activation of specific themes and impulses in human experience.[2]

Since its emergence in the late nineteenth century through the work of Pierre Janet, Sigmund Freud, Alfred Adler, Carl Gustav Jung, and others, depth psychology has brought to light the existence of a hidden order in the unconscious mind, in the form of configurations of complexes, drives, and instincts, conditioning human experience from a dimension of the mind beyond our conscious awareness and beyond

4

the control of our personal will. Depth psychology has also helped the modern individual reclaim something akin to a mythic perspective on life. Jung's theory of archetypes and the collective unconscious—the theory for which he is best known—has been especially influential in this regard, identifying universal dynamisms and motifs in human psychology, evident in the symbolic content of dreams, fantasies, symptoms of psychopathology, myths, fairytales, the arts, and religious ideas. Our personal fantasy lives and dreams, Jung discovered, give expression to a veritable pantheon of universal mythic themes and figures, usually clothed in the familiar scenes of contemporary life. For myth, in Jung's view, is not obsolete, pertaining only to cultures past, but it is a living expression of formative factors and animating powers deep in the human mind. It is an expression of archetypes.

Informed by Jungian psychology, archetypal astrology provides a means of engaging at an individual level with the grand themes and universal motifs of myth and religion, and the ground principles of philosophy and psychology, helping us to recognize and map archetypal patterns in our own experience, for ourselves. It also provides an understanding of cultural cycles and a supporting cosmology or worldview, which can enable us to situate our own life in relation to larger patterns of cultural change and the unfolding historical process. In both these respects, it might cater to the individual's need for meaning in the modern world, providing an expanded understanding of human experience and human nature, and the basis of an individualized spiritual path.

Spirituality and Cosmology

The term *spiritual* is notoriously difficult to define, but in this context it may be understood as connoting our ultimate concerns, the deepest guiding principles of life, and suggesting too a feeling for, and direct experience of, a mystery transcending the individual human personality and personal will. It has much in common with what we ordinarily understand by the term *religion*, of course, except that religion often refers to the organized religious traditions with their denominations and ceremonies, dogmas and moral prescriptions, built up over the centuries. Religion, like spirituality, is essentially to do with a fundamental temper and orientation and mode of engaging with the world. Jung's understanding of the term might be helpful here. "Religion appears to me to be a peculiar attitude of mind which could be formulated in accordance with the original use of the word *religio*, which means a careful consideration and observation of certain dynamic factors that are conceived as 'powers': spirits, daemons, gods, laws, ideas, ideals . . ."—in short forms of archetypes.[3]

Today, notions of a meaningful cosmic order, such as the one posited by astrology, might seem erroneous, antiquated, or merely poetic, of even less relevance to modern life than ancient myths and religions. Science, we tend to assume, has disclosed a universe of an altogether different cast. Under the aspect of scientific materialism, one might behold in the canopy of stars only cold indifference to human affairs, and find in the expanse of space a vast impersonal universe of blind forces and inert matter, arising by chance, without purpose, and destined to move inexorably towards termination. Cosmic processes seem utterly unrelated to the thoughts and deeds of human beings on Earth. As much as modern cosmology might inspire awe and wonder, it remains largely unresponsive to the human need for meaning.

Yet, as many of us realize, this disenchanted picture of the universe is peculiar to the modern era and precludes from its vision dimensions of the mystery of life and human nature undetectable by instruments of observation and measurement. Other perspectives, other sensibilities, take issue with the prevailing assumptions shaping the modern understanding of the nature of reality, and discern that behind the chaos of appearances is an encompassing order—a universal framework of dynamic meaning, purpose, and harmony that reaches into the innermost depths of our being. The study of this universal order has been a prominent concern of myth, religion, and philosophy through the ages, giving rise to great sacred cosmologies and metaphysical visions—"hierophanies," as the historian of religion Mircea Eliade described them.[4] These ancient traditions, to characterize them in general terms, conceive of the universe as a unitary sacred manifestation in which the individual's fate is inextricably connected to the cosmos at large. Far from being rendered invalid by scientific thought, such perspectives embody abiding truths about the nature of reality, truths not detectable by microscope or telescope, or reducible to equations and logic. It is simply that these truths have been lost to the modern mind, for they pertain to dimensions of experience that fall outside of the paradigmatic boundaries of science, and outside of common sight.

Within science itself the prevailing understanding of the nature of reality is far from univocal and incontrovertible. There is no settled theory that accounts for everything, only a fluid juxtaposition of theories yet to be integrated into an accepted coherent vision. Some of these theories, particularly those described as "new paradigm," take us far beyond the assumptions of the classical Cartesian-Newtonian worldview and the dominant paradigms of mechanistic materialism and atomistic reductionism that have so defined the scientific enterprise. Rather, they reveal a universe of interconnection, interdependence, and underlying unity—ideas that have affinities with mythic, esoteric, and mystical conceptions of reality as an undivided whole, in which all things are believed to be united within a single fabric of meaning. Although often mistakenly seen as the epitome of irrationalism and deluded superstitious thinking, from within this emerging perspective astrology might be reappraised, for its assumptions and workings are, as I have discussed elsewhere, rendered plausible, even compelling, in terms of the theories of the new-paradigm sciences and of Jungian psychology.[5]

Synthesis and Application

Over the last thirty years, I have been absorbed in the study of many of these fields—depth psychology, religion, mythology, philosophy, and the new sciences—with the astrological interpretation of a cosmological order a central focus and point of interconnection. In 1999, I set about writing a book exploring the application of astrology to the mythic model of the hero's journey, as formulated by Joseph Campbell, with the hope of demonstrating how astrology, skillfully and judiciously applied, might help us recognize and better understand the deeper animating powers and organizing principles shaping our lives. I was persuaded, primarily by the evidence of my own experience, that astrology could provide an invaluable source of guidance for life, especially as we seek to navigate the challenges of psychological growth and transformation. Yet I was acutely aware that astrology is looked upon with suspicion, if not outright derision, from many quarters, due largely to its perceived incompatibility with the tenets of classical science, which inform our common-sense understanding of reality. For this reason, I felt it essential to address the philosophical question as to how we might understand astrology in terms compatible with a contemporary worldview. Although I had originally envisaged addressing this matter over the course of one or two introductory chapters, as it turned out it was to occupy me through the entirety of what was eventually to become *The Archetypal Cosmos*.

With the first draft of the book manuscript in hand, in August 2004 I arrived in San Francisco from the UK to begin graduate studies in philosophy and religion at the California Institute of Integral Studies. Here, over the course of five wonderfully rich and stimulating years, I had the opportunity to explore in greater depth theories and perspectives treated in my manuscript, and to bring them to a new level of clarity and synthesis. Drawing together the ideas of Jung, Pierre Teilhard de Chardin, David Bohm, Fritjof Capra, Richard Tarnas, Brian Swimme, and others, I formulated the outlines of an "archetypal cosmology," a worldview in which the supposition of an astrological correspondence between cosmos and psyche, between planetary alignments and archetypal patterns in human experience, could be better understood. From that theoretical foundation, based on a synthesis of Jungian psychology and the new-paradigm sciences, I made the argument that astrology could enable us to discover our own unique relationship to the archetypes, the living springs of myth, and that it might therefore provide a new form of mythic orientation for our time.

At the California Institute of Integral Studies, I was profoundly influenced by the work of Richard Tarnas, author of *The Passion of the Western Mind* and *Cosmos and Psyche*, and pioneer of archetypal astrology. Although I had already studied and practiced astrology for many years, Tarnas's approach, which I first encountered in his "Archetypes, Art, and Culture" courses offered in 2004 and 2005, made a powerful impression on me, opening my eyes to the possibility of bringing together astrology and the arts in such a way that each could be meaningfully illuminated by the other. From Marlon Brando and Bette Davis to Bob Dylan and the Beatles, Tarnas provided one striking example after another showing that prominent themes in the life and work of major figures in art and culture can be identified and explored by a symbolic interpretation of the meaning of the planetary configurations at the time of their births, as portrayed in astrological birth charts—a method we will consider closely and employ in the pages and volumes to follow. And just as archetypal astrology can inform our appreciation of works of art, so too, Tarnas demonstrated, art can illuminate and inform our knowledge of archetypes.

As we will see, in astrology the planets, and the configurations they form with other planets, are associated with sets of themes, categories of experience, qualities, states of mind, ways of perceiving and interpreting reality, particular moods and yearnings, and drives and impulses. All these are essential elements of archetypes. By using astrology to understand which of these themes are prominent in our personality and life experience over time, we can recognize the archetypal patterns that find expression through us, that give our lives meaning, that shape our biographical experiences.

8

With a more comprehensive understanding of the archetypal basis and application of astrology in mind, and having published *The Archetypal Cosmos* in 2010, I eventually returned to work on my original writing project, applying astrology as a guide to the pursuit of one's unique individual life path, modeled by Jung's theory of individuation and symbolized in part by the mythic pattern of the hero's journey. For the last several years, working as a professor of depth psychology, my ongoing critical engagement with Jungian ideas has sharpened my appreciation for the central place of archetypes, particularly in understanding transformations in the human personality and the development of consciousness—both key elements of the individuation process, as Jung understood it. More than ever, I am convinced that astrology might prove to be an extremely helpful aid for illuminating the expression of archetypes in this process.

Organization and Aims

This book, divided into four volumes, presents for consideration an approach to life and an interpretive framework that, given a proper introduction, might be of interest to readers who had perhaps not considered astrology before or did not see its relevance to their lives, especially as a guide to deep psychological transformation. Those readers already versed in the language of astrology might, I hope, come to a fuller appreciation of its archetypal basis and its connection to the lineage, principles, and practice of depth psychology as a means of illuminating the workings of the unconscious dimension of human experience.[6] Although these two groups of readers might take special interest in the book, it is written to be accessible to anyone seeking to explore more deeply universal patterns in individual experience and in culture, or trying to navigate periods of change and psychological transformation in their own lives and to come to terms with the inner world.

Volume I consists of four parts, establishing the theoretical framework and method for the exploration of archetypes using astrology. First, in Part One, we will consider the contribution of depth psychology to the modern understanding of human nature. Exploring in detail Jung's theory of archetypes, we will examine their various attributes and forms of manifestation, and consider how we can recognize the presence of archetypes in our experience. This discussion will provide an entrance point to archetypal astrology.

In Part Two, we will explore the main elements of the process of psychological development and transformation that Jung called individuation. Specifically, Part Two sets forth the idea of the individuation process as a "way," considered alongside other models of psychological growth and transformation that are informed by an archetypal understanding of reality and human nature.

Part Three then provides a close examination of the meanings of the Jungian archetypes and other principles of depth psychology in relation to the planetary archetypes studied in astrology. In this section, I aim to make explicit the connection between the two fields, mapping psychodynamic principles onto the pantheon of astrological planetary meanings.

Part Four, concluding Volume I, introduces the fundamental concepts and methods necessary for understanding archetypal astrological analysis—the nuts and bolts of the craft, as it were. It also explores a number of key philosophical concerns, such as the question of fate and free will, which must be addressed when one considers the workings of astrology.

Part Five of the book is housed in Volumes II, III, and IV. Here I undertake a detailed explication of the various combinations of planetary archetypes in astrology. Taking a lead from Tarnas's approach, I draw on a selection of examples of prominent figures in the arts and culture to explore themes associated with specific configurations of planets. The aim here, first and foremost, is to apply the knowledge and insights archetypal astrology affords us to help us engage with life more deeply, more meaningfully, and with greater consciousness. Part Five examines archetypal themes associated with particular planetary combinations (such as Sun-Saturn, Moon-Neptune, and Venus-Pluto) across a range of examples of the life and work of prominent figures and in cultural phenomena. In Volume II, I mostly restrict my analysis to archetypal combinations between Jupiter, Saturn, Neptune, and the first six "planets" (the Sun, the Moon, Mercury, Venus, Mars, and Jupiter) culminating with an analysis of the Jupiter-Neptune and Saturn-Neptune pairings. In Volume III, I focus on the archetypal themes associated with pairings of Pluto and Uranus with the other planets, including the Uranus-Neptune and Uranus-Pluto combinations. Volume IV then explores the array of themes associated with the Neptune-Pluto cycle, in all its depth and profundity, examining the manifestation of these themes in individual and collective experience.

Finally, Part Six, contained within Volume IV, is primarily concerned with collective experience, and the ongoing expression of the myths, religions, and creative visions that shape and sustain our understanding of reality. Building on the Neptune-Pluto analysis, in Part Six I apply astrology to map and describe the archetypal basis of the regeneration and renewal of myth over the last century, surveying cultural expressions and spiritual revelations accompanying the three-planet combinations of Uranus, Neptune, and Pluto.

The book title follows a similar naming convention to several other publications that set forth "spiritual paths" or "ways" to meet life, including Alan Watts's *The Way of Zen*, Michael Harner's *The Way of the Shaman*, and the first two volumes of Joseph Campbell's *Historical Atlas of World Mythology* series, *The Way of the Animal Powers* and *The Way of the Seeded Earth*.[7] Entitling this book *The Way of the Archetypes* is a recognition, in part, of the considerable influence of Campbell's earlier work, especially *The Hero with a Thousand Faces,* on the conceptualization of spiritual life not in terms of participation in a traditional religion or faith of some kind, but as an individual "way," which is in many respects a distinguishing characteristic of contemporary spirituality.[8] The book title, then, was chosen to evoke the sense of the study of and participation with archetypes as a spiritual path in its own right, and to point to the potential of archetypal astrology to serve as a guide to one's own life journey and individuation process. As I look back on my studies of astrology over the last thirty years, I am left with the lasting impression that, conceived in these terms, astrology could help any of us as we seek to better understand ourselves and skillfully move through life. A deep engagement with the archetypes, mediated by astrology, can become a way of life, and a vehicle for the revelation of the mysteries of the psyche and the spirit.

Notes

[1] See Campbell, *Creative Mythology*, 3.

[2] For background on the emergence and fundamentals of archetypal cosmology, see my essay "The Birth of a New Discipline" in Keiron Le Grice, *Archetypal Cosmology and Depth Psychology: Selected Essays* (Ojai, CA: ITAS Publications, 2020). This essay was originally published in the inaugural issue of *Archai: The Journal of Archetypal Cosmology*. Certain paragraphs in the first volume of *The Way of the Archetypes* are adapted from that essay.

[3] Jung, "Psychology and Religion," in *Psychology and Religion: West and East* (CW11), 8, par. 8.

[4] See Mircea Eliade, *The Forge and the Crucible,* 171.

5 See especially, *The Archetypal Cosmos* and my introduction to Part IV of *Jung on Astrology*, republished as "The Colloquy of the Gods" in Le Grice, *Archetypal Cosmology and Depth Psychology: Selected Essays.*

6 The analysis in the book exemplifies the type of research done in the academic field of archetypal cosmology, which, I believe, offers a future direction of development for depth psychology based on the recognition of the cosmological basis of the psychology of the unconscious. Archetypal cosmology incorporates archetypal astrology within a larger focus on the structural order of the universe. It is concerned not only with the archetypal analysis of human experience using astrology, but also with developing and articulating theoretical perspectives to account for astrological correspondences.

7 The proposed third volume of Campbell's *Historical Atlas of World Mythology* series, which remained unwritten upon Campbell's death in 1987, was to be *The Way of the Celestial Lights*, focusing on the significance of astrology and celestial observation since the dawn of human civilization. Campbell was principally concerned with astrology from historical and mythological perspectives, as a source of mythic symbolism and cosmological orientation in premodern cultures. However, in his speculations in the late 1960s and 1970s, in which he contemplated the connections between the "inner space" of the psyche and outer space, and reflected on the implications of the new physics for myth and a potential emerging worldview, Campbell's thinking began to move in a direction consistent with developments in archetypal cosmology, of which archetypal astrology is an essential part.

8 In *The Rebirth of the Hero*, I focus on this aspect of Campbell's thinking, looking at examples from film and biography to explore the different phases of the hero's journey and the challenges we might encounter as we navigate a form of this journey in our own lives. *The Way of the Archetypes* builds on this endeavor, using archetypal astrology to help us gain insights into our own individual myth and the realization of this myth in the fulfillment of our individual life pattern and potential.

PART ONE

Universal Principles

Chapter 1

Encountering Archetypes

Archetypes are universal principles and powers that form the background order of our experience. They are associated with the set of abstract qualities and themes that are intrinsic to what it is to be human—love, beauty, courage, death, joy, suffering, awakening, wisdom, transformation, illumination, freedom, and a sense of the sacred, to name but a few. These are the great universal constants that in their essential nature do not change over time; they are the guiding ideals and core themes of our experiences that shape and inspire human lives from one culture to the next, from one historical era to the next. Our participation with these universals touches our deepest spiritual concerns and aspirations. Indeed, history is filled with accounts of people who have sacrificed everything, including their lives, in the pursuit of these ideals.

The ideal of freedom—to give one example—moves and motivates us all, although it is interpreted and expressed differently by each of us and by each culture. We each partake in the universal quality of freedom even as we set about realizing freedom in our own unique way. *Liberté, égalité,* and *fraternité,* the defining declaration of the universal democratic principles of the modern era, may be upheld as guiding political ideals by many people the world over, but the realization of liberty to the proletariat in eighteenth-century France looks rather different than it does today, with the wealth of freedoms we usually enjoy and claim as our unalienable right. Similarly, although we all experience love, in one form or another, the people and things we love, the objects of our affection, are obviously peculiar to us. Love itself is universal, archetypal; but the expression of love in the specific concrete details of life is unique to us.

Such universals are recognized in the classical descriptions of virtues and vices, a central concern of religion, ethics, and philosophy around the world—in Confucianism and the Buddhism in the East, for example, and in the classical Greco-Roman world and Christianity in the West. The array of virtues articulated in ancient Rome was perhaps the most comprehensive, including *Veritas, Frugalitas, Gravitas, Dignitas, Constantia,* and *Clementia*—truthfulness, frugality, seriousness, dignity, endurance, and mercy, respectively. The guiding principles of human life in Rome, the virtues were to be personally cultivated and passed on through tradition, with each virtue also symbolized in personified form by a particular divinity in the Roman mythic pantheon. Virtues are no less significant in Christianity, of course, which identifies sets of "cardinal" and "theological" virtues, and places particular emphasis on charity, selflessness, and love, reflecting the personal character of Jesus as portrayed by the Church. And in the assemblage of Christian saints we have something akin to a mythic pantheon of deities, with each saint embodying particular qualities and having jurisdiction over specific aspects of life. Certain virtues are also given striking pictorial form in systems of esoteric symbolism such as Tarot, featuring cards including Temperance, Strength, and Justice, alongside archetypal personages such as the Devil, the High Priestess, and the Fool.

Along with the virtues, many traditions detail a litany of vices. The Christian vices, for instance, and their equivalents in other religious traditions, such as the Buddhist hindrances and afflictions, represent archetypal traits that often correspond with particular virtues as pairs of opposites. Perhaps the best-known example, incorporated into Dante's *Divine Comedy*, are the "seven deadly sins": *Luxuria* (lust), *Guta* (gluttony), *Avaritia* (avarice), *Acedia* (sloth), *Ira* (wrath), *Invidia* (envy), and *Superbia* (pride). Related virtues and vices fall together under single archetypal categories, which transcend any moral distinctions between good and evil. For the archetypes do not seem to be inherently moral, at least not in any traditional sense. When dealing with archetypes, the burden of moral decision rests on the individual, guided by reason, ethics, empathy, and the canon of religious teaching.

Archetypes are also closely associated with the basic instincts and drives in human life: the self-preservation instinct, the sexual urge, the drive for power and influence, the life and death instincts, the pleasure principle, aggression, the social instinct, the religious instinct, and others. To see these themes and impulses as the expression of archetypes is to recognize that they are common to all people, and that they exist independently of the individual human will. We do not create these qualities or drives; rather, they exist a priori; they are pre-existing factors that act through us, structuring and pervading the world and our experience of it.

Although we might consciously recognize archetypes in the abstract form of ideals, qualities, and virtues and vices, in their connection to instincts archetypes often function unconsciously in that we tend not to be aware when a particular archetypal-instinctual pattern is stirred, but find ourselves caught up in that pattern, unwittingly swept along by it. The drive for self-preservation, the will to exert and extend power, and the sexual and aggressive impulses are universal aspects of human nature, yet we experience them as our own personal urges and desires, closely bound up with our emotions, which we express and try to satisfy, often acting on them without pausing to question their origin or the motivations behind them, or even to recognize what we are doing. These patterns and drives exert a dramatic yet often unseen influence on us, conditioning human experience and, as Jung's work especially has shown, often curtailing or compromising human freedom.

Ordinarily, we do not have to concern ourselves with archetypes; indeed, life proceeds happily for many people in total ignorance of them. At a certain point of life, however, perhaps reflecting a state of psychological readiness, it might become necessary for us to make known the impact of those parts of our personality, those parts of the psyche, that had hitherto been unconscious, lying outside of the scope of conscious awareness. The call to individuate, to become the person we truly are in the depths of our inward potentiality, requires acute self-knowledge and demands of us that we become conscious of our underlying motivations, that we differentiate them from each other, as we begin to come to terms with the complex reality of the psychological universe within. For some people, this endeavor can become a central component of a spiritual path, perhaps even the predominant focus of life itself.

We might come to recognize archetypes, too, by their effects on us. At certain moments, when the veil between consciousness and the deeper ground of human nature is lifted, we might come into close proximity to archetypes, not only as patterns bound to instincts, which tend to be conservative and blindly repeat themselves, but as creative powers that uplift and inspire. Archetypes are at once spiritual and instinctual, creative and compulsive. Under their influence we can feel ourselves transported, as if to another world or dimension of reality, one of greater intensity and greater emotional charge, far beyond the familiar repertoire of thoughts and feelings we usually entertain. If, for example, we find ourselves stirred by a piece of music or captivated by a brilliant insight or idea, bewitched by beauty or intoxicated by love, or paralyzed by terror or charged with creative inspiration, we might recognize at such times that we have been moved from our depths, touched by something beyond our usual reserves of energy and beyond the normal range of human emotion. A direct encounter with archetypes, in one form or another, seizes us like a possession: we might find ourselves gripped, transfixed, and compelled for better or worse to deeds that we ordinarily would not entertain or feel able to undertake. To come into contact with the archetypes, Jung remarked, is like touching a high-voltage cable. They can release a surge of creative-instinctual power, and deliver a jolting shock to the sensitive human constitution.

The quality of an archetypal experience is often characterized by a sense of the numinous, a term employed by Rudolf Otto and then by Jung to describe an experience of spiritual majesty, fearful mystery, and power—the *mysterium tremendum et fascinans*.[1] These experiences have their origin in the depths of our being; moreover, they seem to emanate from the innermost depths of reality itself. In Indian thought, for instance, something like numinosity is suggested by the term *Brahman*, "the most important single concept of Hindu religion and philosophy," according to Indologist Heinrich Zimmer, which has been translated as "holy power."[2] This is a power, Zimmer goes on to explain, that "is to be found everywhere and assumes many forms, many manifestations."[3] As "cosmic power, in the supreme sense, it moves our conscious personality by premonitions, flashes of advice, and bursts of desire, but its source is hidden in the depth."[4]

The root of the word *numinous* is the Latin term *numen* (*numina* in the plural) suggesting divine power, presence, or will, memorably personified in its multiple aspects in the classical Greco-Roman pantheon of deities—with Zeus and Hera, Athena and Ares, Poseidon and Aphrodite, among their number—and depicted too in many other of the world's mythic traditions. We can thus feel justified in likening archetypes to gods and goddesses of ancient myth. Indeed, to describe the archetypes as gods, as Jung did, well conveys their autonomy, their superhuman power, and their capacity to intrude into the normal course of human affairs, often unannounced and uninvited. As in the experience of the ancients, at the behest of the archetypes we can have the impression that we are merely the mouthpiece of a mosaic of dynamisms and animating impulses, emissaries of energies and ideas originating from a source beyond our conscious volition.

The recognition of the reality of archetypes goes hand in hand with the idea that the human personality is not a singular entity but the composite of a plurality of different centers and sub-personalities, each with relative autonomy, each with its own defining features, ruling ideas, and aims. Although there is usually a fairly stable continuity of identity across these different centers, it becomes evident to us, even with only a modicum of reflection, that we act and think as one person in one environment, at a particular time, and as quite another person in a different environment, at another time. Poet and pragmatist, conservative and revolutionary, hedonist and ascetic live within our breast, periodically pressing their claims for expression, seizing the moment to break to the surface of our awareness between the cracks in the dominant ego personality—the person we normally know and feel ourselves to be. Jungian depth psychology accounts for this multiplicity of personality in the recognition of the archetypal ordering of the psyche, in which the ego, the source of our sense of identity and center of the field of conscious awareness, is recognized as only one psychological center or "complex" among many.

Sometimes even a relatively innocuous change in personal circumstance or wellbeing can expose or bring to the surface aspects of our character that had long remained latent, suppressed, or hidden—to us as much as to others. Weakened by fatigue, ailment, intoxication, or crisis the dominant aspect of our personality, centered on the ego, can lose its secure controlling grip, allowing other selves to present themselves to our awareness, each with its own distinct longings and dreams, qualities and moods, potentials and pathologies. The recognition and expression of these other selves can be a source of great vitality and enrichment, and their integration a primary challenge of psychological growth and development.

The study of archetypes in depth psychology and archetypal astrology, we will see, provides something like an individualized inventory of the archetypal basis of these selves or sub-personalities, enabling us to identify them and then to relate to them with a greater degree of consciousness than we perhaps had before. These approaches can help us to better understand the different ways we are moved and motivated, stirred and "possessed," and to recognize the plurality of complexes that comprise who we are.

Needless to say, this archetypal perspective stands at variance to the currently accepted views of human nature, which tend to call upon theories of genetics and neuroscience, identifying material causes behind personality and behavior, or even rejecting the notion of an innate human nature outright. Yet, as we will now consider, Jungian psychology and archetypal astrology, in their recognition of the formative role of archetypes in human experience, stand within a rich heritage and tradition.

Notes

[1] Thus Jung: "archetypes have, when they appear, a distinctly numinous character which can only be described as 'spiritual,' if 'magical' is too strong a word." Jung, "On the Nature of the Psyche," in *Structure and Dynamics of the Psyche* (CW8), 205, par. 405. For a definition of the term *numinous*, see Otto, *The Idea of the Holy*.

[2] Zimmer, *Philosophies of India*, 74. The description "holy power" comes from Keith.

[3] Zimmer, *Philosophies of India*, 78.

[4] Zimmer, *Philosophies of India*, 79–80.

Chapter 2

A Brief History of Archetypes

F rom the gods and goddesses of ancient Greek myth to the instincts and drives of German Romanticism and depth psychology, the concept of something like archetypes occupies a prominent place in the history of Western thought and culture. In many respects, Jungian psychology represents not so much a new development as a recovery of a perspective lost, the modern reformulation of a perennial archetypal vision in the language of the psychology of the unconscious.

Origins and Evolutions: From the Ancient World to the Modern
The prevailing worldviews of most civilizations have recognized the existence of archetypes in one form or another. The earliest representations of archetypes were mythic: in the world's mythic traditions archetypes were known and immediately experienced as gods and goddesses intervening in human affairs from a heavenly realm or a Mount Olympus, looking down on human beings from on high. Or archetypes were represented by animal, vegetal, or elemental symbolism, associated with the wind, fire, the earth, thunder, the seas, mountains, trees, and other features and forces of the natural world. In astrology—perhaps the oldest symbolic system—archetypal principles take the form of celestial powers connected with the movements of, and the relationships between, the Sun, the Moon, and the planets in our solar system.

With the rise of Christianity, its legalization by Constantine in 313 CE, and its establishment as the official church of the Roman Empire in 380 CE, the classical mythic conception of reality, embodied in the Greco-Roman pantheon of gods and goddesses, fell into decline. Monotheism, the belief in one god, was already enshrined in Judaism. As decreed by the dictates of Yahweh, inscribed on the stone tablets of

Sinai and recorded in the Old Testament, the worship of other deities, such as those of the so-called nature religions, was expressly forbidden; Yahweh alone was to be worshipped. As Christianity spread throughout the Western world and beyond, monotheism replaced or subsumed the polytheism that recognized many gods and goddesses representing different aspects of the divine.

In ancient Greece, the mythic depiction of archetypes as gods and goddesses was gradually replaced by conceptual models, yet models still significantly rooted in the mythic world in which they had their origin. Emerging from earlier cosmogonies, Presocratic philosophy in Greece from Anaximander onwards introduced the notion of *archai* as "first principles" or "originating forms," the fundamental causes of the manifest world of being. Archetypal principles were explained in both mythic and philosophical terms by Pythagoras and Plato who envisaged archetypal Forms or Ideas as eternal universal principles existing in a metaphysical realm behind the temporal flux of the world of experience. These ideal Forms, which include numbers, moral qualities ("the Good, the True, and the Beautiful"), and the prototypes of all existent things (from dogs and horses to chairs and tables), are, Plato proposed, imperfectly replicated or embodied in objects in the world. All dogs participate in the ideal form *Dog* even though each dog is different and unique. All individuals can experience a sense of what is "good" by participating in the metaphysical principle of the Good. And all individuals can recognize an inherent order in the universe because the external world and the human mind are structured by the numinous organizing principles of number.

Aristotle, Plato's student, was concerned with the expression of Forms in nature. For Aristotle, the archetypal Forms exist in the immanent reality of the world, not in a transcendent metaphysical realm. They reside within nature as recognizable universal classes and qualities within material things. The Forms are dynamic and purposive, guiding, impelling, and drawing forth the unfolding development of organisms from latency to actuality, as in the paradigmatic example of the acorn containing within it the latent form of the mature oak tree.

The notion of something like a developmental blueprint that determines the course of maturation and growth pertains to human life too, applying as much to psychology as to physiology. In the early nineteenth century, this idea was taken up by Arthur Schopenhauer who suggested that human beings each have a specific "intelligible character" existing as latent potential, which is to be realized in the known personality or "empirical character" over the course of the lifetime. That is to say, the pattern or design of one's life and personality is pre-given, an idea that has been popularly understood in terms of the realization of a destiny. This might be imagined not as the binding power of immutable fate but as an inborn pattern seeking to be actualized, a life purpose seeking to be fulfilled, an archetypal form progressively unfolding in our experience that shapes the person we are to become, pulling our life in specific directions according to some ascribed goal or purpose—a final cause, in Aristotelian terms. Obviously, this view contrasts markedly with the modern assumption that life and character are wholly conditioned by past causes, determined by external circumstances and childhood experiences, or shaped by acts of will in response to such circumstances. The Aristotelian view subsumes the modern beliefs in causal determinism and the freedom of the human will in its recognition of a greater order of meaning—a formal cause—within which life events take place.

A similar idea impressed itself on Jung. "What happens to a person," he observed, "is characteristic of him. He represents a pattern and all the pieces fit. One by one, as his life proceeds, they fall into place according to some pre-destined design."[1] It was influential too on James Hillman, the originator of archetypal psychology, whose best-known book, *The Soul's Code*, presents an "acorn theory" of human life as shaped by an unseen archetypal power or *daimon* that manifests as a calling or vocation to realize some particular pre-established goal in accordance with an innate archetypal pattern or image.[2]

In Gnostic literature, originating at the beginning of the Christian era, archetypes are recognizable as the oppressive forces represented by the Archons, "the planetary gods borrowed from the Babylonian pantheon," as Hans Jonas notes in *The Gnostic Religion*. In the Gnostic vision, he explains,

The universe, the Domain of the Archons, is like a vast prison whose innermost dungeon is the earth, the scene of man's life . . . . The Archons collectively rule over the world, and each individually in his sphere is a warder of the cosmic prison. Their tyrannical world-rule is called *heimarmene*, universal Fate, a concept taken over from astrology but now tinged with the gnostic anti-cosmic spirit. . . As guardian of his sphere, each Archon bars the passage to the souls that seek to ascend after death, in order to prevent their escape from the world and their return to God. The Archons are also the creators of the world, except where this role is reserved for their leader, who then has the name of *demiurge* . . .

Man, the main object of these vast dispositions, is composed of flesh, soul, and spirit. But reduced to ultimate principles, his origin his twofold: mundane and extra-mundane. Not only the body but also the soul is the product of cosmic powers, which shaped the body in the image of the divine Primal (or Archetypal) man and animated it with their own psychical forces: these are the appetites and passions of natural man, each of which stems from and corresponds to one of the cosmic spheres and all of which together make up the astral soul of man, his "psyche." Through his body and this soul man is part of the world and is subjected to the *heimarmene*. Enclosed in the soul is the spirit, or "pneuma" (called also the "spark"), a portion of the divine substance from beyond which has fallen into the world; and the Archons created man for the express purpose of keeping it captive there. Thus, as in the macrocosm man is enclosed by the seven spheres, so in the human microcosm again the pneuma is enclosed by seven soul-vestments originating from them. In its unredeemed state the pneuma thus immersed in soul and flesh is unconscious of itself, benumbed, asleep, or intoxicated by the poison of the world: in brief, it is "ignorant." Its awakening and liberation is effected through "knowledge."[3]

The notion of Archons as binding powers of fate remains in the modern conception of archetypes in Jungian psychology, but fate is now understood as the compulsive power of instinct, which keeps human beings subservient to unconscious forces seemingly beyond our control. Only by making these forces conscious can we struggle to attain liberation from *heimarmene*, the inborn "bill of debt to fate."[4]

A Gnostic conception of the world was extremely influential on Jung, to the extent that he composed his "Seven Sermons to the Dead" under the name of the Gnostic author Basilides, came into ownership of Gnostic scrolls from the 1945 Nag Hammadi discovery in Egypt one of which was then named after him (the "Jung codex"), inscribed Gnostic imagery in the stone sculptures of his tower home at Bollingen in Switzerland, and even sported a Gnostic ring. The Gnostic insight into the binding grip of Archons was central to Jung's emphasis on the struggle to overcome the hold of unconscious nature over us in the course of individuation, and this idea therefore remains important in how we might understand our own forms of participation with the astrological planetary archetypes. Are archetypes benevolent creative forces that we can participate with in a co-creative engagement with the universe? Or are they oppressive binding powers that dominate us and which must be fought against and overcome through the attainment of psychological gnosis or self-knowledge? Is the universe an ordered mathematical harmony of beauty and goodness, as in the Greek vision? Or is it a realm that imprisons us, and keeps us from our true spiritual home in a transcendent realm of an unknown God beyond the phenomenal world? Or are both viewpoints true to different degrees or from different perspectives?

Meanwhile, in the early period of the Christian era, in a synthesis of Greek philosophy with Christianity, Platonic and Aristotelian conceptions of Forms were reinterpreted in the theological speculations of Saint Augustine (354–430 CE), who turned away from his earlier affiliation with the Gnostic Manicheans in presenting a robust defense of Christianity in *The City of God*. In Augustine's view, as one succinct philosophical commentary puts it, "The Forms (the ideas of the Divine Mind) are rendered intelligible to humans through God."[5]

The recognition of archetypes persisted into the modern era. In the eighteenth century, something like archetypes were conceived in a more limited character by Immanuel Kant as "categories" of the human mind, notably those of space, time, and causality, which are innate predispositions to think, perceive, and unconsciously construct our experience of reality. Kant reasoned that our experience of the world is shaped by these universal modes of cognition and "forms of intuition" inherent in the human mind. In the modern era, if they were recognized at all, archetypes were imagined not as metaphysical principles, but as psychological factors or categories pertaining only to the inner world of the mind. The outer world, Kant reasoned, was essentially unknowable. Human beings could only experience the world as it appeared to their perceptions—a world of appearances, shaped by the categories—not the world as it really is, in itself.

Elsewhere, in the suppressed or forgotten history, lying behind the dominant narrative of the West, paganism remained very much alive, carrying with it a recognition of the magical powers—nixies, fairies, pixies, elves, angels, goblins, and such like—that populate the fairytale and folk imagination. Such entities and powers are reflected in the popular understanding of the word *spirits*. Perhaps these fabled beings were just figments of the primitive imagination. But perhaps, Jung asks, "were there not such beings long ago, in an age when dawning human consciousness was still wholly bound to nature? Surely there were spirits of forest, field, and stream long before the question of moral conscience ever existed."[6] These figures, like the gods and goddesses of mythology, might be understood as personified forms of archetypes.

In the climate of austere Christian faith and Enlightenment rationality of the late nineteenth century, it was left to the occult traditions to preserve and develop the hidden knowledge of the inner world excluded from the dominant Christian worldview and excluded today from our scientific understanding of the world. Astrology itself fell into the tradition of occult knowledge, with its reemergence into Western popular culture in the twentieth century owing much to its transmission by the Theosophical movement, centered on the teachings of Helena Blavatsky, and later by its contact with Jungian ideas.

Science and the Disenchanted Universe

Despite the prominence of archetypes in ancient Greece, which was the origin of modern philosophy and science, in the modern West theoretical models based on archetypes have fallen out of vogue in academia and science. Influenced by interpretations of the ideas of Galileo, Descartes, Newton, Locke, and others, the modern scientific view of the world recognizes only what can be perceived with the senses, aided by scientific instruments. It focuses on the material world, probing ever deeper into the complex structure of matter to understand its composition and thus to understand reality at large. Modern science is atomistic and reductionist in its approach: It breaks things down into their smallest component parts and reduces all phenomena to explanations in terms of the causal interactions of these parts. We see all around us the staggering influence of science and technology in the modern world. But, wedded to these guiding paradigms and models, science discloses only a partial view of the nature of reality. In general, it fails to take into account the larger encompassing context of purposes, meanings, and underlying patterns within which chains of events occur. It is this larger context of meaning that is the focus of archetypal astrology and Jungian psychology.

A legacy of the philosophy of René Descartes in the sixteenth century is the fundamental distinction drawn between the inner world of thought and the outer world of matter. Mind and matter, psyche and cosmos, once believed to be part of an undivided world, henceforth came to be viewed as entirely separate substances and realms interacting causally through the brain. Later, under the accelerating influence of science, the human mind came to be seen merely as an epiphenomenon arising from firing neurons, as nothing more than a spurious derivative of brain activity.

A consequence of Cartesian philosophy, as it came to be interpreted, is that human beings were seen to inhabit two separate yet mysteriously connected worlds: one to be accessed by looking out with the senses, the other by looking within introspectively. Increasingly, the sacred and the spiritual dimensions of life were to be approached and accessed only through human interiority, if at all. The material world was viewed as entirely unconscious, devoid of spiritual value or intrinsic meaning, comprised only of inert matter moved mechanistically by external, scientifically measurable forces.

With the ascendancy of the modern worldview, then, all things and events were understood to be explicable solely in terms of prior causes that can be observed and measured within the material world. The rise of science was accompanied by a decline in other forms of explanation, particularly those based on transcendent universal principles, such as the Platonic Forms. These universals, once thought to be the organizing principles behind the material world, were henceforth deemed to exist in name only, to pertain only to classes of things that could be perceived and named by the human mind. Thus, love was not believed to exist as an autonomous self-subsistent universal principle, as in the Platonic view; rather, love was considered to be a name or label to describe a category of experience. The general idea of love was merely abstracted from particular instances of love observed in the world.

These ideas and developments, alongside the theories of other major figures in the history of Western thought, including Darwin and Freud, have contributed to the disenchanted character of the modern worldview. For many people today the world is no longer experienced as or viewed as spiritual or sacred in essence. A secular, materialistic view of life prevails. Under the influence of classical physics, the universe was thought to be a chance occurrence, lacking any inherent purpose or deeper meaning—a view that largely endures today, in spite of the discoveries of modern physics. The human being is envisaged as a genetically programmed, instinctually driven, environmentally conditioned being, evolved from primates, with a consciousness that has emerged as an accidental by-product of brain complexity, existing in a universe that itself came into being and evolved by chance, without any superordinate design or purpose.

The Psychology of the Unconscious

Although they are no longer principal concerns of philosophy or science, in the early twentieth century ideas akin to archetypes were very much in vogue, and the study of archetypes resurfaced in its clearest form in depth psychology. This new field, with Freud and Jung the central figures, retained the focus of the German Romantic tradition on the irrational depths of inner experience—the emotions, the passions, the will, the instincts, the imagination, questions of meaning and suffering—now studying these phenomena, however, guided by the empirical methodology of modern science. Above all, depth psychology carried forward and significantly developed the idea that there is an unconscious dimension to human experience, and that, consequently, human life is subject to the influence of an overriding will and unconscious drives beyond our conscious control.[7]

Whereas archetypes had earlier been experienced as gods and goddesses or conceptualized as philosophical principles, henceforth they were conceived as psychological factors. Mythic deities, metaphysical systems, astrological principles, and even the religious belief in a transcendent spiritual realm were viewed thereafter as nothing but projections of a psychological reality onto the world and the celestial sphere. The locus of life meaning had shifted decisively from the world itself to the interiority of the human being. This transition was not lost on Jung: "Since the stars have fallen from heaven, and our highest symbols have paled," he remarked, "a secret life holds sway in the unconscious. That is why we have a psychology today, and why we speak of an unconscious."[8]

It is surely more than just coincidence that the unconscious was discovered in precisely the same historical period that brought forth Friedrich Nietzsche's proclamation that "God is dead," symbolically encapsulating the nihilistic consequences of entering the post-Christian era.[9] At almost the very moment when the modern self found itself inhabiting an external cosmos in which all trace of the divine had seemingly vanished, a cosmos utterly devoid of spiritual meaning and purpose, human consciousness immediately plunged into the unsuspected interior depths of the unconscious psyche. In this newly discovered inner world, it became apparent that the ancient gods, although long forgotten and unrecognized, lived on. Thus Jung, in a famous passage, observed:

> We think we can congratulate ourselves on having already reached such a pinnacle of clarity, imagining that we have left all these phantasmal gods far behind. But what we have left behind are only verbal spectres, not the psychic facts that were responsible for the birth of the gods. We are still as much possessed by autonomous psychic contents as if they were Olympians. Today they are called

28

phobias, obsessions, and so forth; in a word, neurotic symptoms. The gods have become diseases.[10]

The gods had not permanently disappeared, they had just become invisible to the modern mind, with its gaze directed outwards, and its vision blinkered to any other psychological reality save for that of its own conscious awareness and rational volition. Without a vital living myth, the modern mind did not and could not readily discern the activity of those powerful dynamic forces formerly conceived as gods. It seemed, in fact, that the only way modern ego-consciousness could be alerted to the existence of autonomous psychological factors outside of its own control was in the form of psychological or physical pathology. "Zeus no longer rules Olympus," Jung remarked, "but rather the solar plexus."[11]

And so it was, through depth psychology's exploration of the symptoms and causes of this pathology, that the gods were rediscovered, no longer as Olympians or celestial powers, but as wholly psychological factors to be approached through human interiority. "All ages before ours believed in gods in some form or other," Jung observed. "Only an unparalleled impoverishment of symbolism," he added, "could enable us to discover the gods as psychic factors, that is, as archetypes of the unconscious."[12]

In the absence of a vital living mythology, and with Christianity increasingly unable to cater to the spiritual needs of the individual, depth psychology found its place in modern culture, first to try to alleviate the symptoms of psychopathology and then later, with Jung's work in particular, to help people find their own sense of meaning and spiritual purpose based not on an outmoded religious orthodoxy, nor even on reason, but rather on a living relationship to the archetypes in the depths of the human unconscious psyche.

Freud and Jung: Psychoanalysis and Analytical Psychology

It was through Jung's discovery of the collective unconscious—a background dimension of the psyche, present in every individual—that the concept of archetypes came to the attention of inquiring minds in modern culture. Freudian psychoanalysis had already done much to illuminate the instinctual basis of human behavior, depicting the human being as the unwitting instrument of unconscious impulses and complexes, ultimately rooted in biology. In Freud's model, the human psyche is something of a battleground between different structural components: the ceaseless instinctual drives of the id conforming to the "pleasure principle," the punitive moral judgment of the super-ego, and the demands and restrictions of the external world. Positioned in the midst of this conflict, the ego, guided by the "reality principle," attempts to fulfill the demands of the id for instinctual gratification under the watchful eye of the super-ego, ever mindful of moral strictures and the necessity of adapting desires to the expectations of civilized life.

Although the concept of archetypes is not present in psychoanalysis, Freud's view of the human psyche as comprising dynamic, autonomous component parts was reflected in Jung's understanding of the close relationship between archetypes and instincts. Beyond this, Freud's recognition of the primary drives of Eros and Thanatos, and the Oedipus and Electra complexes as underlying patterns of human development and behavior, presented a vision of human nature that, even amidst the scientific materialism of the time, recalled in its language and theoretical formulations the mythic sensibility of ancient Greece—a parallel that was more fully apparent in Jung's more explicitly mythic analytical psychology.

Through his exploration of the themes and motifs in his patients' dreams and fantasies, Jung was struck by how these themes bore a striking resemblance to those portrayed in world mythology and religion, and art and culture. Motifs and figures such as death and rebirth, heroes and old wise guides, dark forces and tricksters, were ubiquitously evident, Jung observed, in the products of the human imagination across individuals and cultures. Dreams and fantasies were evidence of an "autochthonous revival" of ancient mythic motifs in the life of the modern individual.[13] He initially called these universal themes primordial images and, later, archetypes, concurring with Lucien Lévy-Bruhl's theory of "collective representations" and anthropologist Adolf Bastian's idea that the myths of all cultures contained universal "elementary ideas," clothed in the local, "ethnic" costumes of that culture.[14] Although Jung claimed that there are archetypes for "every typical situation in life," he focused his attention on a set of major archetypes, ones that are especially prominent during the individuation process—the shadow, anima, animus, hero, mother, child, spirit, wise old man, trickster, rebirth, Dionysus, and the Self.[15] As we will later see, he also explored another class of archetypes based on principles of number and geometry, which are especially significant in astrology.

The human psyche, Jung concluded, is preconditioned by the archetypes; they are the underlying determinants of our experience, the "hidden operators behind the scenes,"[16] as Aniela Jaffé put it, that are expressed in each and every typical human experience, and that provide the background framework of meaning for human existence.[17] Because they are connected to the instincts, the archetypes are, moreover, dynamic motivating centers of human life—"formative principle[s] of instinctual power," as Jung described them.[18] They are purposive, moving consciousness in specific directions, and leading us, if we can come to terms with them, towards greater self-knowledge and wholeness. They are the powers and patterns that impel and define the individuation process.[19]

Consider, for example, the hero archetype, with which we are all familiar in one form or another. As an archetype, we might recognize the hero as a "pattern of behavior," manifest in the characteristic acts of courage, sacrifice, single-minded focus on attainment, the struggle to conquer, and will to prevail at any cost. We might see this pattern in a situation of peril when, without hesitation, the policeman in the line of duty springs to the aid of a comrade, or when the mother instinctively protects her child with no thought for her own wellbeing. We see the hero in the noble yet tragic sacrifice of the young to enlist in a war effort, willing to die a glorious death in service to God and country. We see it in the singular dedication of artists to their creative endeavors and in scientists' unswerving pursuit of truth. For Jung, such patterns are not consciously chosen behaviors but innate responses that become activated in particular circumstances, causing us to think, feel, say, and do things we otherwise would not. They are responses laid down through the course of evolution as "deposits" of "ancestral experiences," which like "riverbeds" channel the flow of libido—life energy—along particular pathways.[20] In acting heroically ourselves, we are expressing an archaic pattern, one that has manifested in human life time and time again, to the point that it is innate, intrinsic to what it is to be human, a governing principle of the "soul's cycle of experience," as Jung put it.[21]

We might recognize the hero too as a mythic image or "archetypal representation"—an "eternal image" that, in Jung's words, is "meant to attract, to convince, to fascinate, and to overpower."[22] Thus, when we see a modern fictional hero—such as a Luke Skywalker, Frodo Baggins, or Katniss Everdeen—performing great and noble deeds in a film, or when we read of acts of heroism in news reports on the affairs of the day, or witness heroic achievements in the sporting world, we might experience a powerful emotional and somatic response. The image touches something deep within us. The experience of the heroic might come upon us with a tinge of the numinous, stirring deep feeling within us, making the hairs on the back of our neck stand on end, moving us to tears, giving us goosebumps.

The archetype is more than an observable pattern or image, for it possesses an instinctual charge, a dynamic compulsion that stirs us to action, pulling us into its sway, often making us blind to all other aspects of experience, all thoughts and feelings that fall outside of the range of the archetype. Thus, the hero archetype sees only challenges to overcome, lands to conquer, or is gripped by an unswerving conviction to realize a goal or to achieve great fame and notoriety. As a "subject with laws of its own,"[23] each archetype perceives the world in its own distinct way, in accordance with its nature, and tends to be oblivious to other possibilities—"blind to its own stance," as James Hillman put it.[24] Under the influence of any given archetype, it is extremely difficult to see beyond it to other feelings, other possibilities, other archetypal worlds.

The hero archetype is one of an array of "transcendentally conditioned dynamisms," to use Jung's description, whose origin lies outside conscious awareness.[25] The capacity to imagine, think, feel, and act in an heroic manner is an a priori condition of human experience. If we recognize its presence in our own lives, we make that particular pattern conscious and thus are less susceptible to the blind compulsion associated with all such archetypes. We can live out the pattern and purpose of the archetype more consciously, and in the process might derive a sense of deep life meaning.

In addition to describing the character of the major archetypes and exploring their significance for the individuation process, Jung gave considerable time and attention to the conceptual challenge of explicating the nature of archetypes themselves. We have already seen a number of Jung's favored descriptions, which give a sense of the complexity of a concept that defies any attempt at singular definition. By the 1950s, late in his life, Jung brought in an entirely different dimension to his understanding of archetypes. Until that time, he had construed archetypes fairly consistently as psychological factors, perhaps, he conjectured, possessing a physiological basis in brain structure—a claim that remains tenuous, at best. Archetypes were conceived as formative principles in the depths of the collective unconscious, located within the individual psyche. The archetypes and the collective unconscious, he thought, are replicated anew within each of us at birth, such that we each inherit a common psychological structure.

Refining his original formulation, however, Jung drew a distinction between the dimension of the archetype that manifests in the psyche (the archetypal image) and the core archetype itself (the archetype *per se*), which is unknowable and is outside the limits of psychological experience: it is "transcendental." We might dream of a wise old man or read of myths and stories of wise figures such as Merlin or Gandalf, and thus come into contact with the archetypal image, but we can never know the wise-old-man archetype directly, as a pure archetype. We see only particular instances of this archetypal figure, and infer the existence of the archetype *per se* from its multitudinous manifestations in human experience.

In a related development, Jung also introduced the notion that archetypes have what he termed a *psychoid* basis. He had realized that in certain circumstances archetypes appear to manifest not only in the inner world of psychological experience (such as in dreams and fantasies), but also in the external world. Their nature seems to straddle psyche and matter, inner and outer, informing and influencing both. These conclusions were prompted especially by Jung's investigation of synchronicities, uncanny "meaningful coincidences" between inner states of perceived meaning and external events. These synchronicities often possess a numinous quality and appear to arise, Jung observed, from a "constellated archetype" in the unconscious.[26] If you were to find yourself passing through a life ending of some sort or perhaps contemplating a venture that was doomed to failure, and at that time you unexpectedly encountered a funeral procession or were surrounded by a flock of crows or ravens, Jung would call this a synchronicity—an episode in which events and circumstances in the external world meaningfully reflect our inner, seemingly private experience. In this example, we might recognize both events, inner and outer, as connected by the activated archetype of death even if there is no apparent causal connection between them.

I have addressed elsewhere the significance of these concepts for developing an archetypal understanding of astrology as a form of cosmic synchronicity. As we will see shortly, the archetypes studied in astrology are general universal principles that appear to pertain to Jung's idea of the archetype *per se,* in that we do not experience astrological archetypes directly, in their pure essence, as it were, but only in their myriad forms of expression in human life. And as implied by Jung's idea of the psychoid basis of the archetypes, astrology rests on an archetypal order manifest in both the psyche and the cosmos, pointing to a unitary reality or ground underlying both. Thus understood, our own deepest nature is seen as rooted within the inner depths of nature itself. The inner depths of the mind, of our subjective experience, and the depths of matter, of the objective world, arise from the same substrate or ground, and the unfolding of this ground is ordered by archetypes. In an earlier work I named this ground the *archetypal matrix*.

Archetypal Psychology

Certain aspects of Jung's psychology were taken up by James Hillman in the late 1960s as he developed his own self-styled "archetypal psychology." Inspired by Renaissance Neoplatonism, Hillman's psychology more explicitly articulated and championed the rich and varied imaginal life of the soul in all its nobility, pathos, beauty, and mythic diversity than even Jung's work had. Hillman affirmed and expanded Jung's vision of the pluralistic archetypal nature of the psyche, granting to the world of the imagination its own vital reality, honoring the multifarious productions of the psyche—its pathology, its mythic figures, and its fantasies—in their own right. Contrary to monotheistic conceptions of the divine, such as the Christian God, and challenging the humanistic idea that the psyche is a function of a singular human self, he believed that the psyche is home to many "persons," and many gods and goddesses, and the ego should therefore give up the illusion of sole occupancy. The realization of the pluralistic or polytheistic nature of the psyche, Hillman suggested, could be achieved by adopting a metaphorical way of experiencing—by cultivating an "archetypal eye" to "see through" the concrete literalisms of contemporary life to the deeper mythic realities these concealed. In our encounter with old age, tradition, conservatism, and the status quo, for example, we might come to recognize qualities of the archetypal senex, the mythic figure of the old man. The goddess Aphrodite lives through experiences of beauty, love, and lust; Hermes is present in our words, our thoughts, our movements, and in the transitional or liminal spaces between things, guiding us across boundaries and thresholds. All aspects of life can take us into the domain of the gods and goddesses, if our eye is mythically attuned. It is a fallacy, Hillman thought, to see such experiences as merely human phenomena, and thus to place them within the range of exclusively humanistic psychology, for the limits of the psyche and the soul are not contained within us, somehow housed inside the body or head, and are not the exclusive preserve of human beings. For Hillman, the soul is not a singular "thing" or entity existing inside the individual person, as in the popular Christian understanding, but a "perspective" or quality within and between all things—an idea conveyed by the ancient belief in an *anima mundi* or world soul. Of course, in spite of Hillman's rejection of Christian conceptions, many of us would want to retain the recognition of a personal, individual soul, expressive of our innermost essence. Hillman's pluralistic revisioning of psychology, however, allows us to reclaim the broader sense of soul as the inwardness that exists within and between all things.

Hillman hoped that an archetypal view of human experience could give soul more authentic expression in modern life and provide a way out of the repressive control of the modern ego, which he associated with monotheism.[27] Hillman realized that psychological conditions such as depression and neurosis are legitimate protestations against the authoritarian rule of the dominant ego and the soulless literalisms of modern life. Thus, symptoms of psychopathology are not something to be treated, corrected, and cured, as in the standard medical model of psychotherapy; rather, such symptoms, Hillman argued, are essential expressions of the depths of the soul and the psyche, which, if affirmed and explored, could provide gateways to a richer, more meaningful life.

Finding myths and archetypes in evidence wherever he looked, Hillman also turned his archetypal eye to the wider culture, in the hope that this might restore a more aesthetic and mythic mode of being, as in the sensibility of the Renaissance. He recognized that gods and goddesses pervade everything—physical symptoms, obsessions and neuroses, works of art, histories and sciences, psychologies and philosophies. As he once said in his own inimitable way, you can't even open your mouth without a god speaking.

Hillman's archetypal psychology serves as a counterbalance, in some respects, to Jung's predominant focus on the role of archetypes in individuation and the depths of psychological transformation. For Jung, archetypes are to be encountered first and foremost in the inner world of dreams and fantasies; they are the agents of transformation, ultimately impelling the individuation process. For Hillman, archetypes are omnipresent, evident as much in the events of daily life as they are in the depths of inner experience; and they have many ends and reasons beyond that of human psychological growth. Yet in unlinking archetypes from individuation, something crucial is lost, for despite their irreducible variety and seemingly conflicting or contradictory modes of expression, archetypes might be understood as functions of the complex totality of the Self, as we will later consider.

Archetypal Astrology

The multi-faceted understanding of archetypes—as Platonic Forms, mythic gods and goddesses, numinous powers and principles, instincts and patterns of behavior, sub-personalities and styles of being—is also integral to archetypal astrology and the broader field of archetypal cosmology.[28] The fundamental assumption informing archetypal astrology is that there is an underlying connection between the expression of universal principles in human experience and the positions and movements of the planets in the solar system. To know how the planets are positioned in relation to each other at particular times is to gain symbolic insight into how the archetypal principles associated with the planets are themselves related to each other, and how they find expression in our lives. The position of the planetary body Pluto, for example, is understood to be meaningfully connected to the expression of themes astrologers associate with the Pluto archetype—rebirth, instinctual empowerment, compulsion, power drives, transformation, and more. Or to interpret the significance of the position of Uranus relative to the other planets is to understand something deeply significant about how themes associated with the Uranus archetype—rebellion, the urge for freedom, awakening, revolution, disruption, birthing the new—are expressed in life. This guiding assumption of a correlation between planets and archetypes might be construed as a logical extension of Jungian psychology applied to the field of cosmology, as noted above, and it finds empirical support from a number of studies, especially Richard Tarnas's extensive research in his 2006 publication, *Cosmos and Psyche*. It is an assumption that, in one form or another, has been at the heart of astrological practice for millennia but one that we are now able to explain and describe more precisely with reference to the principles and ideas of depth psychology.

Indeed, Jungian ideas proved critical to the task of the reformulation of modern astrology in terms of the psychology of the unconscious, for they have been influential on many, if not all, psychological astrologers of the last several decades. The French-American polymath Dane Rudhyar was in many respects the father of psychological astrology, although Rudhyar's visionary work also remained rooted in theosophy and drew liberally on Eastern thought and the emerging field of systems science. From the 1970s, perhaps the two major figures of a Jungian persuasion in astrology were Stephen Arroyo and Liz Greene.[29] Through their many books, and the work of numerous other astrologers of recent decades, astrology emerged anew as a symbolic aid

36

to psychological understanding. From Rudhyar on, Jungian psychology has often been used both to explain and seek to legitimize astrology in a culture suspicious of its truth claims.

The rationale behind the association between the fields lies in Jung's view that the "planets" in astrology are akin to the gods of myth in that both are rooted in archetypes—indeed, in support of his view of astrology as a form of archetypal psychology, Jung coined the term *planetary archetype*. Jung himself had a deep interest in astrological matters, both professionally and personally, judging it to be an early form of psychological understanding and the "sum of all the psychological knowledge of antiquity."[30] He employed astrology as an aid to his analytical work with his patients, and yet he was mindful of the many shortcomings of astrological practice, as he chastised astrologers for giving interpretations that are too literal and failing to conduct empirical studies into astrology.

Jung situated astrology within the transformation of Western civilization in the modern era, viewing it as one of a number of movements that reflected a burgeoning interest in the psychological and the irrational since the late eighteenth century, which stood in a compensatory relationship both to the rationality championed after the Enlightenment and to the decline of religion in the modern world. The modern human had discarded religious conviction in the shift towards rationalism and science, but these did not address the deep inner needs of the soul. Thus arose, in the spiritually destitute individual, a quest for life meaning from areas on the borderland of modern thought—including spiritualism, mysticism, Eastern religion, theosophy, paganism, and astrology.

Jung also devoted considerable time and attention to thinking through how astrology works—that is, trying to understand the relationship of the planets and signs of the zodiac to the dynamics of psychological experience. Jung's views on astrology are far from unambiguous, however, especially in respect of an explanation of astrological correspondence. On occasion, he proclaimed that astrology is an unconscious projection of the psyche onto the heavens, with astrologers seeing in celestial configurations patterns of meaning that really reside within, in the depths of the unconscious mind. Yet he also contradicted this position, especially in his speculations towards the end of his life. For there is much in Jung's own understanding of the psyche and his keen interest in modern physics that supports a cogent theoretical explanation of astrological correspondences as inherent to the deeper order of reality. Jung's writings on astrology, which touch on virtually every aspect of his theories, may be found in the single volume *Jung on Astrology*, published in 2017.

The archetypal nature of astrology—both astrology's lineage in the history of ideas and its conceptual basis in myth, Platonism, and Jungian psychology—has been brilliantly articulated by Richard Tarnas. In *The Passion of the Western Mind* he sets forth a narrative history of Western thought that shows the evolution of the concept of archetypal forms from the Ancient Greeks to the late modern era. Tarnas's second major publication, *Cosmos and Psyche*, then provides a substantial body of evidence demonstrating correlations between the moving planets, as they change their positions relative to each other, and the occurrence of themes and patterns in cultural history. My own work, and that of a number of other scholars and practitioners in the field of archetypal cosmology, has followed Tarnas's pioneering efforts, which have done much to put astrology on a firmer theoretical and empirical footing.

The Sun, the Moon, and the planetary bodies in the solar system are each associated with a particular archetypal principle (a "planetary archetype") and an array of related mythic themes, universal qualities, and instinctual energies. Each planetary archetype might also be mapped on to one or more of the major Jungian archetypes. For example, as noted above, the planetary archetype associated with Pluto is related to themes such as instinctual dynamism, the unconscious depths of the psyche, death-rebirth, transformation, evolution, compulsion, and empowerment. It is connected to the Jungian archetypes of the shadow (containing the repressed instincts and primitive drives), rebirth, and Dionysus, as well as the compulsive, possessive quality associated with all archetypes and the fated quality often associated with the Self. The astrological Moon is associated with the anima (the inner "feminine" principle), and the archetypes of the mother and the child. Saturn is associated with the wise old man or senex, the father archetype, and with the inferiority complex and negative emotions contained in the shadow. Uranus has particular connections with the trickster archetype, especially in its association with creative disruption, and also with the archetypal figures of the rebel and revolutionary, and experiences of liberation, freedom, and awakening. The Sun, pertaining to themes such as the quest for identity, the heroic task of carrying the light of conscious self-awareness, and with the centralizing principle of the psyche, is naturally connected to Jung's concept of the hero archetype and to the realization of the Self. And Venus and Mars, to give two final examples, are associated with the idealized images of female and male contained in the anima and animus, respectively. In short, each of the principles associated with the planets in astrology, which we will consider in detail in Part Four, seems to be related to one or more Jungian archetypes and particular qualities exhibited by these archetypes.

The planetary archetypes are also connected to the gods and goddesses of myth, and to a number of prominent mythic motifs such as those found within the hero's journey. For example, Pluto is associated with Hades, the Devil, Dionysus, Shiva, Mara, Kali, Wotan, the alchemical god-man Mercurius, and a number of other mythic deities, in that they personify Plutonic qualities and themes, such as creative-destructive elemental force and instinctual chthonic power. Pluto is also associated with kundalini energy, the mythic underworld, hell, and purgatory, and the motifs of a "descent into the underworld," dismemberment, and transformation. Neptune is associated with the principles of divine love and universal compassion, personified by figures such as Christ and the Buddha. It is also related to the yearning for paradise, and the quest for mystical experience of oneness or transcendence, central to the esoteric branches of all religious traditions. Saturn relates to the patriarchal authority of Yahweh in the Old Testament, to Chronos and Father Time, to the stern hand of fate, and to the spiritual wisdom and authority of the guru or wise-old-man figure.

Again, as these few examples suggest, each planetary archetype is connected to many different mythic figures from the world's religious and cultural traditions. Each mythic figure represents one or more different aspects or characteristics of the planetary archetypes, which possess universal meanings that cannot be adequately portrayed by any single deity or concept. It has long been recognized in psychologically oriented astrology that the archetypes associated with the planets are, to use Tarnas's terminology, multivalent and multidimensional principles. That is to say, they are indeterminate creative powers that manifest in a wide variety of ways across all dimensions of reality. Although they reflect an unchanging core of meaning, these archetypes do not have singular fixed modes of expression that might be exhaustively described using a few simple keywords. The Saturn archetype, for example, is associated not only with suffering, old age, and death, but also with structure, discipline, and patience. It can manifest as the stern hand of fate or as judgment and criticism, yet it also finds expression as learned wisdom, realism, and a sense of inner authority. One cannot determine from astrology alone exactly how the archetypes will actually manifest in the specific details of life. Astrology pertains to the universal dimension of human experience, to general themes and motifs, and not to the specific form these universals take when manifest in a particular context. We know that Pluto is associated with compulsion and the experience of being driven as if in the grip of fate, but we cannot tell from astrology exactly what this fate is or what particular form the compulsion might take. By studying a variety of examples, however, we might develop a sense for the thematic range and potential of the archetypes, as they combine and interact with each other. We can then use this knowledge as we apply astrology to our own experience.

By studying the planetary order and interpreting its meaning, archetypal astrology provides a way of understanding what particular archetypes are prominent in an individual's life and personality. The moment of birth is held to be especially significant. The patterns and themes of a person's life, manifest in enduring traits of character and the types of experiences encountered, are understood to be symbolically portrayed in the individual's birth chart or "horoscope," showing the positions of the planets at the moment of birth, relative to the place of birth. This is the form of astrology—"natal astrology"— that is most widely known. Many astrologers offer "birth-chart readings," a consultation session in which the astrologer explores the meaning of the various planetary positions, considering variables such as the planets' placements in the "signs of the zodiac" (indicating twelve basic character types or styles of being) and "houses" (symbolizing domains of life or fields of experience), and the geometric relationships, or "aspects," formed between the planets (showing the quality of the relationship between the functions or principles associated with each planet—whether flowing or challenging, supportive or dynamic). Considering all these factors and more, the astrologer will give an interpretation of how the astrological patterns of the moment of birth might manifest in the individual's personality and biographical experiences.

Similarly, astrology can also be applied to collective human experience. Patterns evident in the world at large, in culture and history, are symbolized by the ongoing cycles or "transits" of the planets, year by year, day by day—a method known as "world-transit analysis."[31] Plotting the transits of the planets—their ongoing movements—against a birth chart, one can also consider how changing collective archetypal patterns over time specifically impact the individual's own life—a method known as "personal transit analysis." We will return to consider each of these methods of analysis in Part Four.

In the sections to follow here and in Volume II, I will show how, by employing these methods, archetypal astrology can inform our awareness of the place of archetypes in human experience, and help us to understand the underlying dynamics of our life and personality. To anticipate what will be demonstrated more fully in the chapters to come, I believe that using astrology can help us to recognize the plurality of universal powers and principles within the psyche and thus to come into a more conscious relationship with them. It cannot tell us how to live, or provide a pathway to success and happiness, but it can help to inform our decisions and give some existential orientation to help us become more conscious of how life energy is moving through us. Astrology provides an external frame of reference against which we can map changes in our experience, giving us a larger sense of the timing of major phases and processes in life. Above all, it reveals the workings of a cosmological-archetypal framework that can provide sustaining meaning and orientation for human experience. Such orientation can enhance the depth and mode of one's participation with life at any time but it is particularly valuable during critical phases of the process of individuation when the individual's mode of psychological functioning and way of being in the world undergo a profound transformation.

Notes

[1] Jung, *Psychological Reflections*, 322.

[2] Hillman, *Soul's Code*, 3–40.

[3] Jonas, *Gnostic Religion*, 43–44.

[4] Jung, *Mysterium Coniunctionis*, 230, par. 308.

[5] Solomon and Higgins, *A Short History of Philosophy*, 124.

[6] Jung, *Archetypes and the Collective Unconscious*, 25, par. 53.

[7] The term *psychology* was first used in the late fifteenth century, at the beginning of the modern era. Until the emergence of Wilhelm Wundt's experimental psychology in 1879, psychology was considered a branch of philosophy. Depth psychology, also known as the psychology of the unconscious, emerged as a uniquely modern and Western phenomenon— even if, in the case of Jung's approach especially, parallels can be drawn with certain Eastern religions (see J. J. Clarke, *Jung and Eastern Thought*), Gnosticism (chiefly from the Middle East), and shamanism. The term *psyche* is used in depth psychology to describe the totality of all psychological processes: thought, feeling, sensations, inspiration, fear, desire, transformation, the imagination, spiritual experience, actions, compulsions, pathology, and so on.

The psyche is considered to be distinct from the external world—that is, it is in some sense separate from it, but interacting with it. The psyche possesses its own substantive reality; it is not just a spurious epiphenomenon of the brain, and it is therefore worthy of study in its own right. Indeed it is the medium and precondition of all human experience. It is assumed that the psyche is inextricably connected to biology, although the nature of the psyche-body relationship and the psyche-matter relationship is not settled or clear.

The term *unconscious* has its origins in Friedrich Schelling in Germany and in the Romantic poet Samuel Coleridge in Britain, and refers to those aspects of psychological experience outside of the field of conscious awareness. Depth psychology includes Freudian psychoanalysis and Jungian analytical psychology, and the work of other pioneers such as Pierre Janet, Alfred Adler, Otto Rank, and later Wilhelm Reich. It comes from the German term *Tiefenpsychologie* (coined by Eugen Bleuler). In German, the meaning of *tiefen* is the depths, deep, or low. Depth psychology also has its origins in the philosophy of the unconscious, in the work of C. G. Carus, Eduard von Hartmann, and others.

The critical axiom of depth psychology, and its key contribution to the modern worldview, is that insight that human psychological life is at least partly unconscious, in that there are aspects of the human psyche not under the control of the rational will or even known to us. Our lives are significantly impacted by seemingly irrational motives, feelings, and drives. These can be the cause of unhappiness and perhaps illness, but might also be the source of deeper life meaning and a way to connect to the numinous, to spirit and to soul. From this assumption, depth psychologists of different persuasions employ various methods and therapeutic modalities to bring the unconscious into the field of conscious awareness in order to alleviate suffering, increase self-knowledge, find religious meaning, and to undergo transformation.

Reflecting its origins in healing and medicine, depth psychology retains an emphasis, perhaps even a primary focus, on the alleviation of human suffering, by the curing of a neurosis or a psychosis or restoring meaning to life and contributing to human development—growing, maturing, transforming. It helps individuals to squarely face reality, both that of the external world and the inner world of the unconscious, thereby overcoming delusion and instinctually driven unconsciousness. In some sense, it helps people to become freer by overcoming the negative conditioning of the past, such as problematic experiences as a child in one's upbringing, or early traumas. It aims to facilitate the undoing of repressions and the overcoming of psychological resistances and compulsions.

Today, depth psychology exists as a field in its own right, distinct from academic psychology. In many respects, it has more natural affiliations with the arts, religion, comparative mythology, and alternate approaches to healing than it does with mainstream academic and clinical psychology. Academic psychology has tended to restrict its attention to the study of consciousness, cognitive functioning such as memory or language (as in the work of Chomsky), human development (as in the work of Erikson on the stages of life), moral development (Kohlberg), child development (Piaget), social relationships, and neuroscience. The unconscious does not usually fall within the field of concern of psychology in academia.

[8] Jung, *Archetypes and the Collective Unconscious* (CW9i,) 23, par. 50.

[9] See Friedrich Nietzsche, *The Gay Science: With a Prelude in Rhymes and Appendix of Songs* (1887), trans. Walter Kaufmann (New York: Random House, 1974), 181; and Friedrich Nietzsche, *Thus Spoke Zarathustra* (1885), trans. Reginald J. Hollingdale (London: Penguin, 1969), 41.

[10] C. G. Jung, "Commentary on 'The Secret of the Golden Flower'" (1929), in *Alchemical Studies* (CW 13), 37, par. 54.

[11] Jung, "Commentary on 'The Secret of the Golden Flower'," 37, par. 54.

[12] Jung, "Archetypes of the Collective Unconscious," in *Archetypes and the Collective Unconscious* (CW9i), 23, par. 50.

[13] Jung, "The Concept of the Collective Unconscious," in *Archetypes and the Collective Unconscious* (CW 9i), 44, par. 92.

[14] See Jung, "The Concept of the Collective Unconscious," in *Archetypes and the Collective Unconscious* (CW 9i), 42–43, par. 89.

[15] Jung, "The Concept of the Collective Unconscious," in *Archetypes and the Collective Unconscious* (CW 9i), 48, par. 99.

[16] Jaffé, *Myth of Meaning in the Psychology of C. G. Jung,* 21.

[17] Throughout the *Collected Works*, but especially in *The Archetypes and the Collective Unconscious* (CW 9i), Jung presents a number of arguments for the existence of archetypes by which he sought to make his theory more acceptable within the scientific ethos of his time, with its demands for empirical evidence rather than philosophical speculation or religious belief.

1. Jung situates the notion of archetypes in the history of ideas. For Jung, the archetype is an "explanatory paraphrase of the Platonic Eidos" (CW 9i, 4). Jung's notion of archetypes was not his invention, but part of a long lineage of philosophies that has recognized similar principles. As Jung was at pains to stress, what was unique about his formulation of his theory is that it was not a philosophical postulate but the result of the empirical observation of the phenomena of the psyche, as presented in dreams, pathology, myth, fantasies, and so forth.

2. Jung takes the position that archetypes are closely connected to instincts, and might be construed as "patterns of instinctual behaviour" (CW 9i, 44) comparable to patterns of behavior in animals (CW 9i, 78). If we accept the existence of instincts, his argument goes, it is only a small step to accept the existence of archetypes. He also draws an analogy with the

body: Archetypes, he suggests, comprise an anatomy of the psyche, akin to the anatomy of the body.

3. Regarding the existence of archetypes, he claims that the "authochthonous revival of mythological motifs" in individual experience puts "the matter beyond any reasonable doubt" (CW 9i, 44). He is referring here to the presence of universal motifs in dreams. There are two aspects to this argument: (a) the function of universal motifs in dreams and fantasies is comparable to historical sources (CW 9i, 49–50); (b) we cannot account for the occurrence of motifs, previously unknown to the dreamer, without positing archetypes. See, for example, Jung's discussion of the solar phallus fantasy (CW 9i, 50–53).

4. Jung believes that archetypes account for collective neuroses or psychoses affecting many individuals at the same time (CW 9i, 47, par. 98). Jung's primary example is Nazism and the collective possession state that impacted millions of people in the 1930s and 1940s. If a possession takes place within just one individual, this might be accounted for by personal psychology. But an entire nation—that would require an understanding of the archetypal basis of a collective psychology, common to us all.

5. Jung cites parallels between dreams, fantasies, myths, religious symbolism, and schizophrenic delusions. Because of numerous examples of the same motifs in myth, religion, and literature, such as that of the "divine syzigies," he argues, "we can safely assert that these . . . are universal" (CW 9i, 59) and thus infer the existence of archetypes. Jung adds to this the argument that religious ideas do not lose their power even when ignored by consciousness. For example, the conflict between good and evil continues to exert a compelling attraction on modern people.

6. Archetypes, Jung claims, are responsible for the similarity of human experience, its coherence across cultures, in different time periods. They are responsible for the universal elements of what it is to be human. They are to be imagined as species-specific forms (CW 9i, 78).

7. The existence of archetypal images in childhood dreams proves, Jung argues, that archetypes pre-date consciousness and cannot therefore be creations of consciousness (CW 9i, 66). Here he is trying to prove that archetypes are a priori factors in the psyche, present from birth, or perhaps before.

[18] Jung, "On the Nature of the Psyche," in *Structure and Dynamics of the Psyche* (CW8), 212, par. 416.

[19] Throughout the course of his life, no doubt in an attempt to make his theory more comprehensible to a wide range of readers of various sensibilities and theoretical orientations, Jung proffered many different descriptions of archetypes. I have included in this survey a selection of the most salient.

[20] Jung, "The Relations between the Ego and the Unconscious," in *Two Essays on Analytical* Psychology (CW7), 209, par. 336; and Jung, "Wotan," in *Civilization in Transition* (CW10), 189, par. 395: "Archetypes are like riverbeds which dry up when the water deserts them . . ."

[21] Jung, "Archetypes of the Collective Unconscious," in *Two Essays on Analytical Psychology* (CW7), 95, par. 151.

[22] Jung, *Archetypes and the Collective Unconscious* (CW9i), 8, par. 11.

[23] Jung, *Answer to Job* (Cleveland, OH: Merdian, 1970), 18: "They [archetypes] are spontaneous phenomena which are not subject to our will, and we are therefore justified in ascribing to them a certain autonomy. They are to be regarded not only as objects but as subjects with laws of their own. . . . [W]e have to admit that they possess . . . a kind of consciousness and free will."

[24] Hillman, *Re-Visioning Psychology* (New York: HarperPerennial, 1975), xix.

[25] Jung, *Answer to Job*, 201.

[26] Jung, *Letters II*, 490, and "Synchronicity: An Acausal Connecting Principle," in *Structure and Dynamics of the Psyche* (CW8), 440, par. 847.

[27] See Hillman, *Re-Visioning Psychology*, 41.

[28] Drawing together depth psychology, Greek philosophy, evolutionary cosmology, new-paradigm science, cultural studies, transpersonal psychology, comparative mythology, and religious studies, archetypal cosmology is a culmination, in a sense, of the entire history of the engagement with and study of archetypes across these different fields. In archetypal astrology, psyche and cosmos, inner and outer, are seen as fundamentally related, as different aspects of one and the same reality, informed by a single pattern of self-organization that manifests both as the planetary order in the solar system and the archetypal order in the psyche.

[29] My own understanding of astrology was shaped especially by the writings of Dane Rudhyar and Stephen Arroyo—among the foremost psychologically and spiritually oriented astrologers. My early studies also included the work of Liz Greene, Grant Lewi, Margaret Hone, Isabel Hickey, Llewellyn George, A. T. Mann, Donna Cunningham, Tracey Marks, Bill Herbst, Alexander Ruperti, and others.

[30] Jung, "Richard Wilhelm: In Memoriam," in *The Spirit in Man, Art, and Literature* (CW 15), 56, par. 81.

[31] The term *world transit* was coined by Stanislav Grof. For a definition, see Tarnas, *Cosmos and Psyche*, 102.

PART TWO

The Way of Individuation

Chapter 3

Metaphors of the Way

If we conceive of life as a way, a path, or a journey, we should keep in mind that we are invoking a metaphor that opens to the imagination a certain mode of experiencing, one that shapes how we engage with the world and understand ourselves. Obviously, life defies any of our attempts to define it in singular terms, and is not therefore only to be imagined as a way or a journey. We might equally well describe life using other metaphors—a play, an opera, a story, a school, a prison, a battle, a race, a dream, an illusion, and so on—as many people have.

Yet there is something especially significant in the metaphor of the way, for it has been fundamental to the conceptualizing and envisaging of life throughout history. We need only remind ourselves of the Buddha's formulation of the "middle way" and the "eightfold path" as the means to enlightenment, and Buddhism itself as a "vehicle" that might deliver us to the "yonder shore." Or we might call to mind the Chinese principle of the Tao, often translated as "way." Likewise, in classical Indian philosophy the term *mārga* connotes a way of spiritual realization and metamorphosis, taking several forms, including paths of devotion, duty, knowledge, and contemplation. The motif of a way is prominent in the Mesopotamian Epic of Gilgamesh, dating from around 2100 BCE and perhaps the oldest myth recorded in literary form, which sees its protagonist undertake an epic journey on the quest for eternal life. Homer's *Odyssey*, similarly, presents the adventures of its hero Odysseus as an arduous journey on a quest to return home to Ithaca after years of wandering and captivity, one that has been interpreted as a metaphor for a path of psychospiritual realization. And Dante's *Divine Comedy*, the primary literary expression of the medieval Christian imagination, sees Dante on a spiritual voyage into Hell and through Purgatory on the long ascent to Heaven. Joseph Campbell's classic study *The Hero with a Thousand Faces* is testimony to the ubiquity of the motif of the journey across human culture.

The motif of the way in the form of a pilgrimage is especially relevant to the mystical path, which was brilliantly detailed by Evelyn Underhill in her classic study *Mysticism*, published in 1911. "Under this image of a pilgrimage," she explains,

> the mystics contrived to summarize and suggest much of the life history of the ascending soul; the developing spiritual consciousness. The necessary freedom and detachment of the traveller, his departure from his normal life and interests, the difficulties, enemies, and hardships encountered on the road—the length of the journey, the variety of the country, the dark night which overtakes him, the glimpses of destination far away—all these are seen more and more as we advance in knowledge to constitute a transparent allegory of the incidents of man's progress from the unreal to the real.[1]

"Through all these metaphors of pilgrimage to a goal," she adds, ". . . there runs the definite idea that the travelling self in undertaking the journey is fulfilling a destiny, a law of the transcendental life."[2]

Similar metaphors are applied at a different level to describe the individualism of the modern self. The aspiration to find and forge one's own way through life—to undertake one's own unique life journey—has become increasingly prevalent in the modern world; indeed, in Campbell's view this is a defining characteristic of what he calls the era of individual "creative mythology."[3] With the decline and disintegration of the established religious traditions, for many people spiritual experience has become an entirely individual matter. The popular identification of being "spiritual but not religious" well exemplifies this shift.[4] Whereas the patterns of cultural life, the understandings of the purposes of existence, and the parameters of religious belief were once defined by the dominant cultural myth or religion, today all things are open for question, all options on the table when it comes to how we might live and structure our experience. Spiritual life in modern society is characterized, as Charles Taylor has noted, by the recognition that we are at liberty to choose our own path and find our own purpose—an implicit understanding that has now pervaded the wider culture.[5] Although many of us now take this freedom for granted, the individual choice of spiritual belief and life orientation is a remarkably recent development, only present on a wide scale in the late-modern era.

The motif of the journey, as a model for an individual way of life, is therefore especially resonant with our experience today, indeed perhaps more than ever before, as evident for instance in the broad appeal of mythic books and films structured around this theme, with Tolkien's *The Lord of the Rings* chief among them. Numerous spiritually oriented or "self-help" publications present different possibilities for our choice of life path—the ways of the mystic, shaman, warrior, and artist, for instance, have each formed the subject of popular studies, addressing the pressing need for a source of life guidance and wisdom to help us live creative, spiritually meaningful lives in the modern world. Throughout modern culture, the idea of a "way," as both journey and a manner of living, is now almost ubiquitous; it is the topic of many popular songs old and new, as in Frank Sinatra's classic "My Way," implying a life lived to the fullest on one's own terms, as one chooses and sees fit—a sentiment that has become something of the guiding ideal of the modern self. "There's only one way of life . . . and that's your own," proclaimed English band the Levellers in an indie anthem of the early 1990s, giving voice to the spirit of their own and other generations of youth.[6]

As these few examples imply, the idea of the way is to be understood as a journey or path, but as something more besides: it is also a way of being, a way of seeing, a perspective, an approach to life, a means to achieving something. When we say something has become a way of life for us, we are describing our mode of being in the world, the characteristic form of how we live, how we habitually meet experience.

A way might also often suggest a vocation or calling, something important we have to do in life. The journey undertaken, the work performed, is a means to achieve or realize a task or an aim, consciously chosen or thrust upon us from without. Assuming such a mission often involves going out into the world from our starting point, venturing forth to a destination unknown, and then returning, when we feel we have fully discharged our task. Yet in other cases the journey might not be a literal one, enacted in the world, but a metaphorical one, an inward transformation and shift of perspective within external circumstances that change little. In either case, however, the movement from one point to the other in the fulfillment of this vocation might be imagined as a way.

In a religious sense, a way is also a gateway, a portal to deeper insight or perhaps spiritual revelation, as we read in the words of the Jesus of John's Gospel (John 14:6): "I am the way, the truth, and the life: no man cometh unto the Father, but by me." And crucially, as we see in many of the above examples, a way implies a transformation from one condition to another, taking place over time. This is particularly evident in mystical paths, of course, or myths of transfiguration and rebirth.

In formulating his model of individuation, Jung was advancing another way, possessing affinities with many of the meanings explored above, and one especially suited, he felt, to the psychological needs of the modern individual. To reject or ignore the call to individuate—the imperative to come to terms with the unconscious dimension of the psyche and become the person we truly are—is to fall into inauthenticity and perhaps even into spiritual death; embracing the challenge of individuation might promote a sense of deep life meaning and fulfillment even in the midst of suffering. Reckoning with the archetypes, recognizing them and adapting to their influence on our lives, is a fundamental element of this process.

Notes

[1] Underhill, *Mysticism*, 129–130.

[2] Underhill, *Mysticism*, 132.

[3] See Campbell's discussion of this topic in the fourth volume of *The Masks of God* series.

[4] See Pew Research Center data for information on the increase in numbers of people identifying as spiritual but not religious. For instance: Michael Lipka and Claire Gecewicz, "More Americans Now Say They're Spiritual but Not Religious," accessed April 16, 2021, https://www.pewresearch.org/fact-tank/2017/09/06/more-americans-now-say-theyre-spiritual-but-not-religious.

[5] See Charles Taylor, *A Secular Age*.

[6] The Levellers, "One Way," on *Levelling the Land* (China Records, 1991).

Chapter 4

Archetypes and the Individuation Process

It is a troubling paradox of human existence that we have the tendency to live in a manner that is not in accord with our own nature and we might therefore to fail to bring to realization who or what we really are. Self-loss, "loss of soul," estrangement from our emotions and instincts, and falling into inauthentic ways of being, are, for modern human beings, not only possibilities but probabilities. To be oneself seems like it should be the simplest thing in the world, but in reality, as we all know, it is an extraordinarily difficult undertaking.

Indeed, what we usually take to be our self is only the partial personality we are conscious of—partial because, as Jung discerned, the conscious personality, centered on the ego, is only one aspect of the greater person that we also are. The conscious ego is itself cloaked by an outer persona, an image of the person we would like to be or believe ourselves to be. We can easily take our self-image as our primary reality, and expend much energy trying to actualize the image, to build a life that confirms the fantasy.

We tend to identify with what society and we ourselves consider desirable qualities, unconsciously eschewing those traits of character and aspects of our experience that show us in a less favorable light or that transgress established moral boundaries. Our persona, we can imagine, might show us to be nothing other than the happy possessors of a generous and compassionate nature, exuding an air of confidence and success, with a quick wit and ready smile, perhaps with some concession to certain socially permissible foibles and weaknesses. All other aspects of our personality and life experience incongruent with this ideal image, with the persona, can be unconsciously excluded from awareness such that they do not form part of the conscious identity. Invariably, exclusions include not only darker human emotions and experiences—rage and misery, despair and depression, defeat and death, selfishness and greed, cruelty and evil, and such like—but also a reservoir of vital life energy, unrecognized potentials, and a source of meaning buried within the darkness. What manifests as a troublesome neurotic symptom, for instance, could be the very source of energy we can draw on in undertaking some great destiny or mission that is essential to our life purpose. For our deepest nature can remain veiled, hidden behind the mask we show to others and to the world, and hidden even to us, for in the adult personality it initially falls outside of the limits of our ordinary awareness, and must be searched for, uncovered, and actualized.

Jungian psychology takes issue with the prevalent modern assumption that we are able to create or re-invent ourselves as we wish, making ourselves into the person we want to become. In an age of social media and virtual identities, we can all too easily adopt or create a persona, it is true, furnishing ourselves with the adornments of one imagined role or another, as the occasion demands. Indeed, this capacity is to some degree intrinsic to competent social functioning. But Jungian psychology rejects the notion that true identity is something individually constructed or created by acts of will and imagination, rejecting too the idea that the human being is a blank slate upon which experiences are imprinted. For Jung, our deepest intelligible character—the Self, in Jungian terms—is an "*a priori* existent out of which the ego evolves"[1]; in other words, it has always been there, it is given to us from the first, but it has to be discovered and realized over the course of life. To live a life only in terms of our familiar conscious identity with its cultivated persona is to exist within a structure that is invariably too limited for the essence of what we are and the fullness of our being to be realized. Individuation describes the process by which one moves beyond a life centered on this narrow self, or ego, to a life centered on the recognition and realization of an incomparably deeper dimension of identity and selfhood.

A commitment to individuation is therefore the antidote, proposed by Jung, to the modern sense of alienation and loss of self, for it the process by which one consciously discovers and realizes one's deepest nature beyond that of the personal ego.

Self-knowledge

The quest for self-knowledge is a critical component of individuation. To know ourselves, in the fullest sense, is to come to an understanding of the purpose of our existence. It is to arrive at a realization of what it is that life intends for us. How am I to make sense of the peculiarities and complexities of my life and character? How might I discover an authentic vocation or unique calling? How I am to understand the seeming vagaries of fate that cross my path or the major crises and transitions I will inevitably pass through in life?

We all tend to think we know ourselves fairly well. How could we not? As the years go by, we become all too acquainted with the person we are, our strengths and sensitivities, our quirks and qualities. The face in the mirror is a familiar friend, perhaps a familiar foe. Yet the very notion of the existence of the unconscious implies aspects of our experience and character that we are unaware of, that lie unsuspected in the recesses of our psyche, perhaps only to surface at rare moments, like a breaching whale surging out of the ocean depths—a prominent symbol for the activated power of the unconscious.

For some of us, at critical moments in life the waters of the unconscious can become violently stirred, as the field of conscious awareness becomes filled with strange, alluring fantasies and pervaded by longings and drives that seem to have a life of their own, threatening to overwhelm us, and jeopardizing the integrity of the personality. The whale could swallow us whole, as it might a small vessel adrift on the ocean. Then we have no choice but to try to understand the powerful forces rising within us, to investigate our hidden motivations, and to engage with our fantasies in order to get to the root of the disturbance and turbulence. Plunging into our psychological depths, we might in time realize that we are not the sole commander of the ship steering our course through life, as we had probably assumed up to that point, but one of a crew of different personalities not necessarily all pulling in the same direction. We might recognize too that our mission, our voyage through life, is ascribed to us from another, deeper source—some admiral of the fleet who might chart a course quite at variance with the one we had intended for ourselves, for our imagination for life's possibilities is significantly shaped by cultural conditioning as much as it springs from our authentic inner nature.

Individuation is the process of coming to terms with these unsuspected depths and discerning the cast of characters—the complexes and sub-personalities—present within us. As we become accustomed to the landscape of the psyche, self-knowledge takes on an expanded meaning. We come to discover and embrace our greatest potentialities, those we might have dismissed as unrealistic or unreachable, or disregarded as mere fantasy. We come to learn also of our hidden motives, those we had not dared to face or allowed ourselves to experience. We are led to self-knowledge of our greatest good but also our capacity for evil, as we turn to face the dark side of the psyche. We are compelled to recognize the limits of human willpower and rationality, as we see for ourselves the seeming autonomy of the different voices and motivations within us. And we become able to distinguish the all-too-human person that we are from the universal human, the "great man," or "God-image" within us.

The Realization of the Self

The Self is the term by which Jung refers to this greater human being, the "immortal one," as he described it, which might be distinguished from the ego, the agent of intentional consciousness and decision making, and the basis of our sense of personal identity.[2] The ego is the sense of personhood we reference when we say "I." It describes the sense of ourselves as an independent person with a relatively consistent identity that comes into existence as we develop from infancy to adulthood; it is the self in common parlance.

By contrast, the idea of the Self (often written by Jungian authors with a capital "S"—a convention I am following here) describes an incomparably deeper experience of identity, which in the final analysis is indistinguishable from an experience of the divine. Like the traditional Christian recognition of God's will, the Self represents a greater authority within the psyche, a ruling principle beyond personal willpower and the rational determinations of the ego.

The Self is at once our own innermost deeper being and yet, paradoxically, wholly other, existing outside of our scope of awareness, far removed from our usual sense of identity. Both uniquely individual and universal, the Self is eternal, outside of time, and yet also unitemporal, manifest in a particular moment of history, a never-to-be repeated incarnation in a specific context.

The ego is the reflective function of the Self, in that it is the carrier of the reflective consciousness that allows the Self to become known, to be made actual in a particular historical context, through a particular person. We might say, to put this in more concrete terms, that the ego is to the Self as Jesus is to Christ or Prince Gautama is to the Buddha: Jesus, the personal-historical man, becomes a vehicle for the realization of God as Christ; Siddhartha Gautama, leaving behind his princely existence in the quest for enlightenment and liberation from suffering, realizes his Buddha nature, which becomes manifest through him. Obviously, Jesus, the man, and Christ, the god-man, are not identical, just as we might recognize a distinction between realized Buddha nature and the person Siddhartha. In the New Testament, the difference between ego and Self, between the human person and the universal god-man, is implied in passages in which Jesus draws a distinction between his own will and the transpersonal power of God working through him: "the words that I speak unto you I speak not of myself: but the Father that dwelleth in me, he doeth the works." (John 14:10). We also see the human side of Jesus, his personal ego, in certain places of the Gospel accounts, perhaps especially in his moments of final despair on the cross: "Eli, Eli, why hast thou forsaken me?" (Psalm 22:1)[3] Christ, the Son, as one aspect of the Holy Trinity, represents the incarnate dimension of God, and, like the Buddha, might be considered one particular symbol of the archetype of the Self as the Great Man or the Cosmic Anthropos—the primordial human of Gnosticism.

In the direct experience of the Self, which as far as we know is quite a rare happening, the ordinary human personality can be utterly dwarfed by the presence of the divine, as in the story of Job's encounter with Yahweh in the Old Testament. Its appearance in one's life can often trigger a crisis, a "defeat for the ego," as Jung put it, as one realizes, painfully, the limitations of conventional religious morality and the relative impotence of rational willpower to control oneself and one's life.[4] In time, with good will and no little grace, in a progressive, discerning act of surrender, one might gradually reorient one's consciousness to the Self, recognized as the real power behind the throne of the ego.[5] Or, instead, temporarily identifying with the Self, one can have the sense of titanic empowerment and uplift, as the ordinary human personality is swollen by the influx of numinous energy—one thinks here of Nietzsche's *Übermensch*. Both possibilities, it should be noted, are often alternately or even simultaneously present.

In distinction from its common usage, then, for Jung the Self refers to an experience of deep identity that subsumes and transcends the conscious personality. Although we can remain utterly unconscious of its existence, or aware of it only in rare glimpses, the Self is there all along in the background, as both the origin and goal of our life: As origin, it exists in potential as the greater personality we might become; as goal, this potential is to be realized in the acts of life, as the ego brings the Self to consciousness during the course of individuation.[6] The Self sets the course of life but the ego is responsible for steering the ship, as it were, for actualizing the biddings of the Self in the world. The possibility of choosing a course contrary to one's deeper nature is an ever-present danger, for the lines of communication with the Self are often broken, if they are open at all, or its messages ignored or susceptible to misinterpretation, as the mind is preoccupied with other interests, heeding other voices, lost in the pleasures and problems of life. Invariably, the ego is powerfully conditioned by the environment, as we assimilate a worldview that is not of our own choosing. The ego also tends to live and act primarily out of self-interest (even if this takes the form of altruism—self-interest need not be selfish), shaped by the desire to increase pleasure and minimize pain. To win freedom from the trappings of a false worldview, and to outgrow the defensive conditioning and fearful posture of the ego, is a struggle that might occupy us for a lifetime, if not more. Both these challenges are intrinsic to individuation.

Individuation, then, is a process leading towards the realization of the Self as the emerging principle of psychological order, such that the existential center of gravity within the psyche shifts progressively away from the ego and its associated sense of conscious control of life towards this new center. It is an extraordinarily difficult process to navigate for one's very sense of identity and mode of psychological functioning undergo a radical transformation. It has been described, without overstatement, as a veritable death and a rebirth, demanding of us an heroic journey into the "underworld" of the unconscious realm of the psyche. One cannot simply "let go" and wait for the transformation to happen, for the ego, the I principle, is embroiled in every thought, every impulse, and consciousness has to be wrenched free from its binding identity with this old personality structure and torn free, too, from its domination by instinct.

Although individuation is a natural process of growth and unfolding, in that it is not willed but occurs of its own accord, it demands our full conscious participation. Without this it cannot really proceed beyond a certain point. We are invited, or in some cases obligated, to partake in the reconstitution of the structure of our personality in order that the greater person, the Self, might be born and realized within us. We cannot remain detached observers in this process but are pulled into the maelstrom of transformation. As the old persona dissolves, and the former ego identity passes away, psychological stability is jeopardized, and all perspective, perhaps all control, might be lost. It is therefore of inestimable value during this process to have some kind of external frame of reference that could help to illuminate the experiences we pass through, enabling us to recognize the individuation process for what it is, and identify different aspects of the unconscious as they break to the surface of conscious awareness.

Plurality and Unity

The Self might typically make itself known to us as a "call" to pursue a particular vocation or life path, or as the pull of destiny, or the voice of our innermost conscience or the experience of a higher, fuller reality and perspective, far beyond our usual subjective vantage point. To heed the call, we have to be able to distinguish this voice, this aspect of our psychology, from all others. We must consciously come to terms with all the different archetypal impulses, to differentiate one from the other. This is a labor that requires the sustained investigation of the motives and emotions behind our desires and drives, fears and resistances. It is a task that takes on critical importance if one finds oneself in some kind of crisis of transformation, such that one is pulled into the depths of the unconscious.

In the normal course of things, we can without difficulty recognize a form of psychological plurality within us, in our changing states of consciousness, day to day, hour to hour, even if we usually tend to see these changes in terms of our own shifting thoughts and feelings rather than as arising from archetypes. Yet ascribing such changing patterns of experience to archetypes is a recognition of their autonomy, the fact that they come over us of their own accord, sometimes even in spite of our conscious intentions, as, for example, in the mood that engulfs us that cannot be overcome, or the persistent nagging thought or fear that we cannot repel or reason away. These thoughts and feelings, impulses and images, tend to cluster into "complexes" of emotions, fantasies, and drives, activated in response to particular environmental triggers, and are often linked to biographical experiences and repressed memories of painful episodes or deep impressions from our past. Such complexes, Jung found, center upon archetypal motifs, and present themselves, if we can learn to recognize them, as relatively distinct sub-personalities. Jungian psychology provides an archetypal vocabulary to name these different aspects of our experience, which can help us to recognize these archetypal patterns as and when they arise.

For example, when the hero archetype is constellated in our experience we might feel capable of taking on the world, believing that nothing can defeat us, that no challenge is too great. From within that heroic perspective it seems inconceivable that we could ever fail in our aims, or that we could ever feel the need to seek refuge from life, choosing to withdraw into solitude and quiet contemplation or settling for the life we have. Even death to the hero is a glorious if tragic victory, to be embraced as the meeting of one's fate. Yet when instead the child archetype is prominent, we often feel vulnerable and exposed, or gentle and innocent, absorbed in play and reverie rather than grappling with the world or sacrificing ourselves to some high ideal or great calling. From within the emotional world of the child, which remains alive within us all, an heroic life of struggle is the last thing we would choose to undertake. Worldly achievements and grand missions lose their allure, and might seem empty and futile, as we seek to draw close to our soulful essence and indulge our nostalgic longing for the simple experience of childhood and times past, safe within the home and family life.

At other times still, if the mother archetype is activated, we might find ourselves willing to extend our compassion and care to the world, to draw close to our breast and into our field of concern all those in need, with no thought of our own wellbeing or other life purposes and aims. How different the world looks through the eyes of the mythic Great Mother than it does, say, from the perspective of the archetypal rebel, driven by the compulsion to throw off all restraint, hit the road and taste the freedom of the open air, lured by the promise of distant lands and exciting adventures. And how different it looks too when seen from within the complex of behaviors, feelings, and urges we might group together under the Dionysus archetype, named after the Greek god of the vine: the urge to annihilate ourselves in the intoxicating rush of passion, the desire to feel the wild energy of life coursing through our veins, the blissful extinction of all sense of individual existence through orgiastic merger with a larger whole.

It is easy enough, with the benefit of perspective, to recognize in these descriptions certain familiar aspects of traits and patterns of our character, which form part of the totality of our experience. However, caught in the midst of these different emotional states, this pluralistic vision and awareness of a larger psychological reality can be lost, and we tend then to see the world in absolute terms, through the filtered lens of a single vision. When particular archetypes are powerfully constellated, then decisions made, actions taken, tend not to reflect the totality of who and what we are—the child archetype chooses one course of action based on its own reality, failing to consider the needs of the other sub-personalities; or the hero, conversely, is often impervious to the needs of the child and the soul. Each archetype knows only itself, and claims us for itself. In certain circumstances, an archetype will readily assume authoritarian control of one's personality and one's life, as if it were the only actor on the stage.

From a Jungian perspective, then, a primary component of the depth psychological aspiration to make the unconscious conscious is the recognition of archetypes as the underlying basis of our desires and emotions. Becoming conscious of archetypes implies, first, becoming familiar with their forms of expression and styles of manifestation. We might then, second, be able to recognize when archetypes become activated, "catching" our tendency to unconsciously identify with them. For each archetype, when activated, takes over the sense of "I," passing off its thoughts, feelings, and drives as if they were our own.

Indeed, we ordinarily construe the urges and emotions we experience—to rebel, to be heroic, to mother, and so forth—in this personal manner. It is *our* urge to throw off restraint and restriction or *our* will to undertake a great act of sacrifice or *our* desire to take care of others. That is to say, we *identify* with these feelings and urges as if they originate entirely from our personal psychology. As we have seen, however, Jung's experience in his own life and in working with his patients led him to the conclusion that we should construe the various archetypes—child, trickster, shadow, hero, and so forth—not merely as aspects of our own identity or personal psychology but as autonomous principles, influencing us from the collective unconscious, which is common to us all. This autonomy becomes readily apparent in cases of psychopathology, such as psychosis and schizophrenia, and in the more acute experiences of deep transformation one might encounter during individuation.

During individuation, especially in the critical phase of transformation that Jung called the "confrontation with the unconscious," the rational ego is displaced from its position of authority within the psyche, either gradually or suddenly and dramatically.[7] The captain loses control of the ship, so to speak, and the crew members, perhaps disgruntled from having their opinions ignored and voices silenced for many years, might run amok. Without the ego captain at the helm, control of the personality becomes difficult, if not impossible, to maintain. Mechanisms of suppression, repression, and censorship are impaired or fail entirely, or can be driven to an extreme, in alternating fashion. Then, the multitude of impulses and changing states of consciousness, formerly experienced as relatively harmless or enjoyable aspects of our personality, lending richness to our experience, can become tyrannical rogue forces detached from our conscious personality and disconnected from the larger unity of the psyche. Cut loose, no longer constrained by repression or controlled by a stable ego, archetypes can take on a devilish autonomy and demonic zeal, with utter disregard for aspects of experience falling outside of their view and emotional range.

Even in more stable psychological conditions, identification with an archetype can be problematic, depriving us of our psychological freedom and compromising the integrity of the personality. Identification with an archetype can be a form of escape from the painful challenge of being a true individual, of living authentically. Every archetype comes replete with a complex of recognizable feeling states and behaviors. Some archetypes also have an accompanying persona, a "look," a set of attitudes and postures with which one aligns oneself. If one unconsciously identifies exclusively with the rebel, for instance, one always responds in a way befitting the archetype—every decision is made, every action determined by the modes and styles of that particular pattern that play out unconsciously, living themselves out through us without our realizing. Certain aspects of the archetypal rebel might well be authentic to our own character. The danger, however, is that we can give ourselves away entirely to the archetype. The capacity for an authentic response, requiring conscious reflection, emotional integrity, and taking the creative risk of being oneself is inhibited and stifled by the archetypal pattern, which runs automatically and compulsively. Happiness, under the influence of the archetype, then depends solely on the extent to which we can conform to and give expression to this pattern, gratifying the instinctual dynamism at its core—a happiness that soon becomes hollow. Unwittingly, we find ourselves under the control of the archetype, moved like a pawn on a chessboard by an unseen hand.

Archetypes can pull us into their own schedules for fulfillment, constructing a world in their image. Under the influence of an archetype, we do not see the world as it really is, but through the lens of the particular archetypal vision. That is to say, we "project" onto the world, and onto the people and things around us, fantasies and images associated with the archetype. To the free-spirited explorer within us, the world shows itself as a vast playground, ripe for adventure. The rebel notices only restraints to be defied, barriers to be broken down, conventions to be violated. Through the lens of the child archetype, with its acute sensitivity and permeable boundaries, the world can seem like an alien land of crude crashing noises, violently penetrating our psychic field. To the person in love, the world brings forth its radiance and joy—the skies are blue, the sun shines on us, the flowers bloom, the birds sing; for that time, problematic, painful, and banal elements of reality do not register in our awareness. Through individuation, we might become aware of these projections, and thus see beyond them, recognizing that they are aspects of our own psychology, our *collective* psychology, rather than pertaining objectively to the world itself. By "withdrawing" our projections, we are able to take steps on the path of individuation, coming eventually to a more-or-less realistic view of the world, unobscured by the incarcerating spell of fantasies and illusions arising from archetypes. As a logion in the Gnostic *Gospel of Thomas* states, the challenge is to make "a hand into a hand, and a foot into a foot and . . . an image into an image"—that is to say, to see an image or fantasy for what it is, as plainly as we might see a hand or foot for what it is, to make the image conscious so that we are not blinded by it.[8]

Each archetypal pattern has its own timings too, perhaps even its own sense of time: The intoxicating emotions of the Dionysus archetype crave immediate satisfaction or the absolute annihilation of time itself, the hero strives relentlessly for the occasion of the one great victory, the child yearns to return to or already occupies the timeless world of infancy, the rebel restlessly seeks the fast-paced thrill and excitement of perpetual change and new experience for its own sake. The Self, by contrast, represents a natural pattern of the unfolding of events and experiences, a right time and season for every purpose, one might say, that includes in its proper place the excitement of change, some degree of instinctual gratification, some moments of victory after long struggle, and periods of play, withdrawal, and refuge—yet none of these take absolute precedence. And subsuming all these is a sense of the Self as eternal.

For each of us, if I might put it this way, one critical aspect of individuation is to clearly distinguish between what is from me, pertaining to my personal psychology, and what is archetypal, pertaining to collective psychology. In coming to this recognition, we might then be able to "disidentify" with the archetypes—an exacting and painful undertaking, for it demands that we relinquish attachment to many of our favorite and habitual attitudes, passions, ideas, and ways of seeing ourselves. To state simply what is a complex process, disidentifying implies that we come to realize that, much as we might like to think of ourselves as heroic and rebellious or take delight in the gratification of Dionysian urges, for example, and as much as living in terms of these patterns might seem to be central to our identity, such patterns, as archetypes, originate from beyond the conscious ego. They are not of us or from us; they are not exclusively personal factors but drives, themes, and feelings common to humanity as a whole, and in this sense they are impersonal, collective, and universal.

Disidentifying with all the archetypal powers requires nothing less than ascetic self-discipline and acute psychological vigilance. The archetypes, let us remember, are intoxicating, gripping, enchanting, and fascinating. Their enactment promises instinctual gratification. Inevitably, then, we are inclined to give ourselves away to the archetypes, to identify with them, and abandon ourselves to their impulses. Ascetic self-denial breaks the hold archetypes have over us. By cleaving to a consciously chosen rational position or spiritual ideal, we can create a point of contrast within us to the pull of the desires and fantasies. Setting up this contrast accentuates the "tension of opposites" with the psyche. On the one hand, we know our conscious position, recognizing how in our better judgment, with a sober view of our situation, faithful to our highest ideals, we would choose to think and act. On the other hand, we experience the rush of passions and fears, which grab us and compulsively stir us to action, periodically taking over consciousness. By resisting the overwhelming tendency to act on these urges, however, the fantasies and passions associated with archetypes are no longer blindly acted out and compulsively expressed but contained, held in tension within the psyche where they can be investigated and engaged in dialogue by the conscious ego.

By breaking our unconscious identification with an archetype, we might then be able to relate to it as a subject to an object. We can distinguish between our own will, our consciously chosen stance and view, and what the archetype would have us think, believe, feel, and do. This distinction makes possible the dialogue or dialectical process between the conscious ego and the unconscious, which is integral to Jung's method of furthering the individuation process. Out of the dialogue, which can be mediated by the method of fantasy that Jung called "active imagination," emerges a third position, reconciling the opposites, integrating consciousness and the instinctual power of the archetypes—integrating spirit and nature, as it were. The psyche's capacity to resolve the tensions of opposites in this way Jung called the "transcendent function."[9]

In this manner, we can cultivate ever greater discernment in the recognition of the different impulses and fantasies that compulsively move us, as the ego is progressively differentiated from the archetypes. Discerning the archetypes and instincts, distinguishing them one from another, we might then be able to better attune to the "voice" and directives of the Self.

If the archetypes are imagined as the actors, the *dramatis personae*, on the stage of the human psyche, the Self might be envisaged as the stage director and as the organizing principle of the entire ensemble of characters. The Self constitutes a center point, reflecting the organized totality of the psyche, in which, when realized, all archetypes can find proper expression in relation to the larger whole. The archetypes are not negated or denied in this process. The approach here is not to attempt a rigid control of the archetypes, which would ultimately be futile and misguided, but the aim, rather, is to live out their themes and impulses, allowing them to be expressed in consciousness. To the extent that their expression is in keeping with the purposes and parameters of the Self, the aim is to experience the full power of archetypal energies without being consumed or possessed by them—"riding the back of the Dionysian leopard without getting torn to pieces," as Joseph Campbell described the ideal of a romantic philosophy of life.[10] One needs to live out and express the hero, for example, even allowing the hero to express itself through our life decisions and responses, for that archetype stirs one to great and noble deeds that might otherwise be outside of one's reach. So too, one would wish to be uplifted by the experience of Dionysian rapture of self-overcoming and affirmation of life that it stirs within us. Such experiences in themselves are not pathological—only the unconscious identification with and possession by such archetypal patterns and powers bring danger, and it is the unconsciousness, and compulsion that goes with it, that is to be overcome during individuation.

The asceticism, then, is not a morally motivated end in itself, but a means to self-mastery and transformation, delivering us to a condition in which the archetypes are sufficiently integrated that they find expression spontaneously within the unity of one's life, and egoic control can be gradually relinquished. Rebellion and the urge for freedom remain part of the personality and the dynamic of life but not ends in themselves; they are made subservient to the greater good of the Self. Dionysian ecstasy is part of one's experience, when it naturally occurs, but wild hedonistic abandonment to pleasure or raw emotion is not made the sole aim of our existence, however enticing this might be, or permitted to manifest in a way that can pull us dangerously away from our center and consume consciousness. The compassion and care of the mother continue to be expressed but not at the expense of other, equally valid drives, such as a healthy selfishness or a playful joie de vivre. For our identity is always more than a singular archetypal pattern or role.

The way I am describing here is something other than an Aristotelian "golden mean," intentionally avoiding extremes to keep life in balance. For the psychological balancing comes not primarily from the ego, monitoring and checking these impulses (although this is necessary at times), but by focusing one's energy and attention, first and foremost, on the Self and its vocational directives. Following the Self is not a middle path of moderation; on the contrary, it can lead us to extremes (judged by conventional standards, as least) and pull us far out of our comfort zone. Moreover, the aims of the Self often defy common sense, often appearing irrational from the limited standpoint of human subjectivity, yet they reflect what might be described as a higher "transrational" order or logic. Attuning to the Self, one's individual will can be brought into dynamic harmony with the larger order of things, and one is able to realize one's proper role in life, one's rightful place within the world. Although we might be inclined to see the realization of the Self as the culmination of an exclusively individual path of development or personal realization, the Self, as Jung understands it, transcends the individual and represents a point of organic interconnection with the whole of life. "The Self," he thus proclaims, "is not only in me but in all beings, like Atman, like Tao."[11] To realize the Self through an expansion of consciousness beyond the limits of the ego brings us, Jung remarks, into "absolute, binding, and indissoluble communion with the world at large."[12]

The Self is singular and unitary but it is also complex—a complex unity. To serve the Self does not mean that we do only one thing with our life, pursue only one goal; rather, the ideal of realizing the Self reflects the fact that a particular calling or life task is often central to who we are, to what life intends for us, and that we have to continually choose to follow this calling at the expense of other perfectly valid, alluring, or more convenient options, often, in the process, even defying common sense and good judgment. Something of this kind is suggested by the New Testament parable of the wise fisherman choosing the one large fish, forsaking all the smaller fish. In aligning our personal will with the Self, the wide-ranging plurality of the psyche is brought into relationship with this central concern and life direction. If we can attune to the Self, and give expression to the calling or vocation ascribed to us by the Self, all other archetypes will gradually fall into place. Their energies, rather than manifesting in isolation and at cross purposes, function at a higher level as a unified force in service of the central thrust and purpose of life. The archetypes, we might say, become as satellites around the central star of the Self in the depths of the psyche. Of course, realizing this objective is far from straightforward, and estrangement from the Self and periods lost within the conflict and confusion, passion and pathology of the archetypes are inevitable and unavoidable. Yet, at such times, if the Self can be recollected or experienced as a center beyond the volatility of the instincts, and if one can bring to mind one's sense of calling, this can provide a bulwark against the alluring pull of the instincts and the archetypes, and against conditions of fear, suffering, and despair that accompany the death-rebirth process of individuation. Gradually, over time, a more integrated psyche can develop.

The Opposites and the Evolution of Consciousness

Especially in the modern era, the development of ego-consciousness and free will, its corollary, has enabled us to stray far from the securities of the ingrained instinctive patterns characteristic of animal life and the lives of our early human ancestors. Governed by instinct—the urge to eat, sleep, mate, fight, flee, build, and so forth—actions were sure-footed and uncomplicated, responses carried unquestioned and unconscious conviction, rarely deviating from inherited instinctual scripts. In our primordial ancestors, rational consciousness had yet to decisively emerge, or was present only as only a dim twilight sense of awareness, and life was thus largely unencumbered by the interference of conscious reflection.

The emergence of the ego-complex as the foundation of the modern sense of individual selfhood has been an incredibly complicating factor, however. Today, more than ever before, life is ostensibly directed not primarily by instinct but by reason, by considered thought—or at least that is the assumption and the aspiration. Virtually every act may be questioned, almost every moment requires decision and the contemplation of multiple possibilities, such that we are inescapably burdened with choice, condemned to the anguish of freedom, as the existentialist philosophers realized. Unsure of ourselves, not knowing who we really are, we can find ourselves conditioned from without, yielding to the pressure of circumstance, assimilating the expectations and values of those around us, perhaps even idealizing or imitating those who seem to possess the very conviction and surety we lack.

Jung believed that modern life has fostered the overdevelopment of critical reason, characterized by a "cramp of consciousness" in which the thinking rational ego has become increasingly at odds with the dynamisms of the body, alienated from the larger psyche.[13] Modern human beings have grown distant from their instincts and emotions, unable any longer to live naturally and spontaneously; man, as Nietzsche said, is the sick animal. The instincts, denied or ignored, do not merely disappear, however, but lurk unsuspected in our inner depths, and can return with magnified force, periodically erupting in destructive or debilitating ways. Repressing the natural dynamisms of the psyche, we find ourselves dangerously susceptible to patterns of unconscious possession, projection, or periodic mass eruptions of the unconscious. These outbreaks of the unconscious are most obviously evident in times of war, as Jung noted in his discussion of the re-activation of the ancient mythic figure of Wotan in Germany during World War Two.[14] Alas, such episodes are not confined to the past for, as many recent events testify, wherever and whenever the rule of law and humanitarian principles are rendered ineffective, and external regulations and suppressions are lifted or deemed invalid, barbarism rears its head.

The course of individual development mirrors our collective evolution. As we move from infancy to adulthood, the infant's inarticulate sense of wholeness, naturalness, and unity is lost. The maturing ego gains in power and autonomy, living ever more according to the promptings of rationality and personal will under the pressure of conformity to external expectations and the hard necessities of material circumstance. In varying degrees, this can result in a sense of alienation, estrangement, and inner division, as the natural state of childhood is lost. "Heaven clouds our infancy! Shades of the prison-house begin to close, Upon the growing boy"—Wordsworth captures the inevitable fall into alienation.[15] In certain circumstances, the tension between rational ego consciousness and the repressed instinctual power of the unconscious becomes acute, and the original unity of the psyche is strained to breaking point, and perhaps even ruptures. The result can be neurosis, a state of painful inner division, or in certain extreme cases even psychotic possession or the schizophrenic dissolution of the unity of the psyche into separate parts. Individuation thus requires a healing of the schism within, a reconnection to instinctual life, in an attempt to restore the long-lost wholeness.

With this in mind, we might be forgiven for concluding that the answer to this predicament lies in a reversion to a life of instinct, a return to our natural state. For, indeed, this is an attractive proposition for an alienated ego. There is legitimacy to our regressive longing for the simplicity of childhood or times past, for there is to be found a closer proximity to the unity, wholeness, and naturalness no longer available to modern consciousness. But the direction of evolution cannot be reversed, and the rational ego cannot be willed out of existence or bypassed, at least not without irreparable damage to the integrity of the personality. Moreover, we should not imagine that the emergence of ego-consciousness is an aberration, a mistake to be corrected and repealed. For it appears, rather, to be an essential development in human psychological evolution, accompanying and supporting the appearance of self-reflective awareness—the psychological capacity to know that we know. This development is not to be undone but carried forward. Indeed, a further phase in psychological development now stands before us, a stage leading beyond ego-consciousness to the realization of the greater identity of the Self. Jung's model of the process of individuation charts this transition.

The recognition of the different archetypes in the psyche is a critical step in helping us reconnect with the deeper drives of the psyche, thereby going some way towards healing the split between human consciousness and its instinctual roots. However, as much as Jungian psychology is often associated with healing and reconnecting with nature, for Jung individuation also entails a wounding, a violation, and a struggle to become free of the grip of the compulsion of the instincts; it is a breaking free from the psychological-instinctual hold of unconscious nature over us. Individuation is a "violation of the merely natural man" in that it brings to an end natural life, unconsciously lived.[16] To individuate, we cannot simply follow the path of least resistance by automatically consenting to desires and impulses as they arise, doing what comes instinctively and naturally. Rather, as we have seen, we must consciously engage with desires, hold them in check, investigate them, disidentify with them, and transform them. The natural state is lost in this process but greater consciousness is born. The "animal man" within us—a state of being dominated by unconscious instinct—dies that the "spiritual man" might be born. Overcoming the instinctual power of nature within us, we come back to ourselves, to our own deeper nature, as it were, and are able then to recover a harmonious relationship with nature without—so sorely needed in our time.

The ego, too, as an evolutionary expression of the "animal man," is violated during individuation, suffering one hammer blow after another as it is opened to the Self. Individuation at first increases the tension of opposites in the psyche—reason is differentiated from instinct, good from evil, consciousness from the unconscious, light from shadow, spirit from nature. By wrestling with this tension, however, the opposites, having been thrust apart, might in time be reconciled in the realization of the Self. Thus individuation comprises a pattern of separation and reunion, differentiation and synthesis, plurality and unity, fission and fusion. It is a *complexio oppositorum*, a sacred marriage of the opposites.

Ultimately, individuation does not lead us back to an unconscious existence within nature, back to Eden, as it were, but towards the realization of a new state of consciously attained wholeness, towards the establishment of a "new heaven and a new earth." (Revelation 21:1) This threefold pattern—unconscious unity, alienation, and the quest to recover unity in full consciousness—is suggested in myths portraying an expulsion from paradise or a fall away from divinity, as in the biblical story of Eden, and the quest to return to paradise or to regain a lost golden age—to realize the Kingdom of Heaven, in the Christian scheme. It is a developmental trajectory that is intrinsic to the Romantic pattern of psychospiritual development.[17]

Notes

[1] Jung, "Transformation Symbolism in the Mass," in *Psychology and Religion: West and East* (CW11), 259, par. 391.

[2] Jung, "Concerning Rebirth," in *Archetypes and the Collective Unconscious* (CW9i), 121, par. 217.

[3] See also Matthew 27:46.

[4] Jung, *Mysterium Coniunctionis* (CW14), 546, par. 778: "*the experience of the Self is always a defeat for the ego*" [italics in original].

[5] As Christopher Bryant explains: "The belief that God guides us from the centre of our being can completely transform the idea of obedience to God's will. The duty of obeying God has often been conceived of as though it meant submitting to an authority external to us and over against us. Many have revolted against such an obedience because it seemed to belittle their dignity and proper independence. But if the authority to which I have to submit is within me, then the more I conform myself to its directions the more at one shall I be in myself and the more inner-directed. The more completely and spontaneously I follow the directions of this inner guide the more truly I shall be myself, the more I shall be able to realize and live out my own individual truth" (Bryant, *Jung and the Christian Way*, 44).

[6] In this respect, Jung's idea of individuation might be compared to the humanistic focus on self-actualization, as in the work of Abraham Maslow. For Jung, however, individuation is less about personal self-actualization than the unconscious realizing *itself* through the individual. As Jung declared in the opening sentence of the prologue to *Memories, Dreams, Reflections*: "My life is a story of the self-realization of the unconscious."

[7] Jung, "Confrontation with the Unconscious" (Chapter VI), in *Memories, Dreams, Reflections*, 196–225.

[8] Ross (trans.), *Gospel of Thomas*, logion 22, 24.

[9] For an explanation of the method of active imagination, see Jung's essay "The Transcendent Function," in *The Structure and Dynamics of the Psyche* (CW8).

[10] A comment made by Campbell in *The Power of Myth* interviews with Bill Moyers. See also Campbell, *A Joseph Campbell Companion*, 297.

[11] Jung, "Good and Evil in Analytical Psychology," in *Civilization in Transition* (CW 10), 463, par. 873.

[12] Jung, "The Relations between the Ego and the Unconscious," in *Two Essays on Analytical Psychology* (CW7), 178, par. 275.

[13] Jung, "Commentary on 'The Secret of the Golden Flower'," in *Alchemical Studies* (CW13), 17, par. 20.

[14] See Jung's essay "Wotan," in *Civilization in Transition* (CW10), 179–193, par. 371–399.

[15] Wordsworth, "Ode" in *Intimations of Immortality*, 49.

[16] Jung, *Mysterium Coniunctionis* (CW14), 471, par. 671.

[17] See Abrams, *Natural Supernaturalism*.

Chapter 5

Perspectives on Transformation

We can appreciate, from what we have already covered, just how complex and demanding the individuation process is. To be able to call upon models and frameworks that might enable us to illuminate the way of individuation is therefore of inestimable value. Three such models that I would like to survey here are those of the hero's journey, alchemy, and the transpersonal psychology of Czech-American psychiatrist Stanislav Grof.

Since the publication of Joseph Campbell's *The Hero with a Thousand Faces* in the late 1940s, many spiritually seeking and creative people have derived great benefit from Campbell's exposition of the phases and motifs of the hero's journey. Many people have been helped by the principles and practices of Grofian psychology too. Alchemical perspectives have elaborated and further articulated a Jungian understanding of individuation, which has been so influential on modern conceptions of the spiritual life and individual psychological development. Throughout the better part of my adult life, I myself have drawn extensively on each of these perspectives, as I sought to come to terms with the episodes and experiences of transformation I was passing through. It became clear to me that each model, in different yet related ways, enables us to better understand the presence and expression of the archetypal dynamics of transformation in human experience.

The Hero's Journey

In *Symbols of Transformation* and *Psychology and Alchemy*, among other works, Jung puts forward the view that key aspects of the transformation occurring during the individuation process are symbolically portrayed by myths of the hero's journey. Joseph Campbell presented phases of the hero myth in a loosely schematic manner in his *The Hero with a Thousand Faces*. These myths, he argued, tend to adhere to a certain pattern or template—the *monomyth*, as Campbell termed it—comprising three fundamental stages: separation or departure, initiation or transformation, and return or incorporation. The monomyth depicts, first, the hero's separation from the ordinary daylight world of consensus reality in response to a "call to adventure," which is followed, second, by a threshold crossing, typically marking an initiatory "descent into the underworld" and sequence of transformative experiences on a "road of trials." The adventure culminates with the attainment of a boon or treasure, and subsequent "return journey" in which the hero brings back and disseminates the boon to the culture. The treasure, the "pearl of great price," understood psychologically, might be interpreted as a symbolic representation of the precious gift of individual selfhood, and with it the realization of a unique life destiny and calling—in short, the realization of the Self.

The myth of the hero can be applied to many levels of human experience, reflecting the multidimensional nature of the archetype on which this mythic pattern is based. In certain respects, as certain commentators have noted, an heroic response to life, in its more unconscious and unbalanced forms of expression, brings with it undesirable consequences, serving to perpetuate the domination of nature for economic gain and the totalitarian control and suppression of the emotions. Expressed in an extraverted manner, in service to the consumerist values of our time, and problematically conflated with an exclusively "masculine" response to life, the heroic attitude tends to promote a singular style of consciousness, oblivious to the needs of the larger psyche and ill-suited in certain respects to the demands of our historical moment. Seen in this context, one can well understand the criticism and rejection of the hero myth as an appropriate guiding model for our time. Yet our time also demands heroism in our responses to the many crises and uncertainties we now face. And the hero myth remains intrinsically valuable as a guide to inner transformation. Understood as one aspect of a pluralistic mythic orientation to life, the myth of the hero's journey is especially significant, for it dramatically portrays the experience of the individual in the throes of psychospiritual death-rebirth. Individuation calls forth one's heroism in that it demands the sacrifice of one's former identity. It is heroism in service of the Self, however, not the ego, for ultimately the hero dies as the ego is refashioned and the Self is realized. "The hero," Campbell observes, "has died as a modern man; but as eternal man—perfected, unspecific, universal man—he has been reborn."[1]

Envisaging the way of individuation in terms of the hero myth is not to superfluously or indulgently romanticize what is taking place, for it has very real psychological consequences that can impact the attitude we bring to the process. Given the solitary nature of the spiritual journey, especially in our secular age, the hero myth helps to support individuals as they struggle to find spiritual meaning and to come to terms with the complexities and overwhelming powers of the unconscious for themselves, often without any form of external guidance from society. In deviating from a natural way of being, the individual, unsure of each and every step, risks being swallowed up by the anonymity of collective life, with values and ways of being impressed on us from without. To dare to follow one's own way, to trust in one's own experience, requires resilience, fortitude, courage, and the willingness to risk. It inevitably entails suffering and hardship. Seeing one's experience in terms of the hero myth nerves one to be able to bear the isolation, suffering, and tumultuous emotional states that death-rebirth inevitably brings, and helps one find meaning in the suffering. To conceive of this as an heroic undertaking is therefore entirely fitting.

The psyche itself will constellate and activate the hero archetype in response to the traumatic challenges of individuation, such as those critical moments when consciousness is in danger of being overwhelmed by drives and fantasies gushing forth from the unconscious. In this situation, one may find that the deeds and ordeals confronting the hero in myths have a powerful symbolic resonance with what one is facing in one's life, particularly the act of coming to terms with the unleashed dark forces and intoxicating fantasies of the inner world. Just as in myth the hero embarks on an underworld descent, carrying and protecting the flickering flame of a torch, the sole source of light amidst the darkness, so we must each protect and nourish the precious spark of conscious selfhood, to "kindle a light in the darkness of mere being," as Jung put it.[2] The hero overcomes the dragon or tames the beast within, throws off the chains of fate or brings light into the pits of hell, resisting and repelling the powers of darkness, recovering the treasure buried in the ocean depths, and entering into the *hieros gamos*—a sacred marriage of masculine and feminine, spirit and nature. All such episodes are strongly suggestive of key elements of the individuation process, when the individual may be roused as never before to preserve the integrity of consciousness, even in the face of overwhelming dark forces and insidious threats from all sides.

Later, in Volumes II and III, in describing conn
certain mythic themes and the planetary archetypes,
position to appreciate how archetypal astrology ca
illuminate themes of the universal pattern of the mon
examine, for instance, how the activation of the Urant
our lives can indicate periods of going our own way in life, taking a
chance, throwing off restraint. We will consider how Uranus might
manifest as the awakening call to adventure and trickster-like
disruptions and accidents that unexpectedly alter our life course, all in
service of a deeper telos or pattern. We will explore, too, the function
of Saturn both as a guardian of the threshold or insurmountable
obstacle that bars our way, and as the wise learned guide and internal
voice of authority. And, to give one final example, we will look to the
function of the Pluto principle to understand experiences of instinctual
empowerment, underworld encounters, and deep transformation.

Astrology, it has been astutely said, enables each of us to become the
"priest of our own religion," for it entails cultivating a uniquely
personal relationship to the numinous archetypal factors that have
found expression in religion and mythology through the ages. Astrology
furnishes us too with a source of orientation that might enable us, as we
come into relationship with these archetypal principles, to become the
hero of our own lives, taking upon ourselves the calling and burden of
the realization of the Self, with all that entails.

Understanding one's life experience in terms of the pattern of one's
birth chart and an awareness of the changing planetary cycles can
provide us with a uniquely individual mythology that might be
creatively combined with the model of the hero's journey. This
combination of symbolic approaches allows for a more fluid and
flexible engagement with the model of the monomyth than the
sequence of stages identified by Campbell might suggest, for not
everyone will pass through the phases and challenges of the hero's
adventure in the exact sequence or manner proposed by Campbell or
by other theorists presenting alternative models. Astrology can help us
understand which particular themes and phases are prominent in our
experience and accentuated at particular times in our life.

Alchemical Transformation

The medieval practice of alchemy conjures up images of eccentric old
men in laboratories, concocting strange potions and vapors, in pursuit
of an illusory quest to transform base metal into gold. Behind the
obscurity of the practice, however, and the arcane and often

ⅽnetrable nature of the alchemical texts, Jung discovered in alchemy source of unparalleled insight into the individuation process. The alchemical treatises, he realized, although apparently nothing more than a primitive or fallacious account of the chemical transformations of matter, symbolically depict the series of psychological transformations taking place during individuation. Jung suggested that the alchemists unconsciously projected what was taking place within them, within the depths of the psyche, into the matter they worked on in their laboratories. The intense, even obsessive, nature of the alchemical work, which was solemnly entered into as a religious undertaking, seemed to rest upon and activate a kind of underlying affinity or correspondence between matter and the psyche—an affinity also evident in instances of synchronicity.

Alchemy, we might say, accessed the archetypal nature of the process of transformation. Whether transformation is taking place within matter or within the psyche, the same discernible themes and processes are at work. The alchemists portrayed these processes using a highly unusual combination of chemical and mythic images, describing physical transformations of matter in the laboratory but also related mythic scenes that personify these transformations in human form or using animal and celestial figures—depicting, for example, the transformative experiences undergone by the Sun and Moon, King and Queen, Adam and Eve, and the alchemical god-man Mercurius, often in the form of a dragon or serpent. As the matter was blackened or broken apart, so in the mythic imagination of the alchemist, the King entered a deep depression (a so-called *nigredo* experience), then died and was dismembered. As water was extracted from the physical substance in the alchemical vessel, the alchemists believed the spiritual essence of matter (the *aqua permanens*), was released, implying the liberation of consciousness or "soul" formerly bound up with the instincts in the unconscious. Employing such metaphors, working on the matter in the laboratory became for the alchemist a kind of intense psychospiritual labor of transformation.

The alchemical opus may be considered in terms of a number of overlapping and recurring phases, most significantly the *nigredo* (blackening), *albedo* (whitening), and *rubedo* (reddening). Whereas the *nigredo* is the phase of decay and death corresponding with depression, melancholia, and the descent of consciousness into the underworld of the unconscious, the *albedo* represents illumination and rebirth, the breaking of dawn after the dark night of the soul, as it were. The *rubedo*, completing the ongoing cycle of transformations, symbolizes the reconnection of consciousness with the instincts, passions, and emotions that follows from a re-engagement with life even in the midst of deep transformation.

Within these phases, the alchemist performed a number of operations on the *prima materia*, the initial "base" substance, with the aim of attaining the "gold" of the *lapis philosophorum*, the Philosopher's Stone. Among the more prominent alchemical procedures are *solutio* (dissolution), *calcinatio* (heating, burning), *mortificatio* (death), *separatio* (separation, dismemberment), *coagulatio* (coagulation, becoming solid), *sublimatio* (ascent, rising above) and the *coniunctio* or chemical wedding (the conjunction, union), which, as in the hero's journey, represents a culminating synthesis of the opposites or *hieros gamos*.[3] Utilizing an understanding of these operations, alchemy gives a striking symbolic portrayal of the death-rebirth process, unequalled in its precision and detail.

Alchemy is a bewilderingly complex subject, and I cannot hope to do it justice in this brief overview.[4] What is important from our perspective, in addition to noting its significance for Jung as a symbolic portrayal of individuation, is that the alchemical phases and procedures can be seen as another metaphorical language of archetypes. As such, the various forms of alchemical symbolism might be correlated with archetypal themes studied in astrology. Specifically, by identifying associations of alchemical operations, phases, and symbolic figures with particular combinations of planetary archetypes (Saturn-Pluto, Moon-Neptune, Jupiter-Uranus, and so forth) we might begin to bring the two systems together to give a more comprehensive picture of the expression of archetypes in our lives. By studying astrological birth charts and transits, we will then be able to get a sense, for example, for when particular forms of alchemical transformation are accentuated in our experience.

The historical connection between alchemy and astrology justifies this synthesis of the two approaches, for often the alchemists combined alchemical and astrological imagery in their descriptions of the opus— the work of Michael Maier is a primary example. Indeed, As Edward Edinger has discussed, there is a clear association between certain operations and the classical astrological elements—*solutio* pertains to the element water, *calcinatio* to fire, *sublimatio* to air, and *coagulatio* to earth. Moreover, alchemy, as understood by Maier especially, was to do with the overcoming of *heimarmene*, the binding grip of fate, written in the stars and ascribed at birth. As we have seen, spiritual transformation implied the overthrowing of this "bill of fate," which, in psychological terms, Jung interpreted to mean the realization of conscious freedom, liberating the individual from unconscious patterns of archetypal-instinctual compulsion.[5]

Perinatal Psychology and the Death-Rebirth Process

Despite Jung's best efforts, because of its complexity and obscurity alchemy, as a symbolic spiritual system, remains inaccessible to many people today or ignored entirely. Fortunately, research in the field of transpersonal psychology over the last fifty years has provided other means of understanding the dynamics of the death-rebirth process. The work of Roberto Assagioli and John Weir Perry has been especially important, exploring the nature of mystical transformation, in the case of Assagioli, and powerful visionary experiences associated with psychosis and rebirth, in the case of Perry.[6] Perhaps most significant, however, is the pioneering research and theoretical models of Stanislav Grof, which have been directly influential on the development of archetypal astrology through the work of Richard Tarnas.

Around the same time as James Hillman was developing archetypal psychology in the 1960s and 1970s, Grof, Anthony Sutich, and Abraham Maslow were developing transpersonal psychology—an approach to psychology concerned with the realization of higher human potentials and exploring spiritual experiences beyond the limits of our ordinary conscious awareness or personal psychology. Alongside the prolific transpersonal author Ken Wilber, Grof became recognized as a leading authority in the field of transpersonal studies.[7]

Emerging out of the psychoanalytic tradition that included the ideas and therapeutic modalities developed by Freud, Jung, Adler, Otto Rank, Wilhelm Reich, and others, Grof pioneered his own form of experiential psychotherapy based on the powerful healing and heuristic potentials of "non-ordinary states of consciousness." These non-ordinary states, which are induced either by psychoactive substances or through accelerated breathing techniques, or which arise spontaneously during "psychospiritual crises," are marked by perceptual shifts, powerful fantasies, and somatic experiences, and they provide access to progressively deeper dimensions of the unconscious. What Grof termed the perinatal domain (relating to the psychodynamics and unconscious memories of the trauma of birth) is pivotal to the experience of psychological rebirth.

Whatever else happens to us in life, birth and death are obviously the most significant experiences we can pass through. However much we understand of the process in scientific terms, birth stands at the threshold of a mystery. Contemplating our own history, we know not what comes before, just as the nature of existence beyond death will only become clear to us in the mortal hour. Because it stands before us in life as our inevitable destination, death naturally occupies much of our attention, even as we shy away from the prospect of our own demise. But it is altogether surprising that in depth psychology little attention has been given to the birth experience, especially from the perspective of the fetus. Although it was the subject of Otto Rank's *The Trauma of Birth*, it was not of particular concern to Freud or Jung or Adler. Birth, it stands to reason, must carry at least equal significance to that of death, for it shapes our very being, marking our incarnation into the flesh-and-blood reality of material existence.

Despite the medical advances now at our disposal, which have drastically reduced rates of infant mortality, especially in the developed world, for mother and baby the birth experience remains one of critical danger. Birth, one would imagine, must be especially traumatic for the fetus as its intrauterine life as an aquatic organism, in union with the mother, is brought to a painful and unexpected end. Yet, Grof points out, science disregards the fetus's experience as it is believed that its brain is not developed enough at birth to retain a memory of what happened. However traumatic the experience might be, it will be instantly forgotten or not even imprinted in memory and will thus have no bearing on the subsequent life.

Grof's own research starkly contradicts this assumption. He discovered that in non-ordinary states of consciousness people can undergo the remarkable experience of psychosomatically reliving their own biological birth, even recalling specific details of the delivery that were not known to them in normal consciousness, and were only later to be empirically verified. Furthermore, in reliving the biological birth process, and thereby fully experiencing the previously unresolved trauma of birth, Grof observed that people undergo a kind of "second birth," a spiritual rebirth.

There appears to be an archetypal correspondence between the two birthing processes, taking place on different levels of experience. On the one hand, Grofian perinatal psychology might be seen as making possible a resolution of the unresolved trauma of biological birth, enabling deep, cellular memories of that past experience to arise in consciousness and to be processed and assimilated. On the other hand, it facilitates the process of ego death, and a new birth out of the defensive armoring of the "skin-encapsulated ego" into the fuller reality of the psyche and a more authentic life in the world.[8] The sequence of transformations experienced in the rebirthing process bears striking similarities to the symbolism of alchemy and the Jungian understanding of the transformative process taking place during individuation. In many respects, Grofian perinatal psychology helps us to better understand the psychodynamics of the Jungian rebirth archetype, describing in detail the phenomenology of its various stages while providing a powerful experiential method, mediated by systematic deep breathing or psychedelics, to facilitate the transformative process.[9]

Each stage of the birth process has markedly distinct qualities, themes, and imagery, with an accompanying range of psychological experiences and physical symptoms. Each stage is associated with what Grof calls a "Basic Perinatal Matrix" or BPM, for short. The first phase (BPM I), prior to the onset of delivery, is that of the fetus in its aquatic life in the womb. It is characterized by experiences of oceanic unity, dissolution, non-differentiation, timelessness, and—if the womb experience is a positive one—accompanying feelings of bliss, suggested by images and experiences of the paradise of Eden or of a mythic golden age or blissful ocean scenes.

The second phase (BPM II) reflects the onset of contractions in which the fetus thereafter experiences the womb as an oppressive enclosure, with its world pushing in from all sides, bringing a sense of claustrophobic pressure, with seemingly no possibility of this situation coming to an end. It is connected with the mythic experiences of paradise lost, the expulsion from Eden with the fall of man, the loss of the magical world of *participation mystique* with nature. In reliving this experience, individuals often find themselves seemingly condemned to a world of pain, suffering, exile, hard labor, and alienation, with the accompanying existential sense of "no exit" entrapment, and with the painfully slow passage of time, perhaps even a sense of eternal damnation.

In the third phase (BPM III), the sense of interminable entrapment gives way to an intense life-and-death struggle arising as the fetus is forced along the birth canal. Caught between two modes of existence, and oblivious to the existence of a world on the other side of the process, the fetus finds itself fighting for its life. It marks a state of extreme instinctual arousal, as the sheer struggle to survive releases tremendously powerful aggressive and sexual energies, which in psychological rebirthing experiences function as torturing purgatorial fires of transformation.

The fourth phase (BPM IV) is that of delivery and the birth moment itself, which brings the unexpected release from the intense struggle and entrapment of labor, as the fetus is thrust into a bright new world, bringing with it feelings of euphoric liberation and ecstatic release (or giddy excitement and mania, if rebirth is not fully resolved), symbolized by the breaking dawn, with the coming of light after the long dark night. The movement between these four phases constitutes the ongoing process of psychospiritual rebirth.

In the throes of rebirth, one is in the position of both mother and fetus. As the mother, one is embroiled in the intense, often agonizing, labor of birthing the new self, as the old structure of the ego—its defenses and resistances—are broken down and long-buried emotion is released into consciousness. The body, as a result, progressively sheds its armoring, and the heart is rendered more fully open to experience. Simultaneously, in the midst of this process one feels oneself to be in the position of the fetus, being pushed inch by inch along the birth canal, as the inner being moves out of the old shell of the ego. The process repeats, moving through the perinatal matrices again and again as the rebirth is actualized.

The pain of being born is a continuing process through life. We need to be born out of the childhood psyche and family matrix. We must be born out of the womb of culture into authentic selfhood. We might then struggle to be born out of personal selfhood into our universal humanity and inherent divinity. BPM I is associated with the pull back to a paradise of unconsciousness or pre-consciousness. We need to move into and through the exile, pain, and suffering of BPM II into the turmoil of the instincts and passions of BPM III in order to be born into our fuller being in BPM IV. We are always having to leave behind the comfortable, to resist the pull back towards the paradisiacal womb of unconsciousness.

As this process unfolds, one moves inexorably towards a crushing annihilation, as the deepest defenses and resistances are activated and destroyed. With each mini-death, one becomes more fully at one with life, for a while living more spontaneously, more freely, until the next sequence of death-rebirth manifests. With each completed rebirth, excessive instinctual arousal and empowerment subside and dissipate, and rational egoic control is relinquished. The intense struggle between rational control and instinctual empowerment, between the head and the gut, as it were, is reconciled at the level of the heart.

Working with Grof at Esalen Institute in California, Richard Tarnas realized that the phenomenology and thematic quality of each stage of birth bears striking similarities to themes associated with the planetary archetypes Neptune, Saturn, Pluto, and Uranus, respectively. To summarize briefly what will emerge more fully in our later analysis, Neptune pertains to the undifferentiated unity of the womb and experiences of dissolution associated with the first perinatal matrix (BPM I); Saturn pertains to the suffering, entrapment, and pressure of the second matrix (BPM II); Pluto pertains to the instinctual arousal and death-rebirth struggle of the third matrix (BPM III); and Uranus pertains to the birthing moment and experience of liberation of the fourth matrix (BPM IV).[10] Thus, when any of these four archetypes are prominent in one's life, one tends to encounter transformative experiences associated with the respective perinatal matrix.[11] Each of these planetary archetypes might thus be understood in terms of the dynamics of the rebirth process.

Notes

[1] Campbell, *Hero with a Thousand Faces*, 20.

[2] Jung, *Memories, Dreams, Reflections*, 358.

[3] Edward Edinger describes each of these operations in *Anatomy of the Psyche*.

[4] I cover alchemy at much greater length in *The Lion Will Become Man: Alchemy and the Dark Spirit in Nature—A Personal Encounter* (Asheville, NC: Chiron Publications, 2023).

[5] See Jung's analysis of Michael Maier's "journey through the planetary spheres" in *Mysterium Coniunctionis*, 217–235.

[6] See Assagioli, *Transpersonal Development*, and Perry, *The Far Side of Madness, The Self in Psychotic Process, Trials of the Visionary Mind*, and *Lord of the Four Quarters*.

[7] Among Grof's most significant works are *Beyond the Brain, Realms of the Human Unconscious*, and *The Psychology of the Future*.

[8] The term "skin-encapsulated ego" comes from Alan Watts.

[9] Perinatal psychology is a unique contribution of Grof's approach to psychotherapy and is a central focus of its method of transformation. In this approach, the exploration of the unconscious is not limited to individual biography or the birth experience. Rather, Grof found that in non-ordinary states of consciousness one can gain access to what appear to be memories of historical, collective, cross-cultural, karmic, phylogenetic, and evolutionary events. Furthermore, these memories seem to be organized archetypally and thematically in such a way that traumatic experiences from one's own life, for example, are connected to qualitatively and archetypally similar experiences from our collective past. Within the second perinatal matrix, one might identify with and experience oneself as an animal caught in a trap or as a prisoner of war, for instance, with these experiences reflecting the themes of

that matrix. Deep psychological self-exploration in holotropic states, Grof discovered, provides firsthand experience of the reality of a universal, mythic-archetypal unconscious. For a fuller discussion of the relevance of Grof's psychology to astrology, see Le Grice, *Archetypal Cosmos*, 206-211.

[10] The correspondence between Uranus and biological birth was also proposed by astrologer Donald Bradley, as reported in Donna Cunningham, *Astrological Guide to Self-Awareness*, 93, 95–96.

[11] The connections between the Basic Perinatal Matrices and the planetary archetypes Saturn, Uranus, Neptune, and Pluto are discussed in Grof's essay "Holotropic Research and Archetypal Astrology," *The Birth of a New Discipline. Archai The Journal of Archetypal Psychology,* issue 1. See also Renn Butler's "holotropic astrology" set forth in his *Pathways to Wholeness* and *The Archetypal Universe.* Butler applies Tarnas's approach to archetypal astrology to understand the content of non-ordinary states of consciousness in holotropic and psychedelic therapy.

Chapter 6

Soul-Making and the Symbolic Life

The perspectives and models set out in the last chapter apply most directly to those people experiencing an acute crisis of transformation, or encountering the death-rebirth process in non-ordinary states of consciousness. However, for many people—perhaps even the majority—transformation can occur more obliquely, taking place in the background of experience rather than as a stark "confrontation with the unconscious" of the kind Jung himself passed through. The focus of individuation is then placed, rather, on the discovery of symbolic meaning in life, on accessing the creative power of the unconscious, on the fulfillment of a vocation, or on living more soulfully, discovering and realizing one's individual myth. Of course, these paths are not mutually exclusive and the many different aspects of individuation—including transformation and the search for symbolic meaning—might lay equal claim on us.

Seeking the Symbolic Life

With the West's transition from the Christian era into the modern, the sense of inhabiting a sacred world, a world whose ultimate values and purposes are spiritual, has largely been lost. The acts of life today generally possess only a utilitarian value, in that they are mostly undertaken solely out of practical or economic necessity or for enjoyment. We work to earn money that we might survive and prosper. We strive to satisfy the whim of personal desire, to seek out pleasure and avoid pain. As we undertake our daily tasks, there is usually no sense of being part of a larger mythic, spiritual, or cosmic reality in which we devote our lives to the service of God, as in the Christian view, or engage with the gods and goddesses, as did the ancient Egyptians, Greeks, Romans, and other civilizations. Modern life in the West is almost devoid of meaningful rituals, with the few rituals that remain of a wholly secular or ceremonial nature, lacking the deep significance they formerly carried. Within Catholicism, the Mass is no longer experienced as a living mystery, Jung noted, for the symbols of Christianity do not speak to us as they once did; they have lost their numinous charge. Without meaningful rituals to guide us through our life transitions, we must seek out or formulate our own life meaning.

Reflecting on the psychological consequences of the modern mode of engaging with the world, Jung observed:

> Now, we have no symbolic life, and we are all badly in need of the symbolic life—badly in need. Only the symbolic life can express the need of the soul—the daily need of the soul, mind you! And because people have no such thing, they can never step out of this mill—this awful, grinding, banal life in which they are "nothing but."[1]

> Life is too rational, we have no symbolic existence in which we are something else, in which I am fulfilling my role, my role as one of the actors in the divine drama of life.[2]

> That gives peace, when people feel that they are living the symbolic life, that they are actors in the divine drama. It expresses the desire of the soul; it expresses the actual facts of our unconscious life.[3]

Contrast the experience of the ancient smith or metallurgist with that of the modern steelworker or miner. The former, as Mircea Eliade described in *The Forge and the Crucible*, had a very real sense of working with fire as a kind of sacred magical power, wielding this power in service to nature or to the gods, and occupying accordingly an important place in the life of the community—born into a lineage of smiths, carrying the weighty responsibility of continuing the work of his forebears. The act of forging metal ores was a sacred activity, akin to that performed by the gods, in a reenactment of timeless mythic patterns. The smith was like Hephaestus, and had a relationship to the sacred essence of the material with which he worked. The modern industrial worker, by contrast, lives in a world of corporations and trade unions. Gone is any sense of participation in a sacred activity, imbued with symbolic meaning. Instead, daily labors take place against the backdrop of the inexorable demand for more products, manufactured ever more cheaply and quickly, or under the threat of closure and redundancy. The life of an office worker or a role in the corporate world, with no practical craft or tangible end product, is inevitably even more removed from the sacred symbolic meaning of the kind Jung had in mind, removed even from the natural dynamisms and rhythms of life.

We should keep in mind that the modern way of life is an astonishingly recent development, measured against the evolutionary history of human beings and related hominoids. Life in modern industrial-consumerist societies obviously contrasts starkly with that in traditional, indigenous ones. Jared Diamond gives a sense of this context:

> Traditional societies . . . retain features of how all of our ancestors lived for tens of thousands of years, until virtually yesterday. . . . The shift from hunting-gathering to farming began only about 11,000 years ago; the first metal tools were produced only about 7,000 years ago; and the first state government and the first writing arose only about 5,400 years ago. 'Modern' conditions have prevailed, even just locally, for only a tiny fraction of human history [measured against the 6,000,000 years since the proto-human evolutionary line began].[4]

And of course, the modern era proper, bringing with it the start of the industrial age, is only a few centuries old. In short, the ways of life of contemporary humans in the developed world is a dramatic and novel development, a radical mutation from the established patterns of our evolutionary history. The accelerating pace of change over the last few centuries, especially in our own time, is scarcely comprehensible and has thrust human beings into a reality for which our psychological nature is unprepared. The accelerating pace of change shows no sign of abating—on the contrary. We are moving inexorably into an era of ever-increasing automation in which, with the majority of activities and labors currently performed by human beings soon to be fulfilled by robots and artificial intelligence, we will be further liberated from the hardship and monotony of labor but at the same time deprived of the former source of work, and thus for many people the source of life's meaning and purpose. It will be imperative, in this scenario, that we find creative outlets for unused libido in accord with the direction the life in us wants to go.

Against this backdrop, we can well appreciate the modern experience of rootlessness, loss of meaning, and alienation. The ego-self is a relatively new entity, one that has psychologically broken loose from its moorings, to a large extent, asserting its autonomy, harnessing the power of reason and science in an attempt to master the world. Unconsciously driven by the Faustian desire for ever greater conquest, sensation, and experience, the modern ego often lacks any sense of deep connection to nature and to the spiritual powers and principles recognized by all other human societies. Jung saw the problematic psychological consequences of this transition in the experience of his clients and in the world at large—a phenomenon perhaps even more evident to us today. The call for the cultivation of a symbolic life addresses the need for spiritual and mythic orientation in the new psychological and cultural reality of our time.

By the "symbolic life," then, Jung meant living in a manner that the ordinary events and experiences of our world are seen to carry a symbolic connection to the greater spiritual reality of which we are a part. In going about our daily business and undertaking our work, we might be able to experience ourselves as players in a larger cosmic order or "divine drama," as he put it. We might come to recognize that what we do has significance beyond the sphere of our immediate personal influence, recognizing that we partake in ageless archetypal patterns, connecting us to the vast sweep of human history and our evolutionary origins, connecting us too to the timeless world of myth with its archetypal dramas and adventures.

An awareness of the stories of myth might help to illuminate our understanding of archetypes, as we find resonances between our own experiences—breakdown or depression, rage and rebirth, sorrow and sacrifice, victory and defeat, for instance—and the deeds of the protagonists of myth. It was the fate of Dionysus to suffer death and dismemberment; Icarus, flying too close to the sun, was the victim of his own over-confidence and hubris; Prometheus suffered eternally for his "boon theft" of the secret of fire and creative defiance of the gods; Persephone was abducted to the underworld by Hades—we could refer here to any number of the well-known stories and figures of myth. As numerous depth psychologists have described over the years, these experiences are not just fantastic fictional tales, for they speak to all-too-real human experiences, playing themselves out in our own lives, even if in less overt fashion, through the seemingly ordinary deeds and personal dramas we pass through.

Cultivating the symbolic life through the recollection of life's mythic background liberates us from a limiting entrapment in the literalisms of everyday existence and a narrow preoccupation with exclusively personal problems, making possible a transformation of the mundane world of everyday events into a living sense of participation in a life of greater meaning, in touch with the transpersonal dimension of the archetypes. Living symbolically, our daily activities themselves might remain the same, but, mindful of the myths we are living, we are able to imagine into our life activities in a deeper way. This is not to say we can always live with a sense of mythic enchantment or symbolic meaning—that would be impossible, I think. But we might be able to tune our mode of perception in order that we might "see through" our experiences with an "archetypal eye" to their mythic background. This symbolic-archetypal mode of being and seeing is a natural element of psychological functioning. Thus to evoke it is not to artificially impose myths on life with an act of the imagination but to recognize a lived meaning that is already there, shaping our world and our perception of it, if we could but bring it to awareness and give it priority.

Synchronicity and the Symbolic Attitude
Closely related to the notion of the symbolic life is what Jung calls the "symbolic attitude," in which one adopts "a definite view of the world which assigns meaning to events, whether great or small, and attaches to this meaning a greater value than to bare facts."[5] Symbolic meaning can break through into our world even in the midst of the hurly-burly of things and whir of events. Jung's investigation of the phenomenon of synchronicity, of "meaningful coincidence," led him to recognize that in certain moments the world itself is able to convey symbolic meaning through particular events that meaningfully coincide, often in a startling manner, with our inner experiences. We are wrestling with a particular problem and open a book at random on a page whose content helps us resolve the matter; a daring venture into the unknown is greeted by a herald of white birds and or some other encouraging omen that speaks to us in that moment; the letters on a car license plate or the words of the billboard poster or urban graffiti, never intended for us, of course, communicate a message of profound relevance and significance at just the time we need it.[6] Synchronicities take many forms, but they each reveal something of the inner meaning of our experience and they tell us that the archetypes, from which synchronicities arise, do not only function within, in dreams and fantasies, but permeate the very world in which we live.

Heeding such meaningful coincidences, which are often colloquially referred to as "signs," we can begin to cultivate the symbolic attitude as a way of meeting life, which enables us to become psychologically open to the deeper significance of the events we encounter day by day. What do the particular events of the day and the changes in our environment tell us about our life direction and personal situation? What does it mean, for example, if an alarm unexpectedly sounds as we are contemplating a particular course of action or if our path is thwarted by a series of unusual occurrences (such as perhaps being blocked or slowed down by emergency vehicles or road accidents or the spilt load of a truck)? To the modern mind, such incidents are devoid of meaning beyond the obvious and one would be deluded for thinking otherwise. But Jung believed we might recognize in these events symbolic clues that can help us attune to the intentions of the Self. We might recognize how the circumstances of our life and the events of life, however arbitrary or innocuous these might seem, are aspects of the symbolic ordering of things that at some level are serving our own individuation. "One gives one's mind, as before, to other duties," Jung suggests, "but at the same time one remains alert for hints and signs, both in dreams and in external events, that the Self uses to symbolize its intentions—the direction in which the life stream is moving."[7]

In the absence of a collective myth, these reflections and individual pathways to living symbolically—through dreams and synchronicities, for instance—become increasingly important. Living the symbolic life, and the discovery and cultivation of one's personal myth, might be assisted, I have found, by the application of archetypal astrology to one's life experience, for astrology is based upon a kind of moment-to-moment background ordering synchronicity, in which the changing positions of the planets, relative to each other, are meaningfully coincident with the activation of specific archetypal themes in our experience. Astrology can help us better understand "the direction in which the life stream is moving" and the challenges we might face in seeking to follow the life stream.

As we have seen, in astrology all the planetary archetypes, both alone and in combination, are associated with certain defined themes—we will explore these themes in detail in later chapters. To know which planetary archetypes are prominent in one's life using astrology can therefore help us to understand which themes are accented at particular times. If we know, by studying transit astrology, that Saturn is prominent in our lives for a period of months, we can expect to encounter the range of phenomena and mythic themes associated with the Saturn archetype during that time: somber reflections on aging and the contemplation of one's mortality, experiences of compression and limitation, personal maturation and the assumption of responsibility, a weighty sense of duty and responsibility, a more acute sense of suffering and entrapment, the cultivation of hard-earned wisdom and the pressure to actualize one's destiny or make structural changes—to give but a few examples. To be aware of the constellation of the Saturn archetype in one's life can help to direct one's mind to the myths, meanings, and purposes associated with the archetype and thus raise one's consciousness above the personal and practical struggles of life, as important and absorbing as these are. One continues to suffer, struggle, and strive, of course, but one does so with one eye on the meaning that is being enacted and constellated in one's personal situation. While archetypal astrology can never tell us how to live or make decisions for us, what it provides is a symbolic connection to the shifting energies of the cosmos, such that our individual lives can be seen as aspects of a larger cosmic drama, in which we all play our part. It helps us attune to the great universal themes, associated with archetypes, animating and shaping our lives moment to moment.

Soul-Making and the Archetypal Eye

The process of soul-making, as described by James Hillman, has much in common with Jung's understanding of the symbolic life. Generally speaking, Hillman's approach is more egalitarian than Jung's psychology, however, especially when considering Jung's emphasis on individuation. In its more acute form of a prolonged transformative encounter with the depths of the unconscious psyche, individuation seems to be for the few rather than the many, but soul-making, as Hillman understands it, draws us close to what it is to be a human being, in its concern with the soulful engagement with life, cultivated through imagination and reflection, and through the affirmation of the messy imperfections and contradictions, the pathos and pathology, which make up the human lot. If individuation sometimes demands an heroic, almost superhuman, capacity for self-overcoming and sacrifice, in soul-making, Hillman explains, "action is hindered and one fumbles foolishly in the half-light and the symbolic."[8]

We can get a sense for what Hillman means by soul-making if we contrast it with the ordinary, dominant mode of ego consciousness, with which we are all familiar. The egoic mode of consciousness, generally speaking, is absorbed in the practical concerns of life, struggling with the world and against circumstance, focused on survival and material prosperity, seeking to always be in control and on top of things. This mode of functioning tends to be singular and exclusive, fixated on its goals, caught up relentless striving and activity, and thus allowing little room for the wider range of human feeling or for the free movement of fantasies. It clings to the ideal of health and resists illness and breakdown. It tends to be literal, knowing only the single plane of material concerns, functioning within a narrow field of emotion and experience. Hillman described this mode of being in terms of the archetypal-mythic figures of the hero and the senex (the old), although it should be stressed that it reflects only partial and somewhat pathological elements of these archetypes—a point that, particularly in his critique of the hero, Hillman tended to miss.

Hillman presents soul-making as a "perspective" differing markedly from the mode of functioning described above.[9] Soul-making is characterized by a softer, yielding style of being, one enveloped by reverie and the play of the fantasy life. Dreams and feelings ebb and flow, and foster deep personal reflection. Life is recognized for its soulful beauty. Even suffering, illness, and breakdown are recognized as expressions of the life of the soul, and thus to be accepted and honored, rather than fought against, denied, and corrected. Soul-making might be understood as a reflective and imaginative receptivity to all the experiences life brings our way, gently affirming even the darkest experiences as our own. It is not something one consciously does, so much as something that the psyche does naturally but that can be enhanced by our conscious attention. A capacity present in us all as children, to a greater or lesser extent, the cultivation of soul-making is therefore a question of deepening into this natural psychic process rather than intentionally imposing a way of being on our lives. As Hillman puts it, "our imaginative recognition, the childlike act of imagining the world, animates the world and returns it to soul."[10]

The experience of soul-making often has a poignant quality, bringing the recognition and experience of life as a soulful dream, even in the midst of struggling and suffering. As one engages the shifting play of fantasies, even such fundamental human experiences as individuation and rebirth, so central to the Jungian view of the human psyche, might be understood as one metaphor, one stream of fantasy, among many. Soul-making is thoroughly pluralistic and resists Jung's tendency to give priority to the realization of the Self through individuation as the central aim of life. Soul-making is at home in the pluralistic play of possibilities, disclosed to us by the myriad fantasies and yearnings that come over us. Individuation requires that we prioritize the intentions of the Self over the many other claims the psyche makes on us.

Soul-making, then, is an activity that arises from deep imaginative reflection that makes experience personally known rather than blindly lived. The more deeply we can reflect, and the more we can cultivate an aesthetic and mythic sensibility to aid this reflection, the more alive and more conscious we become, weaving the archetypal tapestry of our experience in the making of soul. Then, experience does not remain unconscious, anonymous, and impersonal—as events that just happen to us—but is made personal, owned, deeply felt, and imagined into.

For Hillman, we can call upon both myth and art to recognize and engage with the particular imaginal figures and fantasies that shape our reality such that we might live out with greater awareness the mythic-archetypal patterns already present in our own experience, affirming them as aspects of the rich totality of the soul. As Jung and Joseph Campbell also stressed in different ways, the artist as mythmaker can portray the "eternally repeated joys and sorrows" that befall each of us, helping us to live our own individual fates more consciously, more meaningfully.[11] Employing a metaphorical way of experiencing, engaging with the figures of mythology and the dramas they enact, serves to open the imagination and deepen reflection. "We may thereby see our ordinary lives," Hillman asserts, "embedded in and ennobled by the dramatic and world-creating life of mythical figures. The study of mythology allows events to be recognized against their mythological background."[12]

For Hillman, as for Jung, myth leads us back to archetypes, which Hillman conceived as "cosmic perspectives in which the soul participates."[13] Each archetype, each mythic figure, has its unique gifts and its pathology, its own range of symptoms, which are intrinsic to its nature. As we have seen, Hillman rejects the medical model of psychiatry, which seeks to cure us of all psychological ills and idiosyncrasies, rejecting too the rational-humanistic drive to control and correct all aspects of the psyche and the Christian ethical impulse to make psychological life conform to an imposed moral ideal. One must engage with pathology and its symptoms as an expression of the gods and goddesses, allowing oneself to fall into the pathology, to "fall apart," if needs be, so that all the parts that comprise who one is might be recognized and honored.[14]

Ultimately, for Hillman, our sufferings and struggles, joys and victories, loves and losses, are more than merely human experiences. These acts are personal, soulful expressions of the movements of the gods and goddesses. These mythic figures are not aspects of human psychology; it is the other way around—a shift of perspective that Hillman terms "dehumanizing." The process of soul-making is not for human ends, but in service of the soul and the psyche, whose archetypal patterns possess their own autonomous reality and being, and live through us, expressing themselves in the world. Soul-making might be understood, then, as an attitude of "hospitality to the gods," by which the ego, usually bound to consensus reality and a literal manner of engaging with the world, is opened to the imaginal-mythic realm of the archetypal psyche.[15] This move invites the gods and goddesses out of their concealment as unconscious factors more fully into the field of our conscious awareness.

The relevance of archetypal astrology to the perspective of soul-making immediately suggests itself. Studying astrology can inform the development of an "archetypal eye," to use Hillman's expression, so that we can become more aware of the mythic themes and dynamisms that are living through us. We can study the planetary configurations in our birth charts, reflect on the archetypal and mythic themes associated with these configurations, and thus become conscious of these themes as and when they arise in our experience. We can also study transits— the ongoing movements of the planets in relation to each other and to planetary positions in birth charts—to better understand themes constellated at particular periods of time. Again, this can enable us to become more aware of what is happening in our lives at these times, to discern the movements of the gods and goddesses, as it were. In engaging with life in this mythical manner, aided by archetypal astrology, we naturally partake in the perspective of soul-making.

Astrology can also inform our appreciation of the arts, helping us to recognize the archetypal themes conveyed by the artist and the artwork. This is a method we will employ in Part Five. By listening to music or watching films, for instance, one can use astrology—a knowledge of the archetypal configurations in the artists' birth charts—to enter into the archetypal complexes and themes evident in these works of art, finding resonances with the expression of these archetypes in one's own life. Opening oneself to the archetypes through the arts, one can become acquainted with the archetypes' distinct themes and prominent modes of expression. Engaging with the arts in this way fosters an informed reflection on one's own experience, such that one becomes aware of how one participates in the great universal patterns, how one expresses them and makes them one's own, incarnating them through one's own life experience.

It is with this in mind that we turn now, in Part Two, to an examination of the Jungian and astrological archetypal principles themselves.

Notes

[1] Jung, *The Symbolic Life*, 274, par. 627.

[2] Jung, *The Symbolic Life*, 274, par. 628.

[3] Jung, *The Symbolic Life*, 275, par. 630.

[4] Diamond, *World Until Yesterday*, 7.

[5] Jung, *Psychological Types*, 476, par. 819.

[6] Thus Jung, in a letter to Dr. S., dated 8 August 1951, notes: "You are quite right to remember the storm that interrupted our conversation. In a quite irrational way we must be able to listen also to the voice of nature, thunder for instance, even if this means breaking the continuity of consciousness" (Jung, *Letters* II, 20–21).

[7] Jung, *Man and His Symbols*, 228.

[8] Hillman, *Senex & Puer*, 41.

[9] See Hillman, *Re-Visioning Psychology*, for his description of soul-making and soul as a perspective.

[10] Hillman, "Anima Mundi," in *A Blue Fire*, 99.

[11] Jung, "Psychology and Literature," in *The Spirit in Man, Art, and Literature*, 89, par. 139.

[12] Hillman, *Archetypal Psychology*, 29.

[13] Hillman, *Re-Visioning Psychology*, 169–170.

[14] For a discussion of "falling apart," see "Pathologizing" in Hillman, *Re-Visioning Psychology*, 53–112.

[15] On the idea of "hospitality to the gods," see Roger Brooke, *Jung and Phenomenology*, 90.

PART THREE

An Assemblage of Archetypes

Chapter 7

Spirit and Soul, Sun and Moon

In the history of Western thought a distinction is made between spirit and soul. We have a basic intuition of what these terms mean, even if they blur into each other, are somewhat vaguely defined, and hard to conceptualize. Understood in religious terms, the word *spirit* has, in the Christian West, come to be more or less synonymous with God. In its more general meaning, however, spirit suggests an active, emanating quality, as implied by the word *spirited* or the idea of spirit as zeitgeist, such as the "spirit of '49." Spirit encompasses overall psychological wellbeing, such as when we say a person is in high spirits or low spirits, but it goes beyond this to include vitality, the flow of the life force, mind, reason, and attitudinal stance—as in the spirit in which we approach something. As Jung has it, spirit "means the sum-total of all the phenomena of rational thought, or of the intellect, including the will, memory, imagination, creative power, and aspirations motivated by ideals."[1] The word *soul*, in distinction, suggests a quality or feeling, often associated with our innermost private depths. If something is soulless, it implies that it is devoid of the inner personal feeling that renders it truly alive—hence Hillman's call to soul-making in the modern world. Whereas spirit is often associated with an energetic aspiration towards the future, soul is more typically connected to the past and to a sense of belonging. In the Christian tradition, soul is imagined as an individual incarnate entity within the body, although as we have seen soul can also refer to the inwardness of all things—the *anima mundi* of Platonism and Neoplatonism. In archetypal astrology, spirit and soul are symbolized respectively (although not exclusively) by the archetypes associated with the Sun and the Moon. As the Sun and Moon are intimately related, the Sun providing the light for the Moon, so are spirit and soul, which overlap in their meaning and function in concert.

Spirit, Consciousness, and Being

In its capacity to illuminate life experience, bringing the world into the field of our awareness, consciousness has long been symbolically associated with light. Light is also often associated with the world-creating and defining power of spirit, of God. The human being participates in the light of spirit, which exists within us, just as the light of the Sun shines down upon us all. In many traditions, the Sun is identified with the major deities (such as Mithras and *Sol Invictus*, in Mithraism and Roman religion respectively). As Robert Bellah, in a discussion of Egyptian "mythospeculation," notes: "Seeing the god . . . as the sun, allows for a sense of human participation in the divine life, for the light of the sun, which surrounds us, is the presence of a god. As one hymn to the sun puts it: 'All eyes see through you. They can do nothing when Your Majesty goes down.'"[2]

In the *Bhagavad Gita*, the Sun is equated with the radiant transcendent light of the eternal Self (*Atman*) and with the figure of Krishna. As one commentary on the *Gita* explains:

> The Supreme Lord Krishna known as *Parabrahma* the source of the *brahman* or spiritual substratum pervading all existence, is the light of all lights, the illuminator of even the sun and the stars. He is shining, resplendently effulgent all things shine from Him, by His light all creation is full of light. Therefore *Parabrahma* is untouched by darkness and beyond all nescience untouched by ignorance. The Svetasvatara Upanisad III.VII. beginning *veda hametam purusam* meaning: The Supreme Lord shines more brilliantly than the sun and by realising Him only one attains *moksa* or liberation.[3]

The Christian tradition, similarly, equates light with spirit, being, and the primordial creative act. In the familiar words of Genesis I:

> In the beginning God created the heaven and the earth.
> And the earth was without form, and void; and darkness was upon the face of the deep.
> And the Spirit of God moved upon the face of the waters.
> And God said, Let there be light: and there was light.
> And God saw the light, that it was good: and God divided the light from the darkness.
> And God called the light Day, and the darkness he called Night.
> And the evening and the morning were the first day.

The light of spirit is here decreed to be connected to the ultimate Good. So too, in Greek philosophical speculation, the light of the Sun is brought into relationship with the Platonic notion of the archetypal Form of the Good. The two traditions, Christianity and Platonism, are joined through the symbolism of the Sun in the thought of Augustine. As Charles Taylor notes:

> Augustine takes over the image of the sun, central to Plato's discussion of the Idea of the Good in the *Republic*, which both nourishes things in their being and gives them the light to see them by; but now the ultimate principle of being and knowledge together is God. God is the source of light, and here is another junction point, linking up with the light in the first chapter of John's Gospel. . . . [T]he light of God is not just "out there", illuminating the order of being, as it is for Plato; it is also an "inner" light. It is the light "which lighteth every man that cometh into the world" (John 1:19).[4]

Accordingly, the realization of the inner light of spirit is often described in terms of enlightenment, awakening, and illumination, as evident in Buddhism, for instance. The Buddha is the enlightened one, the one who awoke spiritually. Likewise, in the transfiguration of Christ, recounted in Matthew 17:2, we read that Jesus' face "shone like the sun." We see a similar idea suggested, of course, in the naming of the historical period of the Enlightenment, which championed the emergence into rational clarity and knowledge out of the shadows of medieval ignorance and superstition. The association between spirit and reason has been there at least since the time of Plato.

These themes and ideas—light and spirit, consciousness and awareness, being and creation, clarity and illumination—all fall within the complex of meanings associated with the planetary archetype of the Sun in astrology. As suggested by the Sun's place within the solar system as the central source of light and the incandescent star that supports all life on Earth so, in astrology, the Sun is symbolically associated not only with the light of consciousness that illuminates the world, and with being, but also with life energy and vitality, with centrality and dominance, and with the power of selfhood and radiance. The archetypal principle associated with the Sun manifests as the urge to be, to be someone, to be recognized, to be noticed, to express, to create.

The moment we wake from our nighttime slumber, and conscious awareness arises within us, the archetypal Sun is activated. Our awareness illuminates the world, our identity is recollected, our will becomes active, and our being centers itself again on consciousness. We focus on the day ahead and the task at hand; we intend, we act, we bring the power of being to bear on our circumstances. The Sun archetype is the principle of selfhood and identity, the central principle of will and intention. It is associated with individuality and the urge to self-expression, with self-esteem and individual pride.

The archetype of the Sun is therefore especially evident in moments when we feel we are truly being ourselves, in those moments when we have a clear sense of our identity and life purpose. It is evident, too, in the feelings of vitality and focused energy that accompany this sharper awareness of self and purpose. One can get a sense for certain aspects of the experience of the archetypal Sun on one's birthday, when the Sun completes its annual cycle and returns to its original place (a "solar return"). The experiences of being the center of attention, of having a stronger sense of our own individuality and our existence, of being in the limelight, and of being celebrated and recognized are intrinsic to this archetype. The experience of the Sun places us at the center of our world, of radiating, pouring our energy into the world. The active, expressive, and intentional quality associated with the Sun archetype gives it an affinity with the Chinese *yang* principle, the active "masculine" force, counterbalancing the yielding "feminine" quality of the *yin* principle, associated with the Moon.

The Ego and Solar Myths

The solar archetype is closely associated with the ego as the central complex of human consciousness. "The refulgent body of the sun," Jung notes, in reference to alchemical symbolism, "is the ego and its field of consciousness."[5] Such is the intimate symbolic association between the Sun and the ego that Jung explicitly connects the development of solar symbolism in myth and religion to the progressive emergence of a differentiated ego-consciousness over the millennia, resulting in the modern sense of identity and selfhood.

In a 1943 lecture given at Eranos, beginning with the proposition that "the Sun is basically a living symbol for the illumination of consciousness," Jung argued that solar creation myths thus refer to the process of "becoming conscious"; just as the Sun rises out of the darkness at dawn, consciousness emerges daily from the dark ocean of sleep and dream, and ego-consciousness, over the millennia, is progressively differentiated from the dim twilight existence that characterizes the primordial condition of *participation mystique*.[6] Like the Sun, the individual human ego, carrier of the light of consciousness, rises up out of the dark primordial mists towards a pinnacle of illumination.

This process ultimately leads, Jung suggests, to the Christian revelation, especially the Gospel of John, and is further developed in the theological speculations of the Scholastics.

> By now we have observed how the Sun god runs through a development in older culture and, in fact, takes on . . . a more and more spiritual shape; and, in the end, this light of the Sun becomes the light of John's logos, which shines out in the darkness and undoubtedly means spiritual illumination and the raising of human consciousness. It is the light of the *gnostis theou*.[7]

For Jung, the course of development of solar myths reflects a dramatic transformation of the human psyche by which the conscious ego emerged as an independent and autonomous self-willing agent, bringing a concomitant progressive strengthening of the human will. The fortification of an independent will enabled human beings to move beyond the *heimarmene* of the ancient world—characterized by fatalism, compulsion, crippling superstitions, and subservience to the will of the gods. As Jung puts it, "The dependency of people of the ancient world on *heimarmene* is [due to] this lack of consciousness that one is in the hands of."[8] In the ancient world, human will, to the extent that it existed at all, was secondary in its power and authority to the will of the gods.

If the emergence of the ego and an autonomous human will is a great cultural achievement, as Jung believes, it also brings with it certain attendant dangers, which he proceeds to discuss. With the development of the individual human subject, a subtle but consequential shift takes place which places singular emphasis upon the willing agent—the "I" principle—utterly disregarding divine will.[9] From the Renaissance and the Reformation on, Jung argues, "the individual no longer said: I *know*, I *will*, but the sound-stress shifted and now he said: *I* know, *I* will. As the human being became conscious of his size and freedom, the undermining of godly authority began."[10]

This psychological transition gave birth to a dualism—between subject and object, God and nature, consciousness and the unconscious, light and dark—that so defines the modern era, for better and for worse. It is a dualism that finds primary philosophical articulation in the work of Descartes. As Jung describes it:

> This freedom of human consciousness, the emancipation of the judgment and will from dependency on what is higher, brought one, I would like to say, one problem into the world—*duality*, a problem that really had never been there before. There had never been the sovereignty of the person in this sense. There had always been higher controlling powers at hand, which put a damper on things. So, this duality brought about a foundation of human consciousness, which had never been there before.[11]

The archetype of the Sun represents this sovereign ego, the ruler or dominant of consciousness. As Cicero describes in "The Dream of Scipio," the Sun is "the lord, chief, and ruler of the other lights, the mind and guiding principle of the universe, of such magnitude that he reveals and fills all things with his light."[12] As sovereign ruler, the symbolism of the Sun is naturally associated with a monotheistic godhead or the king. We see this in alchemy, for instance, in which the alchemists drew on both symbols—*Sol* and *Rex*—to symbolize ego-consciousness. As the ruling dominant of consciousness, in the alchemical drama the Sun and the king are subject to the transformative processes symbolizing the dynamics of individuation, including being devoured, cooked, and dismembered, drowning, dying, and being reborn. The mythic Sun symbolically portrays the fate of the ego.

The solar archetype, then, supports and symbolizes the individual's sense of identity, centered on the ego and, at a deeper level, the Self, for the Sun, as Jung notes, is "the classical symbol for the unity and divinity of the self."[13] In Jungian psychology, the archetypal Sun may be connected to the principle Erich Neumann calls "centroversion" by which psychological energy centers upon itself in the formation of the ego complex and then, at a later point, in the movement towards wholeness and the realization of the Self.[14] Centroversion might be seen as the psychological expression of a more general principle evident through the universe, which cosmologist Brian Swimme calls "centration."[15] We see centration at work when, for instance, a solar system forms around a central star or in the structuring of an atom around a nucleus.

The existential realization of the "I am" accesses the deeper mode of expression of the Sun as the Self, the center of the whole psyche, including consciousness and the unconscious. During those moments when the "I am" is experienced, one's ordinary ego-consciousness connects to a more profound sense of identity, of an age-old, even eternal, being, one that has always been there. Thus Jesus's enigmatic proclamation: "Before Abraham was, I am." (John 8:58) Both the ego and Self, the Sun is associated with Christ, *Atman*, and the incarnate God.[16] The light of awareness of the Sun, expressed in the "I am" realization, is also manifest in what is sometimes referred to as the "witness consciousness," the pure I, or pure consciousness, which is not attached to the stubborn cluster of thoughts and feelings, drives and fantasies, defenses and resistances, that comprise the ego.

For Jung, the light of human consciousness, supported by a differentiated ego, fulfills a singularly important role in the world in that it possesses world-constitutive power: "consciousness has a meaning that is entirely extraordinary. . . . Without consciousness, nothing exists. The world had really been nothing at all until somebody said: that is the world; that *is*."[17] In the 1943 lecture, as in his *Answer to Job*, Jung stresses the critical role of the human in bringing the unconscious divine (the "Dark Father") to consciousness.[18] God, Jung claimed, "revealed a functioning independent human consciousness. Now, the human being is instrumental; he was invented for that. God wanted consciousness so that he could be expressed."[19] It might be understood therefore as a central purpose of human experience to develop a consciousness of the light of spirit. Thus a logion in the Gospel of Thomas reads: "There is Light, at the center of a man of Light, and he illumines the whole world. If he does not shine, there is darkness."[20]

We might notice a parallel here to the work of Martin Heidegger, who calls upon the symbolism of light in the idea of *Dasein* ("there-being"), referring to human existence as a "clearing" in being, illuminating the "lived space" of existence or the life field (*Lebenswelt*).[21] For Heidegger, as for Jung, consciousness bears witness to being, and brings things out of their existential concealment into a known space of awareness.

Logos and Nous: The Archetypal Mercury

As a cosmic or metaphysical principle, the power of spirit, being, and consciousness manifests as *Logos*, the Word of God in the Christian tradition. *Logos* is the principle of divine reason within the cosmos. In the lineage of Greek philosophy, the term has been used to connote reason, argument, discourse, the spoken word, and logic. The implication is that human beings have the capacity to participate in the

THE WAY OF THE ARCHETYPES

divine reason, although this is not necessarily aligned with personal intelligence.

Another Greek philosophical term used to signify something like mind or intellect is *nous*, which is described by Aristotle as "the part of the soul by which it knows and understands."[22] As one philosophical commentary reports, "Aristotle supposes that it is our very nature to desire knowledge and understanding."[23]

In archetypal astrology, *logos* and *nous* fall under the domain of the archetypal principle Mercury, which pertains to the functions of thinking and knowing, reason and rationality, cognition and understanding, articulation and communication. Mercury, the planet, moves in close proximity to the Sun (the two are never more than 60 degrees apart, as measured against the zodiac). Symbolically reflecting this proximity, the function of the archetypal Mercury is closely tied to the forms of expression of the Sun. Human self-reflective consciousness, of course, is intimately bound up with the capacity for intelligence, reason, and knowing. Conscious intentionality requires the capacity for directed thinking, and ego-consciousness is often referred to as "the rational ego" or "rational ego-consciousness"; thought, broadly construed, is the foundation of the Cartesian ego.

Mercury might be imagined as the executor of the intentions of the solar archetype, supporting and articulating our sense of personal identity and the capacity for agency. In Greco-Roman myth, Mercury (the Greek Hermes) was the wing-footed messenger of the gods, conveying the biddings of the Olympians. The archetypal Mercury performs a similar function in human experience, enabling us to perceive, understand, articulate, and communicate the changing impulses and patterns of our experiences. The archetypal Mercury finds expression in the processing of information about the world through the senses, reason and the activity of the critical intellect, and communication with others through speech and writing. Every instant of the perception and assimilation of experience is connected to Mercury, every thought and every word uttered. Each time we read a book or browse the internet, the archetypal Mercury is being expressed. It is connected with information and data, knowledge and education, analysis and understanding. It finds physical expression in letters and emails, phone calls and speeches, newspapers and books. The archetype does not really possess a distinct qualitative emotional or energetic feel and tenor, except perhaps in the fundamental human impulse to learn or the need to understand and communicate. It can be experienced as inquisitiveness or curiosity or the satisfaction of understanding.

The Hero

As we have seen, the archetypal Sun symbolizes life energy, or libido. "The psychic life-force, the libido," Jung notes, "symbolizes itself in the sun or personifies itself in figures of heroes with solar attributes."[24] The Sun archetype and hero are thus closely connected. "The heroes," Jung adds, "are like the wandering sun"; or, again, "the myth of the hero is a solar myth."[25] Re-enacting the sun's descent below the horizon into the darkness of the night, the hero, as we have seen, is the archetypal figure especially associated with the struggle to carry the light of individual conscious selfhood into the depths of the underworld on the transformative journey towards the realization of the Self. The themes of descent, death and rebirth, the underworld, and so forth are more clearly associated with other planetary archetypes, especially Pluto, but the Sun is manifest as the heroic intentional ego-consciousness that undergoes the descent and underworld encounter. It pertains to the active, participatory role of human consciousness in the death-rebirth process.[26]

Especially in the first half of life, the heroic-solar impulse usually propels us on an upward, extraverted trajectory, rising like the Sun towards a pinnacle of clarity and visibility, shining forth in the quest for recognition and attainment. However, the arc of life, like the trajectory of the Sun, bends back towards its source—the darkness of the "maternal ground" of the unconscious, the "feminine" source. The victory of individual ego-consciousness, urged on by spirit, is only fulfilled in the return to soul. Thus Jung's remark in a letter: "This 'noonday sun' is a triumph, and with it the hero's career begins: his voluntary abdication before 'the human and feminine, which by its superiority in love has proved itself equal to the divine.'"[27]

More broadly understood, heroism is at the core of human experience, and we have already touched on a selection of ways this archetype can find expression in life. "Mankind's common instinct for reality," as William James saw it, ". . . has always held the world as a theatre for heroism."[28] The archetype of the Sun thus refers to the hero as the protagonist on the stage of life—a role ascribed to each of us. For the world is so arranged that, in the words of Arthur Schopenhauer, "each is the hero of his own drama while simultaneously figuring in a drama foreign to him"[29] There is but one planetary archetype associated with the Sun, but this archetype is manifest in each individual life, giving rise to the ubiquitous sense of the heroic, infusing us with the sense of the reality, centrality, and importance of our individual selfhood. Ernest Becker equates heroism with the feeling of "cosmic specialness" or "ultimate usefulness to creation," which provides "unshakeable meaning."[30] There are many types of heroism, some of them noble and life-enhancing, others warped or debasing; but at root they each emerge from the solar cosmological-archetypal principle, manifest in the individual as the heroic impulse to find and forge an identity, to express, create, and illuminate. "Our central calling, our main task on this planet," Becker concludes, "is the heroic."[31]

The Moon and the Great Mother

As the astrological Sun represents the singular light of diurnal consciousness, the Moon represents nighttime, nocturnal consciousness, and the domain of the unconscious. This association is borne out by our experience of the Sun and Moon, as human psychological experience shifts in accord with the phases of day and night. At sunrise, with the "birth" of the Sun each day out of the nighttime darkness, our days are full of possibility and promise; on waking, we possess vital life energy to be directed by consciousness and expended in the day's activities. At sunset, our vital energies are mostly exhausted, our conscious focus starts to relax and dissipate, and our sense of identity and being fall back onto something felt, habitual, familiar, less defined—qualities associated with the Moon in astrology. As the Sun sets, conscious individuality itself withdraws from the foreground, disappearing entirely as our waking state passes into sleeping and the unconscious becomes dominant, all taking place under the Moon's watch in the night sky.

The night sky has been poetically envisaged as the matrix or womb of the "maternal unconscious" from which the Sun (consciousness) is born and in which it has its existence. The Moon, as the ruler of the night sky, came to be symbolically associated with the Great Mother goddess as a mythic personification of the mother archetype. These meanings, and an array of derivative ones, are associated with the Moon archetype in astrology—the mother, the unconscious as the matrix of life, pregnancy and birth, nurturing and maternal care, relationality, Mother Nature, and Mother Earth. Whereas the Sun signifies a singular light of a monotheistic godhead, the Moon, as one of many lights in the night sky, is associated with pluralism and polytheism. Whereas the light of the Sun is clear and distinct, but potentially blinding and dazzling, the light of the Moon is softer, more diffuse, more ambiguous, illuminating things in a half-light, reflecting the light of the Sun rather than generating its own—qualities reflected in the Moon's thematic meaning in astrology.

Like the night sky, populated with stars, Jung believed that the unconscious is not a realm of utter darkness, but that it contains sparks of consciousness (he used the term *scintillae* borrowed from alchemy). He also used a "planet simile" to describe the psyche: the ego is like the Sun, the light of consciousness, the daytime light; the archetypes are like the planets or "lights" moving across the dark expanse of space.[32] If we overcome our singular fixation with consciousness, we can come to recognize that the light of the Sun (the conscious ego) is itself situated among many lights in the night sky (the unconscious). It is but one of the heavenly bodies (the archetypes) in the solar system (the psyche)

Reflecting its association with the Great Mother, the archetypal Moon pertains to all forms of relationship based on care, nurturing, and dependency, especially the infant-caregiver relationship. It symbolizes the emotional-relational matrix in which consciousness has its being. It is connected to the past, the womb, childhood, to that which comes naturally and habitually to us, to the felt sense of being, so prominent in young children before the ego becomes established. Indeed, the Moon pertains to the child archetype—to innocence, vulnerability, neediness, and the ebb and flow of changing emotions. This lunar archetype has a yielding, accepting quality akin to the *yin* principle of Chinese thought.[33] Like the Greek goddess Hestia, it rules the hearth and home, and family life; it manifests as the urge to feel comfortable and secure, and to belong. The Moon pertains to the matrix of society, and the security of belonging to a place, family, tribe, community, or to the common crowd, to feel oneself part of the larger human family. It is connected to the prevailing mood of the public, to the common feeling of the people.

The dynamics of the relationship between ego-consciousness and the unconscious might be symbolically understood not only in terms of the Sun-Moon relationship, but also through myths of the hero and the Great Mother.[34] In the Jungian view, the restless wandering of the hero arises as a result of the hero's separation from the Great Mother. To put this in psychological terms, the ceaseless striving associated with ego-consciousness—the quest for identity, the urge to be and to achieve—reflects the ego's separation and alienation from the maternal ground of the unconscious. "Consciousness," Jung notes, "continually in danger of being led astray by its own light and becoming . . . rootless . . . longs for the healing power of nature, for the deep wells of being and for unconscious communion with life in all its countless forms."[35] That is to say, the hero longs for the embrace of the Great Mother, for reunion with the source of life in the unconscious.

In its positive, life-enhancing aspect, the Great Mother is the source of renewal and of the instinctive and intuitive wisdom of nature. To come into relationship with the Mother is to access the vitality and meaning of the archetypes, for the Mother represents the collective unconscious in its entirety.[36] The Mother symbolizes the nourishing ground of life. In its life-negating aspect, however, the same principle can take the form of the Terrible Mother, devouring her offspring, like Kali of the Hindu tradition. The Mother's embrace can smother and stifle, as much as care and support. We unconsciously long to return to the Great Mother, to dissolve into her being and to return to our natural preconscious state, because this frees us from the pressures of individual selfhood, with the isolation, responsibilities, suffering, and restrictions selfhood brings. But just as it would not be healthy for the growing child to return to a condition of increasing dependency on the mother, so, for the adult ego, the yearning for the secure simplicity of unconscious existence is to be eschewed in favor of the preservation of the integrity and autonomy of ego-consciousness. The aim, rather, is to effect a union of the differentiated, autonomous conscious ego with the maternal ground of the unconscious, a union suggested by the motif of the *hieros gamos*, the sacred marriage. To achieve this, we must recover our lost connections with the unconscious as the matrix of feelings and instincts but without losing our identity and capacity for independent intentional consciousness. The process of individuation leads towards the realization of this union, which is to be achieved by the development of the anima function, an archetype, as we will consider shortly, that is also associated with the astrological Moon. The process begins, however, with an encounter with the shadow.

Notes

1 Jung, *Archetypes and the Collective Unconscious*, 208–209. par. 386.
2 Bellah, *Religion in Evolution*, 245.
3 Sridhara Swami's Commentary on the Rudra Vaisnava Sampradaya.
4 Taylor, *Sources of the Self*, 128.
5 Jung, *Mysterium Coniunctionis*, 108, par. 129.
6 Jung, *Solar Myths*, 83.
7 Jung, *Solar Myths*, 86. The Gnostic theou, according to Hans Jonas (*Gnostic Religion*, 285) is the "direct beholding of divine reality."
8 Jung, *Solar Myths*, 88.

[9] The position Jung advances in this lecture is broadly consistent with perspectives in recent work such as Charles Taylor, *A Secular Age* (Cambridge, MA: The Belknap Press of Harvard University Press, 2007) and Richard Tarnas, *Cosmos and Psyche: Intimations of a New World View* (New York: Viking, 2006).

[10] Jung, *Solar Myths*, 108.

[11] Jung, *Solar Myths*, 89.

[12] Cited in Bellah, *Religion in Evolution*, 15.

[13] Jung, *Psychology and Alchemy*, 83, par. 108.

[14] See Neumann, *Origins and History of Consciousness*.

[15] I discuss connections between Swimme's notion of cosmological powers and the planetary archetypes in astrology in *The Archetypal Cosmos*—see Chapter IX: "Individuation and Evolution."

[16] Jung, *Solar Myths*, 112.

[17] Jung, *Solar Myths*, 86.

[18] Jung, *Solar Myths*, 104.

[19] Jung, *Solar Myths*, 88.

[20] Ross, *Gospel of Thomas*, 25 (logion 24).

[21] See Heidegger, *Being and Time*. For an excellent study of the ideas of Heidegger in relation to Jung, see Roger Brooke, *Jung and Phenomenology*.

[22] Aristotle, *De Anima* iii 4, 429a9–10; cf. iii 3, 428a5; iii 9, 432b26; iii 12, 434b3), cited in Christopher Shields, "Aristotle's Psychology," *The Stanford Encyclopedia of Philosophy* (Winter 2020 Edition), Edward N. Zalta (ed.), URL = <https://plato.stanford.edu/archives/win2020/entries/aristotle-psychology/>.

[23] Aristotle, *Metaphysics* i 1, 980a21; *De Anima* ii 3, 414b18; iii 3, 429a6–8), in Shields, "Aristotle's Psychology," *The Stanford Encyclopedia of Philosophy*.

[24] Jung, *Symbols of Transformation*, 202, par. 297.

[25] Jung, *Symbols of Transformation*, 205, par. 299.

[26] Perhaps with this in mind in his representation of the course of the individuation process Jung called on the metaphor of the sun's journey across the sky, designating the first half of life as the period in which the ego, like the sun, emerges from the darkness of the unconscious and reaches its noontime zenith. Noon, when the sun begins its descent, represents midlife, the onset of the second half of life, the moment of transition, when the ego turns to begin its return journey of descent towards the source. The strict association with particular points of life in Jung's model is somewhat contentious, but of significance for us here is the connection between the journey of consciousness, the hero motif, and solar symbolism.

[27] Jung, letter to Erich Neumann, 28 February 1952, *Letters II*, 42.

[28] James, quoted in Becker, *Denial of Death*, 1.

[29] Schopenhauer, quoted in Arthur Koestler, *The Roots of Coincidence*, 108.

[30] Becker, *Denial of Death*, 5.

[31] Becker, *Denial of Death*, 1.

[32] For Jung's "planet simile," see *Jung on Astrology*, 33.

[33] A dialogue in Jung's Red Book alludes to the secret identity between the soul and the mother: "I, your soul, am your mother, who tenderly and frightfully surrounds you, your nourisher and corrupter" (Jung, *Red Book*, Appendix C, 582).

[34] See especially Jung, *Symbols of Transformation,* and Neumann, *The Great Mother.*

[35] Jung, *Symbols of Transformation*, 205, 299.

[36] As Jung observes: "Wisdom dwells in the depths, the wisdom of the mother; being one with her means being granted a vision of deeper things, of the primordial images and primitive forces which underlie all life and are its nourishing, sustaining, creative matrix. (Jung, *Symbols of Transformation*, 413, par. 640).

Chapter 8

Shadow, Super-ego, and Senex

Perhaps the most well-known of all the Jungian archetypes, the shadow is Jung's term for the dark side of the human personality—all those aspects of our experience that are deemed taboo, morally unacceptable, or socially undesirable, and which therefore are often repressed, existing outside of our conscious awareness. Jung describes the shadow as the complementary counterpart to the light side of the personality. Where there is light (of conscious awareness) there is shadow. Life consists of pairs of opposites, and thus psychological darkness can never be avoided or banished, any more than we can do away with night and live in perpetual daylight. Good presupposes evil, for every positive there is a negative, for every high a low. The primary distinction of light and dark, day and night, conscious and unconscious is symbolized, as we have already seen, by the solar and lunar archetypes in astrology. Yet in facing the darkness within oneself during individuation, one first encounters archetypal themes and experiences pertaining to the shadow.

There is an enduring fascination with the dark side of life and with the taboo, for we sense in the darkness and forbidden a source of power not available to us consciously. If we dare to explore the darkness, we encounter there a range of experiences that, because they arise from primitive and uncivilized drives, are often more vital, more authentic, than the experiences that compromise our socially conditioned reality, with its concessions to societal expectations, and its moral strictures and restraints, responsibilities and duties. In dreams, the shadow can often take the form of a dark figure or threatening beast, relentlessly pursuing the dreamer. In the arts, an imagination for the shadow has given rise to creations of classic and popular explorations of dual personalities, such as *The Strange Case of Dr. Jekyll and Mr. Hyde*, *The Incredible Hulk*, and more recently *Fight Club*. We see in each of these examples the dark inner other as an autonomous figure, often undervalued, denigrated, or denied, and bringing with it the fear of the loss of control, of unleashing of forces of evil, chaos, and destruction. The Joker of the Batman films is another example of this kind. The shadow figure is typically wild and primitive, not abiding by or constrained by the laws of civilized life, and yet it is the source of tremendous power and potential for good as well as for evil, containing the very power one needs to draw on in meeting one's fate and the living of an authentic life. The shadow is primitive for it represents areas of our experience and aspects of our personality we have not faced and consciously engaged with, thus remaining undeveloped. The shadow is also the weak and inferior side of the personality, embodying traits one finds it difficult to accept in oneself, for they often pertain to areas of life in which we feel we have fallen short, failed, and not lived up to what is expected of us by society, and that we have therefore avoided or denied. Thus the shadow is sometimes personified, Jung notes, by the figure of the dwarf—a figure who is small, maimed, overlooked, and often despised but, like the unconscious that stands behind it, is incredibly potent. In each case, the shadow is comprised of a combination of traits excluded from the conscious personality that, if assimilated, would round out the individual's character.

The assimilation of the shadow is far from straightforward, however, as the dark power within is usually unavailable to the conscious personality hermetically sealed inside the walls of the ego structure. One can only gain access to the submerged and repressed power of the unconscious and begin to acquaint oneself with the existence of the other archetypes through first facing up to one's insecurities, weakness, and inferiority that comprise the personal shadow. Then, as Jung remarked, "if we step through the door of the shadow we discover with terror that we are the objects of unseen factors"—namely the pantheon of archetypes.[1] In this sense, the shadow is the passageway, running through a fissure in the ego structure, that leads to the realm of the collective unconscious.

In relation to the astrological planetary archetypes in astrology the shadow maps onto a number of different principles, but it has the strongest associations with Pluto, Saturn, and Uranus. Those aspects of the shadow pertaining to unrecognized and uncivilized drives, the instincts, the bestial and subhuman, the capacity for wanton destruction—in short, the dark underworld of the instinctual unconscious—fall into the domain of Pluto. Aspects of the shadow pertaining to moral judgment, inferiority, weakness, suffering, pain, guilt, and sin have clear associations with Saturn. And the capacity of the shadow (in its relationship to the trickster) to trip us up and cause us to blunder pertain to Uranus. We will consider further the compelling attraction of the feeling and expression of power and the underworld encounter, relating to the planetary archetype Pluto, in a chapter to follow. And the shadow dimension of Uranus will be addressed in our later discussion of the trickster archetype. But let us turn our attention first to the aspects of the shadow to do with moral judgment and inferiority—traits that are related to Saturn.

The Shadow and the Ego Structure

Although the archetypes are all always operative in life, and cannot therefore be said to manifest in any kind of linear sequence, in a "confrontation with the unconscious" the shadow is the first archetype encountered. For Jung, facing the shadow is the "apprentice-piece" of individuation, an initiatory challenge that calls forth our moral courage, and from which we are inclined to recoil in fear, embarrassment, guilt, or defeat.[2] The shadow contains the repressed contents of personal experience and is thus, at one level, synonymous with what Jung calls the personal unconscious. Everything we have not been able to face and assimilate in our biographical experiences—our personal complexes and repressed memories, for instance—reside within the personal unconscious. As the name implies, we are usually unaware of the existence of these parts of us. If, however, due to some psychological crisis, one's persona is no longer adequate to cope with the demands of life, repression can fail and the persona can "dissolve"; one can experience a "collapse of the conscious attitude," as Jung put it.[3] Then, we must turn to face the shadow and begin the path of individuation if we are to move beyond the crisis, live authentically, and further our psychological development.

Facing the shadow can be a humbling experience. We are forced to admit that we are not—or not only—the competent, accomplished person we perhaps believed ourselves to be, but that in certain aspects of our character, we are undeveloped, primitive, weak, and inferior, unable to live up to the standards we adhere to and aspire to. The shadow, and the Saturn principle with which it is associated, is the Achilles' heel, the point of weakness and vulnerability in our personality, from which we ordinarily unconsciously shield ourselves. The ego structure initially forms and develops around the area of weakness, as if to protect us from experiences and emotions we find too painful to assimilate. As we grow, we gravitate towards our strengths, to those talents that come naturally and the areas of life in which we are comfortable and competent. Meanwhile, we unwittingly push to one side experiences that bring pain and discomfort. Such a situation can persist long into adult life, perhaps even indefinitely. But life intends that we become whole, and circumstances might thus arise that send the structure of our world and our personality crashing to the ground like a Tower of Babel, shattered by some divine lightning bolt issuing forth from the Self. Amidst the ruins, the long-concealed sore spot and weaknesses are exposed, and might be faced and passed through, if we can muster the moral courage and will.

While it remains unrecognized and unaccepted, the shadow can undermine the conscious ego's posture and well-meaning plans and intentions. The shadow sabotages our conscious aims; the weakness we cannot or dare not face trips us up, exposing the ego to aspects of life it would rather avoid. Until we have been able to face up to the challenge of Saturn, life constantly brings our frailty and vulnerability before us, attracting circumstances and events that call forth the shadow and opportunities for its recognition, acceptance, and integration.

The encounter with the shadow represents something like a biblical "fall" from ignorance and a psychologically naïve innocence into a fuller experience of life's inherent suffering, and the associated feelings of misery, depression, guilt, sin, and judgment. It is a fall into painful alienation, separation, and entrapment—an experience that seems to be an inevitable consequence of incarnate earthly existence. Through the shadow, we might come to apprehend, with direct immediacy, the self-perpetuating misery of *samsara*, to use the Buddhist term.

Understandably, then, encountering the shadow brings with it feelings of fear, trepidation, shame, embarrassment, guilt, foreboding, and even dread. No longer shielded by repression, one is confronted by a morass of acutely painful emotions that had been festering below the surface of consciousness, perhaps for years. It demands considerable courage and resilience to prevent oneself turning away from these feelings, for who among us would want to spend our waking hours wading through the dark residues of the pain of a lifetime? Even to allow these emotions to fully enter consciousness, however, is far from straightforward, for we would obviously prefer not to be subject to them, and for this reason we tend to automatically resist them and unconsciously repress them as they arise. The encounter with the shadow thus only becomes possible when repression fails or can be systematically overcome. To assimilate the shadow demands that we break down deeply ingrained resistances, undo repressions, and in so doing die, a little at a time, to the rule of the old ego.

If the personality becomes too one-sided, identified with a narrow persona, the shadow grows in power. A reservoir of unlived life energy accumulates in the unconscious, straining almost to breaking point the functions of repression and censorship, which protect the integrity of the ego and sustain its boundaries. In such a condition, the narrow ego personality effectively becomes a kind of prison, with consciousness trapped in an oppressively limited existence encased within the walls of the ego, and resistant to the influx of new life, but with pressure bearing down on it from all sides. As a result, the personality crystallizes and ossifies. By inhibiting the flow of life energy, the ego structure can foster alienation, and deliver us to a wasteland situation, as the conscious personality becomes walled off from the world, like an empire ruled by an old king, whose kingdom has become barren, left to ruin and decay. The alchemical figure of the king personifies the ego in this condition. Like a tyrant ogre, the ego clings to the established order as if its existence depends on it, ruling with an iron fist, devouring new life before it has the chance to blossom, desperately attempting to remain in control, and to fortify a collapsing, decaying empire.

In its limiting, life-resistant mode of expression, Saturn is associated with all these themes and experiences: the old and the established order, fear and negativity, separation and alienation, boundaries and structures, crystallization and decay, atrophy and contraction, judgment and inferiority, resistances and repression. At root, Saturn is associated with the principle of negation, the "no" response to life, often manifesting as a turning away from the pain of life in an unconscious attempt at protection and self-preservation. Freud sees such resistance as the cause of human illness and suffering: "Human beings fall ill of a conflict between the claims of instinctual life and the resistance which arises within them against it."[4]

The personal shadow represents the escape-route from the alienated condition of a defensive ego; it is the chink in the ego's armor, the crack in the structure of the walls of the dominant personality, through which consciousness, if it is willing and able to endure a prolonged uncomfortable and painful psychological experience, can find a way out, leading to an experience of the larger reality of the psyche. "The shadow," Jung reflects, "is a tight passage, a narrow door, whose painful constriction no one is spared who goes down to the deep well."[5] In this respect, it might be imagined as something akin to the experience of the contracting womb and birth canal described in Grofian psychology. Indeed, as we have seen, Tarnas and Grof discovered that the second perinatal matrix is closely associated with the Saturn archetype. All experiences of entrapment and limitation, when we feel imprisoned in a life situation and our escape route blocked, pertain to Saturn. The entrapment serves a constructive purpose, however, for it forces us to face ourselves. It is only by a willingness to bear the claustrophobic constriction of facing the acutely painful aspects of one's personality and life experience that one can be transformed, and emerge in time from the domination of the old, autocratic ego. For it is in our area of weakness and inferiority that the ego has little or no control. As painful and belittling as the experience of the shadow is, it leads us into virgin territory, as it were, outside of the rigid grip of the old ego. Through the shadow, we may tunnel down into the vast expanse of the unconscious.

Facing the Saturnian dimension of life through the shadow, what was once a weakness can in the fullness of time become a strength. The collapse of the conscious attitude and the encounter with the shadow present the opportunity to rebuild the structure of one's life on firmer foundations. Our former weakness, the area of life causing us the most difficulty and discomfort, and demanding of us the greatest effort to come to terms with, can then become the cornerstone of the new personality, the foundation on which the Self might be realized. What is more, the labor and long struggle with our weaknesses draws forth moral qualities and Saturnian virtues—patience, discipline, humility, hard-earned wisdom, self-knowledge, and deep understanding. It enables us to develop backbone, steadfastness, and maturity. Saturn manifests as a moral burden placed on us, the cross we have to bear, and the positive limitation that provides grounding and structure for our lives. If one can come to terms with the Saturnian dimension of experience, the millstone around one's neck can become a burden gladly borne. Saturnian virtues are hard-earned but of enduring value.

The Super-ego and the Weight of Tradition

As we have seen, the shadow is created by an implicit moral judgment as to what aspects of our psychological experience are compatible with our persona, and what is socially acceptable, and morally permissible, legitimized and sanctioned by the social group to which we belong. The function of moral judgment is well represented by the Freudian concept of the super-ego, the "introjected" moral conscience acquired from our upbringing, which throughout childhood was represented and enforced by parents, teachers, and other authority figures. As an internalized function, the super-ego is in the role of judge and arbiter, determining which aspects of experience are congruent with our moral code and societal expectations, and which are to be excluded and disowned. To bring together Freudian and Jungian perspectives, we might say that the judging super-ego, executing the functions of moral censorship and repression, effectively creates the complex of emotions, memories, fantasies, and drives that together comprise the shadow. In the super-ego we also see crucial elements of the archetype of the father, which represents the "principle of the spirit," initiator into life in the wider world, and embodiment of the moral law, whether of society and civilization, or, at another level, the law of one's own deeper being representing a conscience derived not from the values of the social group, but from the Self. In Freudian psychology, the super-ego, as the conscience and introjected moral authority, stands in opposition to the uncontrolled and uncivilized desirousness of the id. As Jung puts it, "The father is the representative of the spirit, whose function it is to oppose pure instinctuality."[6]

To come into relationship with the shadow during individuation feels as if it requires a moral transgression, going against the dictates of the super-ego as paternal and societal authority. We are obliged to allow into consciousness, and to accept as our own, impulses, emotions, and images that are starkly counter to the person we consider ourselves to be and that violate our ingrained ethical standards and moral boundaries. For most of us in the Western world, these boundaries are significantly shaped by Christian beliefs and ethical imperatives, reflecting Christianity's sharply defined categories of good and evil, light and dark, and its accentuated emphasis on sin and guilt. We are each subject to a range of implicitly accepted assumptions about how we should live, often pertaining to a deeply instilled work ethic and to the duties and responsibilities placed on us that we feel, rightly or wrongly, we must fulfill. In these matters, we feel acutely what society, family, and our peers demand and expect of us, and in what ways we are lacking in our capacity to meet these requirements. Saturn and the shadow pertain to those aspects of life in which we are exceptionally sensitive or that we deem gravely important—as much as we might like to pretend otherwise, or as much as we might mask any insecurity and self-consciousness behind some confident image, over-compensating for the weakness, inferiority, and seriousness that we might not even be able to admit to ourselves. Adler's notion of the inferiority complex is relevant here, of course, for it is recognized that a sense of inferiority will tend to foster a compensatory drive for greatness, superiority, power, and achievement—an individual "will to power."

Freud described the super-ego as "an agency that observes and threatens" to punish the ego.[7] As an "observing agency," like a sentry or prison guard, the super-ego "enjoys a certain degree of autonomy" and can function unconsciously.[8] It is therefore not subject to the individual's conscious control through acts of will. We cannot stop it proffering judgments or make it cease from its punitive assaults. For Freud, the super-ego rests on a real structural arrangement of the psyche; it is not just a personification of conscience.

The super-ego, Freud adds, is often severe and cruel; "it abuses the poor ego, humiliates it," applying "the strictest moral standards" as it "represents the claims of morality" and brings with it a sense of guilt related to conscience.[9] The super-ego "represents the demands of a restrictive and rejecting character" in distinction from, and often in outright opposition to, the life-affirming, ever-desiring id.[10] Unsurprisingly, then, the super-ego's attacks on the ego can, in characteristically Saturnian fashion, give rise to melancholia.[11] The oppression of the super-ego brings with it guilt and anxiety, hypercriticism and depression, which weigh heavily upon us.

Despite this seemingly wholly negative character, the super-ego possesses a positive dimension too, for it also serves to promote the aspiration towards an "ego ideal," reminding us of the exacting standards we should meet and pushing us to actualize our best self. As Freud puts it, the super-ego is the "vehicle of the ego-ideal by which the ego measures itself, which it emulates and whose demand for ever-greater perfection it strives to fulfill."[12] It is, he adds, the "representative of every moral restriction, the advocate of striving towards moral perfection," and thus is crucial for "the higher side of human life."[13]

As the "vehicle of tradition," the super-ego is passed on generation to generation.[14] Freud explains: "The past, the tradition of the race and of the people, lives on in the ideologies of the super-ego, and yields only slowly to the influences of the present and to new changes."[15] Thus, the super-ego, like Saturn, is of a conservative nature, adverse to change, representing and enforcing the status quo and carrying forward tradition. In these respects, the super-ego might be compared to Friedrich Nietzsche's notion of the "thou shalt," the moral imperatives and expectations that impinge on us and oppress us (the "values of a thousand years," as Nietzsche put it), and which, in his view, must be overthrown if we are to win through to authentic freedom.[16] In Gestalt psychology, Fritz Perls's concept of the "top dog" might also be mentioned here, referring to the aspect of human psychology that enforces and commands, issuing imperatives—"you should do this," "you must do that"—to the "under dog" side of the personality.

For Nietzsche, the principle of the "thou shalt" embodies the oppressive side of tradition and established values. Yet we can recognize too that the assimilation of all that is best in tradition is an essential aspect of psychological development—essential both for personal maturation and for competent participation in social and cultural life. One cannot bring forth one's unique gifts in a way that is valuable to others unless one is aware of what has come before. To put this another way, one cannot truly individuate until one has assimilated the wisdom and learning of the past. But one cannot individuate either unless one is able to go beyond the boundaries of established values and learning to move into the field of one's own authentic experience.

All of the above phenomena are associated with the Saturn archetypal principle: limitation, suffering, judgment, authority, rules, censorship, repression, fear, inferiority, established values, resistance, guilt, embarrassment, and sin. Saturn finds expression in the moral commandment and the laws of the land. In myth, it takes personified form as the threshold-guardian that, as a symbol of our own fear and resistance, obstructs us, barring the way to authentic experience and the acceptance of our life adventure, and preventing the realization of our deepest nature, until we are able to pass beyond it. Psychologically, as we have seen, Saturn is closely connected to fear and the self-preservation instinct, which manifests in psychological form as the structure of the ego, with its characteristic defensive posture, serving to shield us from the world and from the painful reality of the full range of psychological experience. Saturn is present in old, life-resistant forms and structures; it pertains to boundaries and obstacles, and a cleaving to established rules as to how we should live and what we ought to do. It is the hard hand of the father, the ruling authority that must be assimilated and ultimately overcome if we are to win through to our own original experience and individuate. In sum, we can see that Saturn pertains to an array of experiences intrinsic to both the Jungian archetype of the shadow and the Freudian super-ego.

The Wise Old Man and Senex Consciousness

Because of the challenging or problematic nature of many of the phenomena and experiences associated with Saturn, this archetypal principle is a maturing influence in our lives, grounding us in the practical realities and necessities of the world, pushing us to the actualization of our innate potentiality, exerting upon us the pressure that will enable us to cultivate discipline and control, restraint and responsibility, temperance and good judgment. Saturn constitutes the very tests and trials that forge the moral character of the youthful, aspiring ego. In this respect especially, it is the astrological principle most clearly associated with the Jungian archetype of the wise old man, "the superior master and teacher"[17] who, Jung observes, "tests the moral qualities of others,"[18] and elicits insight and wisdom. "The wise old man," he continues, "appears in dreams in the guise of a magician, doctor, priest, teacher, professor, grandfather, or any other person possessing authority."[19] Popular forms of this figure, featured in literature and film, readily suggest themselves—Gandalf in *The Lord of the Rings*, Yoda and Ben Kenobi in *Star Wars*, for instance—but it is important to keep in mind that the archetype finds expression directly in our own experience, as a personification of the guiding intelligence or superior knowledge of the unconscious that can come to our aid in the hour of need. This archetypal figure might manifest, for instance, as an uncanny "voice" in our dreams, announcing what is to pass, reflecting the vantage point of the total psyche. The interventions of the old man—in myth, dreams, literature, and in immediate personal experience—can be likened to the mythic motif of "supernatural aid."[20] Thus Jung: "The old man always appears when the hero is in a hopeless and desperate situation."[21] The magical appearance here pertains more immediately to Neptune, as we will shortly consider, but the specific character of this archetypal figure is expressive of Saturn. He is an authority figure, embodying the wisdom of hard experience, from which he is able to provide guidance to the aspiring hero, symbolizing the ego: "The old man knows what roads lead to the goal and points them out to the hero."[22] The old man also slows things down, hindering the youthful, perhaps impetuous hero, eager for the adventure ahead and the promise of attainment. Saturn is connected to the principle of Time and the Greek god Chronos, for this principle often impedes us, slowing down progress, making us work step by step for any advancement and reward. The gifts of Saturn often come late, in the fullness of time, when one has reached a place of calm maturity and detachment, and worked long and hard at overcoming one's weaknesses and assuming the burden of responsibility that life places on us. Through the slow unfolding in time, Saturn matures and ripens, bringing things to completion at the right moment. Saturn has associations too with the Freudian "reality principle," to which the ego is impelled to adhere.[23] When well integrated, Saturn can furnish one with the ability to squarely face the truth of one's reality, doing what needs to be done, with an unhurried sense of the right timing of things.

Another Saturnian aspect of the wise old man is the capacity for stern criticism, recalling a prominent feature of the Freudian super-ego. As if to puncture any sense of inflation or complacence, the wise old man can find faults and flaws that push us towards greater standards of perfection and consistent effort. Likewise, in myth and popular portrayals in the arts, the old man as mentor and teacher can set his young disciples seemingly pointless tasks and tests, whose value often only becomes apparent in retrospect, when the training manifests as the learned skill and wisdom necessary for the life adventure. The wise old man archetype represents the capacity of the psyche and the world to impose on us this kind of hard discipline, bringing the ego to greater maturation, pushing us to do what we must, frustrating us that we might cultivate the Saturnian virtues of patience, consistency, and discipline. Saturn can manifest as the hand of fate knocking us back on track, impressing on us what it is we really must do to live authentically. In its combined expression as both shadow and wise old man, Saturn in astrology shows that which is most limiting, that which we have to struggle against over and over again, are the very experiences that give to life a structure and meaning. Jung refers to the wise old man as the "archetype of meaning."[24]

More generally, the wise old man is closely connected to the senex archetype, whose qualities, as James Hillman has described, might be observed throughout our experience as aspects of Saturn:

> Saturn is at once archetypal image for the wise old man, solitary sage, the lapis as rock of ages with all its positive moral and intellectual virtues, and for the Old King, that castrating castrated ogre. He is the world as builder of cities and the not-world of exile. At the same time that he is father of all he consumes all, by living on and from his fatherhood he feeds himself insatiably from the bounty of his own paternalism. *Saturn is image for both positive and negative senex.*[25]

In line with Hillman's emphasis on the *anima mundi* and his application of archetypal psychology outside of the therapy room, seeing gods and goddesses and archetypes in all things, he gives an exhaustive account of the many forms of "senex consciousness" and all aspects of reality pertaining to the Saturn principle. For Hillman, the senex archetype "expresses all that is old, ordered and established."[26] It is "slow, heavy, chronic, leaden: these qualities produce weight."[27] Like Jung, he recognized that "personifications of this principle appear in the holy or old wise man, the powerful father or grandfather, the great king, ruler, judge, ogre, counsellor, elder, priest, hermit, outcast and cripple."[28] "Some emblems," he adds, "are the rock, the old tree, particularly oak, the scythe or sickle, the time-piece and the skull."[29] Saturn and the senex are personified as the god Chronos, as Father Time, and as the Grim Reaper. In Meister Eckhart's view, one Saturnian theme—time—is inextricably connected to another—the obstacle or barrier, which separates us from our divine nature. "Time is what keeps the light from reaching us. There is no greater obstacle to God than time."[30]

We can see Saturn as senex in everything that is old—an old stone wall or an ancient monument, a medieval church or castle, the ruins of a Roman fortress or the long traditions of great universities. Saturn represents not only psychological structures—as in the structure of the ego—but any kind of structure or boundary, such as the skeletal structure, or dividing walls, or perimeter fences, or buildings as the infrastructure of the city. It is manifest in political establishments, governments, legal courts, and institutions. It is expressed in psychological heaviness but also concretely in the heaviness of material things; it is the principle that pulls us down or anchors us or grounds us in practical realities. Saturn is present as the force of gravity and in the denseness of solid matter, which, like the nature of the Saturn archetype, is enduring and slow to change. The hard facts, the literal, and the concrete substance of things also fall under the domain of Saturn, as do conservatism, traditionalism, and the status quo.

In alchemical terms, as Hillman notes above, Saturn/senex pertains to the process of *coagulatio* by which the liquid form of the alchemical substance becomes solid, assuming a definite tangible form, or becoming stuck, blocked, damned up, weighed down. Saturn makes things real, gives them realized physical form. But this form can become set in stone, rigid, and life resistant—hence the alchemical commitment to the ongoing process of dissolution and coagulation: "*solve et coagula*" as the alchemical dictum decrees.

In another obvious alchemical association, Saturn finds expression in the operation of *mortificatio*, bringing the "death" of the established form of the matter, often personified as the death of the old king. It is therefore evident too within the *nigredo* phase of the opus, with its melancholy blackness and suffering, leading to the death experience. And we meet Saturn again in the alchemical vessel itself, which serves as the containing structure for transformation, much as the structure of the individual psyche and the limitation of circumstance serve as the containing structures of psychological transformation during the individuation process.

Many of the psychological meanings of Saturn can be associated with the reality of death, and the fear of death, considered by certain thinkers to be the primary underlying motivation in human life. Unsurprisingly, then, Saturn is associated with a range of psychological conditions, both common and pathological, that have been the focus of exploration in psychotherapy and psychiatry. As Hillman notes, "melancholy, anxiety, sadism, paranoia, anality, and obsessive memory ruminations reflect this archetype."[31] An encounter with death is significant for soul-making, in Hillman's view, and existential philosophers and psychologists stress the importance of facing one's mortality for living authentically. An encounter with death serves like nothing else to put one's attention on what is most important in life and to make us aware of our limited time on the planet to do what it is we must—a noble manifestation of the Saturn archetype.

Notes

[1] Jung, *Archetypes and the Collective Unconscious*, 23, par. 49.
[2] Jung, *Archetypes and the Collective Unconscious*, 29, par. 61.
[3] Jung, *Two Essays on Analytical Psychology*, 156–171.
[4] Freud, *New Introductory Lectures on Psycho-Analysis*, 72.
[5] Jung, *Archetypes and the Collective Unconscious*, 21, par. 45.
[6] Jung, *Symbols of Transformation*, 261, par. 396.
[7] Freud, *New Introductory Lectures on Psycho-Analysis*, 76.
[8] Freud, *New Introductory Lectures on Psycho-Analysis*, 75.
[9] Freud, *New Introductory Lectures on Psycho-Analysis*, 76.
[10] Freud, *New Introductory Lectures on Psycho-Analysis*, 86.
[11] Freud, *New Introductory Lectures on Psycho-Analysis*, 75–76.
[12] Freud, *New Introductory Lectures on Psycho-Analysis*, 81.
[13] Freud, *New Introductory Lectures on Psycho-Analysis*, 82.
[14] Freud, *New Introductory Lectures on Psycho-Analysis*, 84.
[15] Freud, *New Introductory Lectures on Psycho-Analysis*, 84.
[16] Nietzsche, *Thus Spoke Zarathustra* ("Of the Three Metamorphoses"), 55.
[17] Jung, *Archetypes and the Collective Unconscious*, 35, par. 74.
[18] Jung, *Archetypes and the Collective Unconscious*, 225, par. 410.
[19] Jung, *Archetypes and the Collective Unconscious*, 216, par. 398.
[20] See Campbell, *Hero with a Thousand Faces*, 69–77.

21 Jung, *Archetypes and the Collective Unconscious*, 217, par. 401.

22 Jung, *Archetypes and the Collective Unconscious*, 221, par. 405.

23 As Freud explains, the ego is positioned between the external world, the id, and the super-ego. The ego is a portion of the id, modified by coming into contact with external reality. It has a reality-testing function. The ego "has taken on the task of representing the external world to the id—fortunately for the id, which could not escape destruction if, in its blind efforts for the satisfaction of the instincts, it disregarded that supreme external power" (*New Introductory Lectures on Psycho-Analysis*, 94). The ego dethrones the pleasure principle (which rules the id) and replaces it with the reality principle. "The ego stands for reason and good sense while the id stands for the untamed passions" (*New Introductory Lectures on Psycho-Analysis*, 95).

24 Jung, *Archetypes and the Collective Unconscious*, 35, par. 74 & 37, par. 79.

25 Hillman, "Senex and Puer: An Aspect of the Historical and Psychological Present," in *Senex & Puer*, 38 [emphasis in original].

26 Hillman, "On Senex Consciousness," in *Senex & Puer*, 243.

27 Hillman, "On Senex Consciousness," in *Senex & Puer*, 249.

28 Hillman's characterization of the senex here draws on themes associated with his own birth-chart combination of Saturn and Neptune—see Volume II (especially 242–244, note 6 to Chapter 20) for a discussion of the expression of this archetypal complex in Hillman's work.

29 Hillman, "On Senex Consciousness," in *Senex & Puer*, 243.

30 Meister Eckhart, quoted in Huxley, *Perennial Philosophy*, 197.

31 Hillman, "On Senex Consciousness," in *Senex & Puer*, 243.

Chapter 9

Uranus and the Trickster

The capacity of the unconscious to usurp our sense of personal control, derail our plans, and sabotage our intentions and chosen life directions is represented by the mythic figure of the trickster, whose prevalence in world mythology supports Jung's treatment of this figure as a major archetype or principle in its own right. In certain respects, as Jung notes, the trickster is equivalent in collective mythology to the shadow in personal psychology in that both are inferior and primitive, comprised of aspects of our character and of life that have remained unconscious and are therefore undeveloped.

Functions of the Trickster: Disruption, Awakening, Liberation
Especially evident in the trickster figure is the capacity of the larger psyche to trip us up, to cause us to blunder and fall, through sheer unconsciousness of our actions and motivations. The thoughtless deed, the slip of the tongue or ill-chosen word, the unfortunate timing of an action, and the seemingly accidental intervention of chance are all expressions of the trickster principle. Attributing such phenomena to an archetype implies there is an essential element of universal human experience, an aspect of the unconscious that ever lies outside of human control and reveals the limitations of the ego. The archetypal character of the trickster suggests furthermore that behind these happenings there lies a hidden logic or purpose. The "psychopathology of everyday life"—slips of the tongue, jokes, forgetting of names and words, leaving things behind—is often indicative not just of a failure of repression, permitting unconscious wishes to manifest, as Freudian psychoanalysis has described, but is also expressive of an unseen purpose at work in the unconscious. Chance and circumstance are the means by which the unconscious manifests from without, as much as the unconscious speaks to us within through the symbolic language of dreams.

The trickster figure symbolizes life's refusal to bend to our will or conform to our plans, or to be accommodated within neat rational categories and orderly structures. Joseph Campbell characterized the trickster as the "disruptor of programs."[1] The structures and strategies erected to protect us from the vagaries of fate, from our own shadow inferiority, and from feelings of long-repressed pain are particularly vulnerable to the intrusions of the trickster. When this archetype is activated, the highest tower, the securest job, and the best-laid plan can be wiped away in the blink of an eye, for the trickster will destroy that which stands in the way of authentic life, "liberating" us from circumstances, habits, attitudes, and relationships that inhibit free expression, or awakening us to the existence of patterns that bind us. The energy in the shadow that we cannot face or acknowledge, and thus cannot integrate and live consciously, seems to "set up" a situation in which we stumble.

In this respect, the trickster serves to save us from ourselves—that is, from the human proclivity towards misguided attempts at self-protection, denial, and avoidance—and is therefore also connected to the archetypal figure of the savior, as Jung notes. "He [the trickster] is a forerunner of the saviour, and, like him, God, man, and animal at once. He is both subhuman and superhuman, a bestial and divine being, whose chief and most alarming characteristic is his unconsciousness."[2]

The trickster archetype puts us into relationship with the original wholeness of the psyche, which is instinctive and natural, but lacking in self-conscious awareness. Through the trickster our own unconscious nature breaks through into the field of human activity and awareness, disrupting and awakening, breaking apart and liberating, that we might step into more authentic modes of being in the world. The unconsciousness of this figure is evident in its association with the darkness of the shadow; in this respect the trickster is prerational and inferior to human consciousness, lacking a developed moral sense. In describing Yahweh as a trickster, Campbell notes the immorality and reprehensible fickleness and brutality of a deity who allows human beings to build monuments and towers, for instance, only to strike them down on a whim if they become too high, or even to flatten entire cities of those who not bend the knee in worship to him. These actions cannot be justified morally, and often seem nonsensical, but experience suggests that a secret order or intention is often at work in episodes reflecting the presence of the trickster. This archetype represents the "dynamic of the total psyche to overthrow progress," as

Campbell puts it.[3] But what is overthrown is invariably progress towards goals that are not in accord with the aims of the Self.

Much as we might resent such unwelcome intrusions, then, and much as these seeming accidents might be incomprehensible to us at the time, appearing as anything but meaningful or purposive, if we can open ourselves to a deeper logic or order working through them, we might come to appreciate the trickster as an aspect or function of the Self. Indeed, at root, the trickster might be construed as the expression of God's will or the Tao, as it comes up against human will. Jung's personal understanding of God makes this very point: "This [God] is the name by which I designate all things which cross my willful path violently and recklessly, all things which upset my subjective views, plans and intentions and change the course of my life for better or worse."[4]

The trickster also manifests at thresholds of transition, as here too the ego is not in control, when the psyche falls into a state of volatile but creative chaos. Moments of death-rebirth (in the transition from BPM III to BPM IV in the Grofian scheme) bring liberation and sometimes manic highs, but until the new mode of being and psychic structure have become established and settled, firmly connected with ego-consciousness, the unconscious can still have the upper hand and one can act without really knowing what one is doing. Trickster-like upsets and blunders can, in this case, serve, if only retroactively, to re-awaken us and to reintegrate consciousness with the completion of the rebirth experience.

Freedom and Rebellion

All these capacities, functions, and traits fall in the thematic range of meanings of the Uranus principle in astrology. Thus many astrological texts associate Uranus with the principle and experience of freedom and liberation—although this liberation is not always welcome at the time. If one identifies with the urge to freedom, and with the rebellious emancipatory feelings it engenders, one can express Uranus in acts of rebellion and protest against all that inhibits and constrains, all that is unfair or uncomfortable. Uranus is prominent in the archetypal character of the rebel, the freedom-fighter, the protester, and in the adolescent energy of revolt and creative experimentation. Unconsciously expressed, Uranus is to do with the experience of instinctual freedom—the freedom to do as we wish, to act in an unconstrained manner that we might follow our natural impulses and desires. As Freud observed, it is precisely this experience of freedom that is sacrificed in exchange for the orderly security that comes from living in civilized society, with its rules and structures.

When inhibited or repressed, the unrecognized urge for freedom might manifest in undesirable form—perhaps somatically as the injury or bodily spasm or neurotic twitch that gets in the way of life, stopping us from functioning as we wish. The same impulse, if we unconsciously identify with it and act it out, can keep us in a state of restless excitement, constantly distracted by novelty and new external stimulation, seeking change for change's sake, revolting against any constraint or orderly way of being.

Creative Genius, Individualism, and Revolution

We have focused our attention thus far on the disruptive, and sometimes destructive, dimension of the trickster, and its capacity to jolt us and awaken us as it unexpectedly crosses our path, often heralding the breakdown or collapse of a life structure. But equally the Uranus principle in astrology may be recognized in moments of creative inspiration and revelatory insight. It finds expression in creative impregnation and the birthing of ideas, seemingly from a higher dimension of consciousness, such as in the "aha" moment of scientific discovery. As such, the Uranus principle is closely associated, Richard Tarnas has observed, with the figure of Prometheus in Greek myth, symbolizing the liberating genius, bringing the boon of creative insight and new knowledge to humanity just as Prometheus stole the gift of fire from the gods.[5] Uranus often manifests in human experience as the spark of brilliance or creative genius that impregnates us with progressive and inventive ideas, inspiring us towards a better future and liberating humankind from tyranny and oppression.

In astrology, Uranus is especially associated with the liberating power of science and technology, and the pioneering spirit of invention, helping us to move beyond established limits and outmoded truths into realms of unexplored experience. Equally, the archetype is associated with revolution and revolt against the ruling order. Indeed, the planet Uranus was discovered in close coincidence with the French Revolution, the paradigmatic example of political revolution and the progression of civilization towards the embrace of democratic ideals. The very notion of the free individual, autonomous and self-defining, creative and self-aware, is closely related to the meaning and experience of the Uranus principle. It is therefore manifest in the individualism that so defines our age, with everyone doing their own thing, overthrowing all forms of tradition and the past, but often in the process forsaking the much-needed connection to sustaining values and ways of being that form our cultural heritage and that provide a sense of rootedness. The Uranus principle often finds expression over and against Saturn.

At another level, however, Uranus is manifest not as mere individualism, which can be superficial, emphasizing differences to enable a person to stand out from the crowd in the cultivation of a social persona, but also as the drive behind individuation that furthers the realization of the Self, as an expression of genuine individual character and original selfhood. The Uranus principle manifests as the urge to go our own way in life, to go off the well-trodden path and seek out authentic individual experience. It gives a special attunement to the irreducible uniqueness of the individual life, as a never-to-be-repeated phenomenon.

Similarly, the experience of freedom, associated with the Uranus archetype, can manifest at different levels. At the level of the persona, freedom might often mean the liberty to style and present oneself as one sees fit or to identify with the fashions, life roles, groups, and movements that one chooses. At the level of the ego, the same impulse manifests as freedom of choice, the capacity to create one's own meaning and to live one's life as one wishes, to exercise choice and will, free from oppression by outside forces. At the level of the Self, freedom implies becoming the person one truly is, beyond the personal ego, a transition that also requires acceptance of limitation and the binding pattern of one's life. Egoic freedom must be forsaken as a new form of freedom arises, as one relinquishes the rational personalistic control of one's life in an act of submission to the greater authority of the Self. This submission also has much to do with the experience of Neptune, as we will see.

More broadly, Uranus is evident in the experience of "otherness" and the perspective of the outsider or bohemian, living to the beat of a different drum.[6] Uranus represents the minority viewpoint, the avant garde, the radical idea years ahead of its time, and the outlier position or anomaly that disrupts and destabilizes the status quo or settled truth, demanding recognition and integration into the conscious values of a culture. Just as trickster experiences associated with Uranus can disrupt the ego's plans and force one to reckon with the life aims of the Self in the unconscious, so, at a societal level, the same archetypal principle stands behind those experiences that do not conform to what is expected, cannot be accommodated into neat rational categories, and fall outside of the boundaries of normal life. Uranus acts to break things open; it is manifest in the experience of the breakthrough, birthing the new and thus contributing to an ongoing evolution in human experience. As Tarnas has argued, the dialectic between Saturn and Uranus principles has been essential to the evolution of Western thought and civilization.[7]

In terms of the psychodynamics of the unconscious, the Uranus "breakthrough" motif manifests as the sudden emergence or irruption into consciousness of new psychic contents. It manifests too in the experience of enantiodromia, the sudden reversal of one psychological position or opposite to its other pole, as in the arch rationalist succumbing to a fit of childish irrational emotion. In terms of Grofian perinatal psychology, as we have seen, Uranus pertains to the birthing moment in the transition from BPM III to BPM IV. It is therefore associated with the moment of the breaking dawn and the birth of new light amidst the darkness.

In astrology, the action of Uranus is often likened to a flow of electricity. The experience of the Uranus archetype can leave us feeling charged or wired or jolted, for it manifests often as an unexpected lightning bolt of energy. It tends towards extremes and sudden, unpredictable shifts, which can catalyze creativity and help to awaken us from settled habits or a state of existential slumber, promoting a leap forward in consciousness and the periodic release of creative energies into the field of human endeavor. The same principle seems to be at work across all levels of life. As I have described in *The Archetypal Cosmos*, the Uranus principle can be equated to the cosmological power of emergence, as identified by the cosmologist Brian Swimme. "Emergence, the capacity to create new forms . . . is active when the universe brings forth galaxies, stars, and solar systems, or when new species come into existence."[8] In short, as a multidimensional principle emergence may be recognized in virtually all the themes discussed above in relation to Uranus.

Notes

1 Campbell, "Joseph Campbell—Mythology of the Trickster."
2 Jung, *Archetypes and the Collective Unconscious*, 263, par. 472.
3 Campbell, "Joseph Campbell—Mythology of the Trickster."
4 Jung, "Letter to M. Leonard," 5 December 1959, in *Letters* II, 525.
5 See Tarnas, *Prometheus the Awakener*.

[6] A point made by Donna Cunningham in *An Astrological Guide to Self-awareness*, 93–107.

[7] Tarnas, *Passion of the Western Mind*, 492–493 (note 10 to Epilogue). In this note, Tarnas describes the Promethean principle, pertaining to the Uranus planetary archetype, as "restless, heroic, rebellious and revolutionary, individualistic and innovative, eternally seeking freedom, autonomy, change, and the new."

[8] Le Grice, *Archetypal Cosmos*, 249.

Chapter 10

Dionysus, the Will-to-Power, and Rebirth

We turn now to consider a number of archetypes, and philosophical and psychodynamic principles, connected to the planetary archetype Pluto, looking first at the Plutonic dimension of the shadow.

Passing through the "narrow passageway" of the personal shadow, one encounters a deeper dimension of that archetype—the collective or transpersonal shadow, which can be envisaged and experienced as the "underworld" of the unconscious. In the collective shadow reside all elements of experience incompatible with the culture's or even the civilization's values—taboo drives and appetites, impermissible thoughts and feelings, evil and the deep-rooted primal urges common to all of us. The shadow at this level contains the monstrous and subhuman, the bestial and demonic, the primitive and barbaric. The moral challenge of facing the weakness and painful emotions of one's personal shadow becomes that much greater when one is forced to gaze into the abyss of the darker side of human nature. It might be preferable to avoid this dimension of experience entirely, to keep it securely locked away in a vault within the unconscious, such that we could live more or less oblivious to its existence. But the shadow is the source not only of evil, but of much that brings to life vital enrichment and tremendous animating power—indeed, the repressed instinctual power of the unconscious is the motive force that drives transformation; perhaps for this reason the way of individuation leads to the instinctual underworld. And even if we attempt to ignore it, the primitive instinctual forces of the Plutonic underworld find ways to emerge and erupt into human experience—in compulsions and manias, barbarism and violence, lusting and destructiveness. Unless positively expressed, the power of the Pluto archetype can eat away at one, like a devouring serpent.

The Id and the Underworld

The Pluto archetype is closely related to the instinctual dimension of the shadow, and its meaning encompasses too the Freudian id (*Das Es*), the "dark, inaccessible part of our personality" and "a cauldron full of seething excitations," as Freud described it.[1] It is in the id, according to Freud, that somatic influences and instinctual needs find "psychical expression" for it is "filled with energy reaching it from the instincts."[2] For Freud, the id is a realm of chaos, with no particular directed will, organization, or purpose, save for that of the satisfaction of the instinctual urges and thus the attainment of pleasure. The id is motivated solely by the pleasure principle, seeking pleasurable forms of satisfaction for its ceaseless cravings. Thus Freud is able to conclude: "Instinctual catharsis seeking discharge—that, in our view, is all there is in the id."[3] The purpose of psychoanalysis is to undo repressions and make the instinctual drives conscious such that they can be discharged.

The impulses and images in the id, in Freud's judgment, are "virtually immortal" in that the id's energy never ceases and continually seeks discharge. It is not bound by human value judgments or ethics, and thus it continually hits against the moral constraints of the super-ego. It is the task of the ego, under the moral pressure of the super-ego, and mindful of the demands of living in the external world, to find acceptable forms of satisfaction for the id.

Pluto pertains to the instinctual underworld of the unconscious, conceptualized as the shadow and the id. It pertains to the appetites and desires, passions and compulsions. It is associated with primitive drives of a sexual or aggressive nature that live beneath the surface of consciousness, periodically threatening to erupt, empowering and unconsciously manipulating us, taking possession of consciousness, pulling us into the underworld of the primitive and uncivilized realm of human experience. In its unregenerate form, it might be envisaged as the simmering cesspit of lust, violence, evil, and chaos lurking behind the veneer of civilization, respectability, and—increasingly today—political correctness. Ironically, as Freud revealed, the Plutonic id empowers the very censorship and repression, associated with the super-ego, that bear down on the uncivilized urges within the id.

Dionysus and Instinctual Possession

A number of these Plutonic qualities are represented and expressed by the mythic figure and archetypal principle of Dionysus, although in other ways Dionysus is also strongly associated with the Neptune planetary archetype. According to the classicist Edith Hamilton, he was, for instance, "the god of holy inspiration who could fill men with his spirit"—a distinctively Neptunian attribute, as we will later consider.[4] Yet the Plutonic nature of Dionysus is equally prominent. The Greek god of the vine, Dionysus could lead his followers to revelry and wild abandon, inspiring ecstasy and madness, stirring animalistic passions and effecting a union with the powers of nature. As Hamilton describes, the Maenads or Bacchantes that followed Dionysus and were inebriated by his wine, became "frenzied." "They rushed through woods and over mountain tops uttering sharp cries, waving pine-cone tipped wands, swept away in a fierce ecstasy. Nothing could stop them. They would tear to pieces the wild creatures they met and devour the bloody shreds of flesh."[5] The intoxication, madness, and mystical aspects of Dionysus are predominantly Neptunian themes, but the wild devouring and destructive possession state is unmistakably Plutonic.

Jung's understanding of Dionysus was shaped to a significant extent by his study of Nietzsche. Reflecting on Nietzsche's *The Birth of Tragedy*, he observed:

> The Dionysian impulse . . . means the liberation of unbounded instinct, the breaking loose of the unbridled dynamism of animal and divine nature; hence in the Dionysian rout man appears as a satyr, god above and goat below. The Dionysian is the horror of the annihilation of the *principium individuationis* [associated with Apollo] and at the same time "rapturous delight" in its destruction. It is therefore comparable to intoxication, which dissolves the individual into his collective instincts and components—an explosion of the isolated ego through the world. . . . His individuality is entirely obliterated. . . [C]reative dynamism, libido in its instinctual form, takes possession of the individual . . . he is nothing but sheer Nature, unbridled, a raging torrent, not even an animal that is restricted to itself and the laws of its being.[6]

To put this in terms of personal experience, Dionysus is an archetype we can recognize in states of frenzied passion. It is present again in the gnawing sense of emptiness that comes from desiring ever more, of needing ever more stimulation, fulfillment, pleasure, and power. Dionysus, as one aspect of the more inclusive Pluto principle, is like a bottomless pit that can never be filled and that craves incessantly. The inexorable nature of Pluto's desiring and willing can be the cause of much unhappiness, and its relentless driving desirousness is often ill-suited to more sensitive human needs and emotional states, and to our moral commitments. The impersonal power of the archetypal Pluto cares little or nothing for human sensitivities and the cries of the soul.

For Jung, Dionysus pertains to the raw, uncivilized power of the "maternal abyss" of the unconscious, for "the 'terrible mother'," Jung notes, ". . . unbridled and unbroken Nature, [is] represented by the most paradoxical god of the Greek pantheon, Dionysus."[7] Pluto, as Dionysus, relates to a possession state in which the individual is, for a time, utterly consumed by instinctual power, taking the form of intensified emotional charge and the urge for self-annihilation and abandonment to the wild, intoxicating elemental force of nature, a power usually excluded from ordinary experience. "Dionysus is the abyss of impassioned dissolution, where all human distinctions are merged in the animal divinity of the primordial psyche—a blissful and terrible experience"—Jung recognizes the attraction and the danger.[8] The experience of Dionysus is blissful because, in the upsurge of emotional-instinctual power, we are carried away and feel ourselves reconnected to the passions and urges that throb and pulse through our veins, connecting us to a primordial life energy beyond that of our individual will. We feel ourselves part of some greater power, riding the back of the intoxicating passion of high emotion. The experience is terrible because in this frenzied possession state, individual differentiation is lost and the integrity of consciousness is jeopardized. One can give oneself away to the Dionysian rapture and thus the autonomy of the ego is utterly annihilated. The spark of consciousness of our separate ego-self is lost, and with it all morality and higher life goals can be abandoned too.

For this reason, the experience of and expression of Dionysus is often rendered taboo—the history of the West reveals a sustained suppression of the Dionysian in favor of the Apollonian order, Christian moral values, and Enlightenment rationalism. The result, of course, has not been the elimination of Dionysus—on the contrary, for Dionysus is now everywhere we care to look in our violent, politically unscrupulous, and over-sexualized culture.

Robert Johnson, a prominent interpreter of Jungian ideas, identifies ways in which Dionysus finds expression in our experience, mostly unrecognized, and often in warped or surrogate form: "He [Dionysus] lives in the thrill we feel when we read about the latest terrorist bombing, the latest arson fire, the latest political assassination."[9] "With no sacred means of expression we can express our need for Dionysus only symptomatically," he adds, in all forms of social pathology, brutality, violence, perversions, war, and lust.[10] This archetype impels us

135

to the inexorable pursuit of more satisfaction, more power. Dionysus stands behind the periodic yearning for everything to collapse, in our mostly unspoken and unrecognized wish to utterly annihilate the order of our world so that we can return again to the vital feeling of our uninhibited animal nature. It causes us to vent on behalf of our natural wild impulses that suffer repeatedly at the hands of our civilized ways of life.

Outbreaks of horror and vengeance well up from the Dionysian underworld of energy associated with Pluto, hell-bent on retribution for oppression and the violence done to our animal nature. Elements pertaining to Pluto are also to be found personified in the Germanic god Wotan, the god of "storm and frenzy" whose resurgence in the German psyche in the 1920s and 1930s, Jung believed, was the archetypal cause behind the rise of Nazism and the catastrophe of World War Two.

Rather than act out these Plutonic drives unconsciously, Johnson suggests that we might engage them ritually, intentionally making space in our lives for the expression of Dionysus, as exemplified, for instance, by the socially sanctioned revelry and abandon of the carnival celebrations of the Mardi Gras, or in rock concerts and sporting events. However, while ritual might help to let off Dionysian steam, as it were, and make us feel better by honoring the god, Dionysian energy also serves another end: it pushes us inexorably deeper into experiences of transformation and rebirth. A deliberate catharsis of this energy through ritual, while bringing temporary release and balance to the psyche, might prevent or delay the onset of psychological death-rebirth as a key aspect of the individuation process.

Ritual expression, therefore, is not always effective or desirable. One cannot summon Dionysian energies at will nor always channel them into convenient forms of expression. The archetypal drive has its aim and its reason that cannot be made subservient to the human will or accommodated into conventional activities. Indeed, as it seeks out transformation, the psyche might see to it that we find ourselves in circumstances in which Dionysian energies are powerfully stirred but unable to be expressed. The thwarted energies, with no immediate outlet, must therefore be contained, held in check, or are repressed, which then provides the psychological energy and imbalance needed for transformation. The unconscious becomes powerfully charged with a reservoir of unexpressed life energy, which serves as the fuel for transformation. Thus, the expression of Pluto mutates from Dionysian ecstasy and wild abandon to the will to transformation and rebirth.

Descent and Rebirth

Dionysus is connected to the death-rebirth mysteries of Eleusis and is one among several mythic figures (alongside Osiris, Attis, Adonis, Persephone, and Christ, among others) that partake in the archetypal pattern of the dying and rising god, whose essential form is evident in the myth of the corn spirit. As a god of the vine, Dionysus suffers the fate of the corn spirit. Dying each autumn, he is dismembered, to be reborn again in spring. As Hamilton describes: "his death was terrible: he was torn to pieces, in some stories by the Titans, in others by Hera's orders. He was always brought back to life; he died and rose again . . . [in a] joyful resurrection. . . ."[11]

The pattern of dying and rising relates to Jung's description of the rebirth archetype, a pattern that is universally evident in human experience. "Rebirth," Jung claims, with good reason, ". . . must be counted among the primordial affirmations of mankind."[12] This archetype manifests, for example, in the ideas of resurrection in Christianity and of reincarnation in Hinduism and Buddhism. Rebirth can be effected, he notes, through rituals, such as the Mass, a form of vicarious participation in the rebirth inherent in life; through rites of passage as in premodern societies; or through the spiritual exercises performed in mystical traditions. One can be temporarily reborn through losing oneself in the greater power of a group or crowd, or through identification with a god or hero, as in Jung's discussion of the resurgence of Wotan in Germany or in Nietzsche's identification with Dionysus. The type of rebirth with which Jung was most concerned, however, is that elicited by individuation or "natural transformation," which can bring about a reorganization of the structure of the psyche and an expansion of consciousness through the assimilation and integration of the dark side of the psyche—the unconscious.[13] As we have seen, the rebirth is from an identity exclusively centered on the ordinary "I," the ego personality, into the Self, "the larger and greater personality maturing within us . . . that other person who we also are and yet can never attain to completely."[14] "Nature herself demands a death and a rebirth," Jung believed, and the human being cannot escape these demands.[15]

Pluto pertains to the principle of transformation itself, for it is associated with the entire sequence or cycle of birth, sex, death, and rebirth. We have already considered the perinatal dynamics of the birth experience, with the intensified instinctual arousal of erotic and aggressive drives and the life-and-death struggle during delivery. The Plutonic dimension of experience later manifests, from adolescence on, as sexual libido. According to psychodynamic theorist Michael Washburn, as the ego develops during childhood and into adolescence, the power of the "Dynamic Ground" of existence is repressed from awareness.[16] The ego becomes ever more separate and autonomous, and sexual desire arises as a compensatory urge for union and the annihilation of ego boundaries, with the experience of orgasm temporarily overcoming the separation intrinsic to individual selfhood and unconsciously restoring the lost unity with the ground. Just as sexual orgasm brings reunion at the level of instinct, individuation aims at a higher union, as it were, at the level of spirit.

As an adult, one experiences Pluto as passion and appetite, for sex or power or pleasure (as in Schopenhauer's notion of the will and the Freudian notion of the id). Under the experience of the archetypal Pluto, one is driven, gripped, empowered, perhaps even possessed, seeking to gratify the instincts and satisfy one's cravings. The Pluto principle can be experienced as desperation, for it manifests with an extremity and intensity under which we feel that everything is on the line. It possesses an all-or-nothing and life-or-death quality.

Pluto has a strong connection to the base and instinctual—to aspects of life lived at a primitive level, including that which has remained underdeveloped within us, such as drives and urges that have seemingly failed to mature in step with the rest of the personality. It is the work of individuation to transmute and sublimate some of this "lower" energy to "higher" creative ends—as in Freud's view of the redirection of the desiring id to cultural goals. By bringing primitive desires to the surface of consciousness, these drives can be integrated into life, such that in time they lose their compulsive quality. Until this integration takes place, however, Plutonic drives can often be experienced as desperation and grasping, fuelled by instinctual arousal. The farther one goes into the experience of rebirth, the more desperate and insistent the instincts become.

Pluto manifests in another form as the will-to-power, the inherent impulse to attain and express ever more power and influence, which Nietzsche considered the primary motivating force of human experience—although it is perhaps better seen, in polytheistic terms, as one among many life motivations. Directed back upon oneself, the will-to-power manifests as the drive for "self-overcoming," the overcoming of one's limits and resistances to life, dying to what one was, as one embraces the long-repressed power of the Dionysian principle.

We might find in the Dionysian experience "a motion embracing the whole world," as Jung puts it, with a "flood of overpowering universal feeling which bursts forth irresistibly."[17] In this sense, the Dionysian principle stands behind the Nietzschean ideal of the *amor fati,* the "love of fate," giving rise to an absolute and unconditional affirmation of life.[18]

The Daimon and the Evolutionary Power in Nature

Considering these various psychodynamic, esoteric, and mythic concepts and symbols, we can begin to get a sense for the range of themes and experiences associated with Pluto, many of which are prominent in depth psychology. Indeed, Pluto is the principle of depth itself, pertaining to all that is deep, all that belongs to the underworld. Depth psychology, coming from the German term *Tiefenpsychologie,* is so named because of its focus on the dimension of human experience that lies beneath our conscious awareness. In this context, we can appreciate the association of Pluto to the theme of the descent to the underworld in myth. Pluto is the archetype that pulls us down into the depths, that consumes and devours us. It is associated with Hades, ruler of the underworld, and the Devil in Christianity.

In a larger context, on a cosmological and metaphysical scale, Pluto is associated with the Shiva-like power of destruction and creation, dramatically evident in the unleashed power of nuclear explosions, which physicist Robert Oppenheimer, who first harnessed nuclear power in nuclear warheads, likened to the role of Shiva in Hindu scripture ("Now I have become Death, the destroyer of worlds."). According to Heinrich Zimmer, Shiva represents "the destructive power of the Universal God, who, under the form of Shiva-Rudra (*rudra,* "The Howler," "The Roarer"; this was the Vedic name of Shiva, and refers to his world-annihilating aspect), periodically annihilates the created universe."[19]

Pluto symbolizes the elemental power of nature, which Tarnas frequently describes as "titanic."[20] The titanic elemental energies from the pre-human world associated with Pluto, the buried power in the inner depths of nature, touch all our lives both individually and collectively. Like Dionysus, Pluto represents the immanent power of nature, manifesting in and through the material world of space and time as the inexorable, relentless driving force within nature, ever destroying and consuming, seemingly blind and without purpose, yet at another level manifesting as the motive teleological power of evolution. For the drives of Pluto are not merely blind urges and purposeless passions. The power of the daimon works through our experience of willing and desiring, through that to which we are compulsively drawn. Pluto then expresses itself as a fateful calling or the pull of destiny shaping our lives through our passions. Pluto represents the experience of being in the grip of a greater will that draws its power from the depths of nature, moving us on occasion to superhuman acts of titanic achievement or sometimes to bestial and abhorrent deeds. It can lead us to self-destruction and unconsciousness or into the depths of transformation and resurrection. The role of conscious discrimination in dealing with Pluto is critical. The Self as daimon can be ruthless and all-consuming, and needs to be balanced with the human qualities of love and moral discernment.

In a brilliant discussion of the nature of a time-bound divinity in *The Perennial Philosophy*, Aldous Huxley gives what can be read as a vivid portrayal of the nature of the Pluto principle:

Whenever God is thought of as being wholly in time [i.e., a wholly immanent divinity, present within nature], there is a tendency to regard Him as "numinous" rather than a moral being, a God of mere unmitigated Power rather than a God of Power, Wisdom, and Love, an inscrutable and dangerous potentate to be propitiated by sacrifices, not a Spirit to be worshipped in spirit. All this is only natural; for time is a perpetual perishing and a God who is wholly in time is a God who destroys as fast as He creates. Nature is as incomprehensibly appalling as it is lovely and bountiful. . . . God as manifested in the universe is the irresistible Being who speaks to Job out of the whirlwind, and whose emblems are Behemoth and Leviathan.[21]

He continues:

God in time is manifestly the destroyer as well as the creator; and because this is so, it has seemed proper to worship him by methods which are as terrible as the destructions he himself inflicts. Hence, in India, the blood sacrifices to Kali, in her aspect as Nature-the-Destroyer; hence those offerings of children to "the Molochs," denounced by the Hebrew prophets; hence the human sacrifices practised, for example, by the Phoenicians, the Carthaginians, the Druids, the Aztecs. In all such cases, the divinity addressed was a god in time, or a personification of Nature . . . the devourer of its own offspring. . . . Sublimated traces of these ancient patterns of thought and behaviour are still to be found in certain theories of

140

Atonement, and in the conception of the Mass as a perpetually repeated sacrifice of the God-Man.[22]

We see in these passages several prominent themes attributed to Pluto: the "unmitigated power," the destruction and creation, the acts of devouring and consuming, and the elemental force of nature and of God.

Mercurius and Alchemical Transformation

In Christianity, Dionysus assumes the guise of the Devil, carrier of the chthonic, instinctual, orgiastic, demonic energies of the passions and appetites, which have no place in the prevailing conceptions of God and Jesus as wholly beneficent figures of light and love and purity. It is for this reason that Jung considered the Christ image in some ways inadequate as a symbol of the Self, for although Christ is a god-man, a greater universal being, he represents only one half of the psyche, excluding darker qualities, the earthly and material, the passions and the instinctual forces of nature. In short, many of the qualities and energies associated with the archetypal Pluto are excluded from the Christian conception of the divine.[23] Thus Jung turned to alchemy, and the god-man Mercurius, as a "compensatory counterpart" to Christ. By including the dark side of the psyche, Mercurius constitutes a more complete symbol of the Self. Whereas Nietzsche set up the mythic figure of Dionysus as an adversary of Christ, a figure representing the instinctual energies and will-to-power denigrated by Christianity's emphasis on altruism and moral goodness, Jung sought to reconcile this polarity in the paradoxical nature of Mercurius who is at once divine and instinctual, a representative of the "dark spirit of nature," the *spiritus vegetavius*.[24] The Gnostic figure of Mithras, the lion-headed man, is similarly better able to reconcile the human and the animal, the spiritual and the instinctual.

In the symbolic language of alchemical treatises, Mercurius often takes the form of a serpent or uroboros (the serpent or dragon consuming its own tail), symbolizing the capacity of the instinctual power of nature to ever devour itself in blind, incessant willing and desiring—qualities pertaining to Pluto, as we have seen. As a symbolic figure closely related to Pluto, Mercurius as serpent or dragon also manifests as the power of the instinctual unconscious that is to be contained, transformed, and overcome during individuation. Like Pluto, Mercurius is both the substance to be transformed and the agent of transformation, for the contained instinct also empowers and instigates the death-rebirth process.

Pluto is related to the alchemical substance sulphur, symbolizing the motive force of willing and desiring that animates human life, and the instinctual compulsion that unconsciously has us in its grip. Much of the work of alchemy has to do with the overcoming of this compulsion and the winning through to freedom from ingrained patterns of unconsciousness, conceived by the alchemists as the binding compulsion of fate.[25] Again, such themes are of central relevance to understanding Pluto.

Fire is a prominent symbol of Pluto, too, suggesting the activity of the Pluto archetype to transform through the "heat" of instinct that is directed inward. As we have seen, the element fire is evident in the alchemical process of *calcinatio*, which, like the purgatorial fires of the Christian mythic imagination, has the effect of releasing, purifying, burning out, destroying, and transforming. Stanislav Grof refers to this capacity of the psyche to purge through intensity and extremity of expression as "pyrocatharsis."[26]

In sum, then, Pluto pertains to the entire realm of the instinctual unconscious and the experience of being driven, impelled, possessed, and perhaps devoured and destroyed by the upsurge of energies from our depths. Yet it pertains also to the capacity to be transformed through the encounter with these energies, by coming to terms with the underworld of the unconscious. Pluto aims at transformation through death-rebirth such that we might become vessels for the expression of the evolutionary creative-destructive force of nature. Transformed, we might then willingly participate in the fulfillment of what may be understood as the inexorable power of fate.

Notes

[1] Freud, *New Introductory Lectures on Psycho-Analysis*, 91.
[2] Freud, *New Introductory Lectures on Psycho-Analysis*, 91–92.
[3] Freud, *New Introductory Lectures on Psycho-Analysis*, 93.
[4] Hamilton, *Mythology*, 74.
[5] Hamilton, *Mythology*, 67.
[6] Jung, *Psychological Types*, 138–139, par. 227.
[7] Jung, *Symbols of Transformation*, 401, par. 623.
[8] Jung: *Psychology and Alchemy*, 90, par. 118.
[9] Johnson, *Ecstasy*, 18.

[10] Johnson, *Ecstasy*, 25.

[11] Hamilton, *Mythology*, 75.

[12] Jung, *Archetypes and the Collective Unconscious*, 116., par. 207.

[13] See Jung, "On Rebirth," in *Archetypes and the Collective Unconscious*.

[14] Jung, *Archetypes and the Collective Unconscious*, 131, par. 235.

[15] Jung, *Archetypes and the Collective Unconscious*, 130, par. 234.

[16] Washburn, *The Ego and the Dynamic Ground*, 138–141.

[17] Jung, *Psychological Types*, 143–144, par. 234.

[18] As Nietzsche writes in *Ecce Homo*: "My formula for greatness in a human being is *amor fati*, that one wants nothing to be different, not forward, not backward, not in all eternity. Not merely bear what is necessary, still less conceal it—all idealism is mendaciousness in the face of what is necessary—but *love* it. ("Why I Am So Clever," in *Ecce Homo*, in *Basic Writings of Nietzsche*, 714.

[19] Zimmer, *Myths and Symbols in Indian Art and Civilization*, 181.

[20] See Tarnas's discussions of Pluto throughout *Cosmos and Psyche*.

[21] Huxley, *Perennial Philosophy*, 197–198.

[22] Huxley, *Perennial Philosophy*, 201–202.

[23] See Jung, "Introduction to the Religious and Psychological Problems of Alchemy," in *Psychology and Alchemy*, 3–37, pars. 1–42.

[24] Jung, *Mysterium Coniunctionis*, 97, par. 127, & 225, par. 298.

[25] See Jung, *Mysterium Coniunctionis*, 128, par. 151.

[26] Grof, *Psychology of the Future*, 48.

Chapter 11

Animus and Anima, Masculine and Feminine

We have already addressed the centrality in Jungian psychology of the dynamic movement of energy between opposites, especially in connection with the pairings of spirit and soul, solar and lunar, conscious and unconscious, and light and dark. In facing the unconscious, another pair of opposites is to be reckoned with—the "divine syzygy," pertaining to the archetypal inner masculine and feminine, which Jung calls animus and anima, respectively.[1] These too, as we will now consider, may be mapped onto different elements of the planetary archetypes recognized in astrology, most especially onto the archetypes associated with Mars and Venus.

Classical Jungian theory holds that the conscious personality of a man is compensated by the "feminine" nature of the unconscious, taking the personified form of the anima. Conversely, within a woman, according to Jung, there exists a "masculine" unconscious, in the form of the animus, compensating the "feminine" nature of a woman's conscious personality. Jung believed that men carry around within them an inner image of the female ideal as the anima, which is projected onto women in romantic relationships, just as women bear within them the animus as an inner image of the male ideal, projected onto men. We find ourselves compulsively drawn to those people who embody our anima and animus traits; indeed, as popular wisdom decrees, the search for the beloved, for one's other half, might bring to one's experience a sense of wholeness and completion. For Jung, however, these inner principles of masculine and feminine are to be realized within oneself in the course of individuation; anima and animus are to be participants in the realization of a sacred marriage of the opposites.

While this classical model of feminine and masculine, anima and animus, remains of value, clearly today we live with the awareness of a more complex and fluid understanding of biological sex and gender, and of sexual orientation, which calls for a progressive revisioning of

Jung's initial theory. Many Jungian commentators have been led to conclude that the functions ascribed to the anima and animus exist within each of us, regardless of biological sex or gender identity (a view supported by astrology) while not overlooking important differences that remain between men and women, and differences in psychological orientation and disposition across individuals. The following discussions of anima and animus should be read with these crucial caveats in mind.

The Animus: Opinions and Critiques

In its initial form of expression, before it is brought into relationship with the conscious ego during the course of individuation, the animus tends to manifest as "irrational opinion" that takes two primary forms. First, the animus presents all manner of ideas, beliefs, and views that have a certain inexplicable quality of absolute truth and conviction, appearing to unequivocally explain any given life situation, providing a sense of misplaced surety and guidance for life decisions. The animus effectively serves as the mouthpiece for and instrument of a kind of folk psychology, as Jung explains:

> The animus is rather like an assembly of fathers or dignitaries of some kind who lay down incontestable, "rational," *ex cathedra* judgments. On closer examination these exacting judgments turn out to be largely sayings and opinions scraped together more or less unconsciously from childhood on, and compressed into a canon of average truth, justice, and reasonableness, a compendium of preconceptions which, whenever a conscious and competent judgment is lacking (as not infrequently happens), instantly obliges with an opinion.[2]

An accepting unconsciousness underlies all animus opinions, whose general all-embracing character is the very antithesis of critical self-reflection. Until we have given sustained attention to the formulation of a worldview, questioning the assumptions and ideas by which we understand ourselves and interpret our life experiences, we are invariably subject to generalized ideas that are not our own and that have been unconsciously assimilated from our parents and peers or from the wider culture. Animus opinions and explanations often sneak through our critical awareness undetected, for they are often taken for granted by those around us, seemingly describing the "way it is." I am thinking, for instance, of statements such as "you only live once" or "life's what you make it," which are proffered by many people and which might enter our consciousness when we are pondering major life decisions. Anyone can be the mouthpiece for such opinions, which come from what Heidegger called the "they"—the anonymous mass

Because animus statements are often sweeping in their scope, they tend not to support the kind of critical self-awareness and independence of thought that are crucial for individuation. One simply accepts such statements; one does not question. Critical thought is somehow bypassed and one thus lives another's truth, or perhaps even a long-perpetuated falsehood.

Despite their questionable foundation in actual truth and fact, because they reflect the authority of consensus of the social group animus opinions can together comprise a formidable arsenal of arguments and assertions, which might be personified in dreams in the figure of a critical or opinionated man or group of men. As a kind of personality, Jung remarks, the animus comes across as "mannishness, argumentativeness, obstinate self-assertion, and the demon of opinion in every possible shape and form."[3] Yet in truth, Jung adds, "the animus is not a real man at all; he is a slightly hysterical, infantile hero whose longing to be loved shows through the gaps in his armour."[4] The animus here is an "infantile hero" because the archetypal figure has not yet been realized as an inner principle of heroic autonomy, independence, and creativity. Because the animus is initially wholly unconscious, it remains in an immature state and therefore primitive in its functioning.

To call into question such assertions one must first be able to catch them as they arise and recognize them for what they are by testing their actual validity when applied to one's own particular life situation. One must critically examine each of these assertions, subjecting them to reason and measuring them against one's own evolving living truth. To defy such beliefs in the living of one's life is to go against the grain of consensus opinion and the accepted ideas and patterns of collective life, and thus to dare to stand in one's own authority and independent judgment. One must be willing to stand alone.

When engaged consciously in this way, the animus can be transformed in its mode of expression to a psychological function that supports autonomy of judgment and independence of spirit in creativity and action. The initial unconsciousness of the animus calls forth the development of critical reason and truly individual judgment. When one has worked through much of the canon of uncritically accepted generalized inherited assumptions, one stands firmly in what one knows to be true. The animus becomes differentiated and developed in its function. In this respect, the development of the animus might be likened to the cultivation of "right understanding" in Buddhism and to the act of "judging righteous judgment" in Christianity, and recognized as playing a central role in the attainment of self-knowledge.

The second unredeemed mode of expression of the animus is hypercritical judgment. The animus can sit on one's shoulder as a fierce inner critic, whose criticism, however, partakes in the same unconsciousness that gives rise to the incontestable opinions and half-truths described above. Marie-Louise von Franz, Jung's foremost follower and collaborator, described an experience of just this kind of unconscious hyper-criticism stemming from the animus. As she was beginning work on a book project, she was overcome with the belief that the endeavor was of no worth and that she should abandon the project immediately rather than waste more time on it. Having accepted this assessment, that night she had a dream of being jabbed with a sharp pencil wielded by a man.[5] As she reflected on the meaning of the dream the next day, she came to the realization that it was not she, Marie-Louise, who had thought the writing project of no worth, but the animus, functioning as a largely autonomous sub-personality. "It" or "he" was presenting the critical assessment of her work (jabbing her with a pencil), which she had unquestioningly accepted as being her own judgment, and a correct one.

As we have seen, archetypes tend to appropriate our sense of identity, the sense of I, and thus to pass off beliefs and ideas, feelings and desires, as if they were our own. Thus, it initially appears it is not the animus as a separate center or function presenting its opinions, but that the ideas and beliefs come from us. Hypercritical responses are accepted in the same manner, perhaps until the personality revolts against the critical barrage and one breaks free of the tyranny, creating the psychological distance from which it is possible to see the criticism then as something external, something other than an expression of one's true self. Such rebellion can be the opening to the recognition of the animus as an autonomous function existing outside of our personal will and separate from personal identity. Again, in facing up to the barrage of inner criticism, and being forced to determine for oneself whether the criticism is valid, one can develop the animus and then benefit from its creative function in life. One might then exhibit an unshakeable confidence and authority, impervious to outside criticism. In this sense, the animus manifests as the spirit of independent creative strength and understanding.

Animus Personifications and the Inner Masculine Ideal

In personified form, according to classical Jungian theory, the animus can be envisaged as the inner hero in the female psyche, a knight in shining armor, riding in to sweep the unconscious maiden off to some other kingdom in which responsibilities and cares are banished, and dreams fulfilled. Like a substitute father, the animus-hero is able to provide safety and security (or at least that is the fantasy), while simultaneously bringing intellectual stimulation and erotic satisfaction. More generally, and gender considerations aside, this figure is seen in the form of hero worship, arising from the universal human need for figures who possess the strength and courage one might come to discover and assimilate within oneself, if one could come to terms with the archetypes during individuation.

In personified form, the animus undergoes various mutations as one matures. Initially, at a basic level, animus fantasies might center on the strong man, with an attraction to physical strength and courage. Later, the animus figure can become the man of power, such as a political figure or ruler or successful businessman. In another form, attraction can focus on the intellectual, with the powerfully developed intellect now coming to carry animus projection, just as, finally, the inner masculine ideal might be personified by the spiritual guru, representing qualities the individual's psyche needs to develop and assimilate.[6] Ultimately, the aim, however, is the withdrawal of all projections so that the animus is not carried by other people but developed as a function and capacity within oneself. One will not be as compulsively attracted to displays of strength and power in others, whether of body, mind, or spirit, if one has assimilated these qualities for oneself.

In astrological symbolism, the animus pertains most especially to the planetary archetypes associated with Mars and Mercury, with elements too of the Sun and Saturn. The archetypal figure of inner masculine hero falls within the domain of Mars, for the Mars principle is associated with qualities such as strength, aggression, anger, daring, action, striving, and conquest. The astrological Mars finds expression in the form of the archetypal warrior, whose character is manifest in the daily battle of life, fighting the good fight, and in the ardent pursuit of one's goals in the world. We see Mars energy in athletics and sports, as a kind of surrogate or sublimated war; Mars as the warrior is evident especially, of course, in various forms of the martial arts, prevalent the world over—karate and jujitsu, taekwondo, kung fu, boxing, wrestling, sumo, samurai, ninja, and going back to the gladiators of ancient Rome. Even the simulated combat of computer games partakes in Mars, for this archetypal principle pertains to competitiveness in every aspect, such as the cut and thrust of business, or political sparring. In depth psychology it is recognized in the "instinct of aggression" and in ego-strength. The animus as Mars pertains at one level to the "obstinate self-assertion" of which Jung wrote, but in more refined form it is evident as inner strength and independence. These "masculine" traits, as they are commonly decreed, need not be projected onto others, but realized within as fundamental aspects of one's own psyche.

Mercury, as we have seen, pertains to the realm of ideas, thought, and speech, through which the animus often makes itself known. Irrational opinions and an unconsciousness of one's ideas about the world reflect a deficiency in one's relationship to the Mercury principle, a deficiency that might be overcome through the differentiation of the animus during individuation. Then, the Saturnian critical element of the animus, not unlike the Freudian super-ego discussed above, might mutate and evolve too, such that one's critical faculties support and shape one's creative life rather than impede or suffocate it. As noted above, by working through the ideas and beliefs that present themselves to consciousness, even the severely critical judgments, one can in time begin to stand with strength, grounded in one's own clearly considered convictions. The oppressive Saturnian-senex element of the animus, which often develops out of the father archetype or introjected moral values of one's culture, might then take on the form of the wise old man or come to embody the spiritual reason of a Virgil in the *Divine Comedy*.

We see here then a combination and conflation of particular qualities in the single archetype of the animus: As the inner ideal of the masculine and as the drive for self-assertion, the animus invokes Mars; as ideas, thoughts, and opinions, it invokes Mercury; as an inner critic and unconscious inner authority, it invokes Saturn; and in its association with heroic fantasies it touches upon the domain of the Sun archetype. By these definitions, all of us possess a relationship to animus themes—some of us more consciously, depending on our preferred and established style of consciousness; and some of us more unconsciously, if other, opposite qualities are more intrinsic to our sense of identity. In all cases, however, the differentiation of the animus function remains essential for individuation to unfold.

The Anima and Astrological Principles

Equally, if not more, crucial for the progression of the individuation process is the archetype of the anima, to which Jung devotes considerable attention throughout his body of work, perhaps even to the partial neglect of the animus. As we have seen, Jung considered the encounter with the anima to be the "master-piece" of individuation, surpassing in its importance, subtlety, and difficulty the encounter with the shadow—the "apprentice-piece."[7] A relationship with the anima only becomes possible after one has first turned to face the shadow darkness and made efforts to hold the shadow before one's gaze, turning the light of consciousness onto the excluded dimensions of psychological experience and thus opening oneself to the reality of the unconscious. Then, out of the shadow darkness, another figure emerges into the foreground of one's fantasy life—the image of the anima, often personified in female form. "The inferior personality," Jung notes, "changes into the feminine figure that stands immediately behind it."[8] The utter darkness of the shadow yields, giving way to the dark feminine beauty of the anima, which might ultimately serve as a psychological function that makes possible a relationship with the Self.

The astrological principles most associated with the anima are Venus and the Moon. Venus is associated with romantic love, Eros, beauty, pleasure, joy, happiness, liking, desire, affection, and the romantic and erotic dimensions of the feminine; and the Moon, as we have seen, is associated with the mother, the realm of feeling, and the soul. These themes and elements co-exist in Jung's understanding of the anima.

In its connection with happiness and *joie de vivre*, the anima has clear associations with the Venus principle, which is operative in our likes and loves, our pleasures and enjoyments, in happiness and in joy, and in wanting and desiring. That which we find pleasing on the eye, that which promotes harmony and accord, balance and proportion are Venusian, as are the appreciation of and the creation of beauty, whether discerning aesthetic evaluations or judgments based solely on surface appearance. Venus can be superficial, taken in by appearances, and it inclines us, when this archetype is active, to indulgence and vanity, treats and rewards. It touches us in small moments of simple pleasure throughout the day, yet on a metaphysical level Venus is also connected to beauty in the Platonic sense as Form or Idea, part of the Platonic ideal triumvirate of archetypal forms: "the Good, the True, and the Beautiful." As a psychological function, Venus is associated with the experience of liking and evaluating based on one's tastes and preferences or on how much pleasure or discomfort something brings. Above all, the Venus principle is evident in our romantic relationships and friendships as the basis of attraction and the giving and receiving of love.

Beyond this association with Venus, the anima is also the principle that connects us, one the one hand, to the realm of the mythic-archetypal unconscious and an enchanted existence. In this role, it has affinities with the archetypal-astrological principle of Neptune, which governs myths, dreams, illusions, ideals, enchantment, and magical allure. On the other hand, the anima is closely bound up with the sphere of the instincts, appetites, and primitive drives in the depths of the unconscious. In this sense, the anima possesses elements of the astrological Pluto, whose nature we explored in the previous chapter. All these aspects of the anima become apparent during the course of individuation.

Irrational Feeling and the Wellsprings of Life

Initially, the anima manifests as irrational feeling, in distinction to the irrational thinking associated with the animus. We might recognize the bursts of irrational feeling in the consuming mood that overcomes us in spite of our rational protests and well-intended efforts to shake it off. We might recognize it too as touchiness and over-sensitivity and the "saccharine sentimentality" that can take hold when circumstances (typically the dynamics of interpersonal relationships) invite the anima's involvement.[9] The engulfing mood or episode of touchiness demonstrates the anima's autonomy and the ego's ineffectiveness in mastering the anima—its inability, that is, to control feelings and overcome the instincts through reason and willpower alone. Indeed, an overdevelopment of rationality and a controlling will can be the very conditions in which the anima might burst forth uninvited, hypnotizing us with alluring fantasies and desires that pull us unprepared into the abyss of the dark underworld of emotion and instinct.

If the claims of the anima are ignored or unrecognized, as not infrequently happens, life can become stale and deeply unsatisfying, for the world seems to offer little to stir one's feelings or to permit the fulfillment of one's deepest desires. If the anima's needs are not met, we might encounter this archetype as a form of childish emotional protest and a refusal to participate in a world that does not conform to our deeply rooted wishes and images about how life should be. The anima is closely associated with the heart's desire, which is often at odds with our rational plans for life and common-sense strategies for how to live. It is described by Jung as the "archetype of life" or the "natural life-urge," which is "beyond all meaning and all moral categories"[10]; it is experienced as the feeling of truly being alive, a feeling that elicits an embrace of life. "The anima wants life," as Jung puts it.[11] It is thus closely associated with the principle of Eros. To connect to the anima is like prospecting for buried water in a barren desert and tapping into the eternal wellsprings of life. The anima is the life-giving springs of water that renew and reinvigorate. It is the animating force of desire that moves us to action and pulls us, through the nigh-irresistible lure and promise of a fullness of being and intensity of feeling, into the sphere of relationship and emotional entanglements. Happiness, as we usually understand it, has much to do with the expression of the anima.

In Greek mythology, we find deities who portray the romantic-erotic dimension of the anima in the form of Cupid, Eros, and Aphrodite. In Indian mythology, the equivalent figure to Cupid is that of *Kāma*, "the Hindu god of love," Heinrich Zimmer explains, "who, with flower-bow and five flower-arrows sends desire quivering to the heart."[12] The "heavenly damsels" of Indra's palace, known as Apsarases, are also compelling embodiments of the anima. As Zimmer notes: "These ever youthful, ever charming damsels form the seraglio of the inhabitants of Indra's paradise. They are the ever desirable, ever willing mistresses of those blessed souls who are born into Indra's heavenly world . . . . Apsarases represent the 'Innocence of Nature,' 'Delight Without Tears,' 'Sensual Consummation Without Remorse, Without Doubts or Subsequent Misgivings.' They are the initiating priestesses of the ever-new ancient mystery of the mutual attractiveness of the sexes."[13]

Further anima figures, in the form of nymphs, nixies, fairies, witches, and sirens, populate myths and fairytales, Jung notes, and these well represent the magical allure and danger of possession and destruction associated with the anima, calling to mind its connection with Neptune and Pluto, respectively. The lure of the anima, of our desire and feeling nature, is like a witch's spell or the song of the sirens, whose seductive melodies are impossible to resist, for they promise an experience of bliss usually denied to us in the ordinary course of daily life and relationships. The siren call, like falling in love, can touch us so powerfully and completely that it causes us to be willing to risk everything, perhaps even life itself, for the rush of renewed joy, zest, and Eros. When the anima is powerfully activated, it can usurp reason and good sense, taking over decision-making and distorting our perception of the world. In this respect, a case of anima possession can be likened to a "seizure" or to a mythic encounter with a goddess. Today, the anima, Jung notes, "no longer crosses our path as a goddess but, it may be, as an intimately personal misadventure," or, he adds, "perhaps as our best venture."[14] It can be our best venture because the possessive lure of the anima is not without deeper meaning or purpose, for it represents, even if in veiled or distorted form, the claims of the soul, buried deep within our emotional world and desire nature.

The Mother and Feminine Being

In early psychological development, the anima is initially bound up with the mother archetype, just as the animus is with the father. In the family romance of child psychology, according to classical depth psychology, the mother is the primary object of the boy's love affection (as in Freud's understanding of the Oedipal complex), with the mother fulfilling the role of both nurturer and beloved, just as the father is protector and beloved for the young girl (as in the Freudian Electra complex). During the course of psychological maturation, the anima and animus begin to function as distinct archetypes, with the romantic ideal images associated with these archetypes projected onto people outside of the family, as the adolescent forms love relationships that will lure him or her into necessary participation with the wider world, and away from the womb of family life and childhood.

In adult life, the anima continues to find expression most immediately in the sphere of relationships, especially those of a romantic and erotic nature, by means of projection onto another person, the object of one's affections, who appears to be the source of the very anima qualities waiting to be discovered within oneself. In folk wisdom, the search for the beloved is thus construed as a search for one's soul mate or other half, who would bring to one's life experience a wholeness we ordinarily lack and bring the fulfillment of our dreams of a happy life—this is what the anima would have us believe. And, indeed, the heightened sense of feeling alive, fulfilled, and complete with the blossoming of a new romance might be understood in part as a result of the activation of the anima and animus archetypes.

Yet throughout, the anima retains its close connection to the mother. When it becomes activated in adult life it can stimulate a nostalgic longing for the past, to periods of life when we were more in touch with our feelings, when life energies flowed more freely, more instinctively. Often, even as life progresses on the outside, deep within the feelings can remain stuck in an earlier life phase or fixated on the happy times of years gone by. Symbolically speaking, the anima can lure us towards a regressive union with the mother, and a return to the magical and comfortable womb of childhood free of the pressures, suffering, and limitations of ego-consciousness. With an undeveloped anima, still bound up with the mother-child relationship, it is difficult for us to accept the world as it really is or to give ourselves fully to life in the here and now.

The mother is but one form of the anima, which represents, Jung notes, all the "outstanding characteristics of a feminine being," and is therefore personified by a variety of female figures, depicted as anything from impersonal objects of sexual desire and romantic figures of the cultural imagination (such as Helen of Troy) to religious icons of spiritual purity and angelic benediction (such as the Virgin Mary)—each expressing a combination of traits associated with the Moon, Venus, Neptune, and Pluto.[15]

The Differentiation of the Anima

At a base level, the anima is closely bound up with instinctual desires and appetites. Especially when the anima is denied, through repression or excessive rationalization and egoic control of the personality, it tends to manifests in a crude and unsophisticated form. The compulsive urge to experience the rush of life, to feel the pulse of desire, then manifests predominantly through the sexual instincts, perhaps through pornography or licentious sensual indulgence and lusting. The anima here bleeds into the Dionysian archetype and the Freudian id, governed by the pleasure principle, with the voice of the soul and the more sensitive feelings lost within the wilder emotions and instinctual urges. To put this in astrological terms, here Venus and the Moon are laced with Pluto, consumed by the mire of the instinctual underworld. At another level, the feelings and desires associated with the anima become attached to an image of female beauty, with the particular carrier of one's romantic projections embodying the vital life energy and animating power of the anima. The anima initially represents the reward or "solace for all the bitterness of life" and "compensation" for life's struggle, offering the emotional gratification we feel we deserve in the face of the hardship of life and the pressures of functioning as a separate ego.[16] In this form, the anima is personified by the femme fatale figure or the muse, who possesses an enigmatic, *"je ne sais quoi,"* enchanting quality, and who is therefore readily the object of fantasy projections.

As the desire nature is progressively differentiated—that is, as we come to terms with the demands of the emotional world and become more conscious of the motivations behind our desires—the expression of the anima in dreams and fantasies changes form, reflecting an inner evolution that is crucial for individuation. The satisfaction of the anima at the level of instinct gives way to, or exists alongside, the desire for romantic fulfillment or the pursuit of our dreams and ideals in the world. In this respect, the anima possesses a *maya*-like capacity for spinning a web of illusory desires, which pulls us into entanglement with the world. The anima, or soul, Jung notes, "makes us believe incredible things, that life may be lived," and in this respect it is the function that, at a metaphysical level, brings the material world to life: "With her cunning play of illusions the soul lures into life the inertness of matter that does not want to live."[17] The anima in the individual psyche connects us to the *anima mundi*, the soul or spiritual essence within the materiality of the world, for the individual soul exists within the soul of all things.

In alchemy, the great task of the alchemical opus is to liberate the soul, the "slumbering spirit of nature," from its entrapment in the "chains of *physis*," and to reunite the soul with the transcendent dimension of spirit. The Queen or *Luna*, as symbols of the anima, are to be united with the King or *Sol*, in a *hieros gamos* of feminine and masculine, unconscious and conscious.

As in this alchemical myth, it is the work of individuation to liberate the anima, as soul, from its entrapment in the realm of instinct, by differentiating the voice of the soul from the insistent demands of the passions and the appetites, which can easily pull us onto a path of destruction unconsciously in search of revitalized feeling and the renewal of life. If indeed the anima represents the heart's desire, we must remember that the heart desires many things, some of them conflicting and contradictory. Individuation entails the differentiation of these desires in order that we can recognize our own true emotional response. If it can be recognized and heeded, this authentic feeling response—the "still, small voice" of the soul—is an unerring guide to the living of life and it makes possible a connection between the conscious ego and the Self. If the anima becomes a differentiated function within the psyche during the course of individuation, it can serve as another center or viewpoint alongside rational thought, a function that enables us to attune to the biddings of the Self through intuitive feeling. A differentiated anima enables us to feel into the "rightness" of things, to determine what is the right course of action, irrespective of reason and common sense or of the pressing and urgent demands of the moment. The anima thus becomes a mediator between the ego and the Self, serving as a psychopomp or guide to the unconscious and a guide to life, like Beatrice in the *Divine Comedy* or Ariadne, the Cretan princess who, in Greek myth, helps Theseus escape from the Minotaur's labyrinth. Moving through the encounter with the shadow into the sphere of the collective unconscious, the amorphous darkness of the unconscious begins to reveal a plurality of archetypes. The anima is the function that reveals this plurality, and enables us to navigate it.

For all the irrationality associated with the anima, Jung explains, "something strangely meaningful clings to her, a secret knowledge or hidden wisdom."[18] It might become apparent to us, as we begin to know ourselves and understand our deeper motivations more clearly, that behind the irrational moods of the anima a higher purpose is at work. One behaves in an unreasonable manner, seemingly at the mercy of wholly irrational emotions, but, it might be seen in retrospect that such moods and feelings reflect, albeit in a distorted way, what it is we must do if we our to live in a manner that is faithful to the Self. The anima is attuned, one might say, to the Tao of things, in that its feeling responses reflect the higher ordering of the Self, beyond the awareness of the rational ego. Behaving in a reasonable manner, according to the dictates of ethics and the conventions of social intercourse, or aspiring always to be fair and equal in our dealings with others in relationships, for instance, will often lead us to act out of step with a principle of deep intuitive feeling within us that knows what we need more than we ourselves do, for it is attuned to the greater "way of things." The obstinate feeling, moodiness, touchiness, and so forth might thus reflect the protest of our feeling nature against the rational, moral, or socially acceptable standard in the living of our life. The differentiation of the anima pertains to a process by which we learn to recognize, cultivate, and heed this feeling voice within us, which then becomes established as a psychological function, existing alongside rational reflection, to be called upon in the making of decisions and the orientation of our life. As Jung's research into synchronicity suggests, the unconscious at times seems to have an apparent foreknowledge of future events and thus knows what we must do, the course of action we must take.

The anima, one might say, "knows" what one's life destiny is, even if only in an inarticulate way. Yet the impulses and fantasies associated with the anima can often appear fantastical or unrealistic. They often make no rational sense and put us on a very uncertain path, perhaps entailing risk seemingly without any guarantee of reward. We can find a whole host of impelling reasons not to take the anima fantasies seriously, so we continue with life, putting them to one side. However, one invariably then finds that from time to time one is inexplicably moody or irritable, despite one's best efforts not to be. If one's partner is an obstacle to the anima's goals, romantic projection onto the partner falls away, unconsciously replaced by negative projections. These occurrences seem to be happening of their own accord for reasons totally unrelated to any deeper purpose. So accustomed are we to directing our lives according to reason and common sense that we grow distant and often disconnected from our deeper feelings. As time goes by, with the rational ego necessarily developing as an autonomous principle of self-determination, the realm of feeling becomes less accessible to consciousness, and it becomes unconsciously centered on the anima principle. One's true feelings become buried under a morass of contradictory emotions and desires, and it is the work of individuation to pick through this tangled mess.

The encounter with the anima is the "master-piece" of individuation because the workings of the anima are so subtle. We are so closely identified with our feelings and desires that it is extraordinarily difficult to avoid falling under their sway and being hypnotized by the anima's promise of emotional fulfillment. In facing this archetype, however, by exploring the seemingly irrational feelings associated with the anima, we might in time establish a connection with a source of life wisdom beyond the knowledge of the conscious ego, beyond reason and logic—a life meaning that is personified by the archetype of the spirit, often in the figure of the wise old man, that might come to the aid of the ego if it becomes ensnared in its own machinations and rational plans, unable to emancipate itself.

Notes

[1] For a discussion of the syzygy, see Jung, "Concerning the Archetypes, with Special Reference to the Anima Concept," in *Archetypes and the Collective Unconscious* (CW9i).

[2] Jung, *Two Essays on Analytical Psychology*, 207, par. 332.

[3] Jung, *Symbols of Transformation*, 304, par. 462.

[4] Jung, *Symbols of Transformation*, 304, par. 462.

[5] Marie-Louise von Franz had natal Mercury conjunct Mars. Mercury here pertains to the writing and to the pencil, Mars to the man and the jabbing with the pencil. The harsh judgment is reflected also in tendencies associated with her natal conjunction of Saturn and Pluto.

[6] This sequence of transformations of the projected animus has been set out by Jung and von Franz. See, for example, von Franz, "The Process of Individuation," in *Man and His Symbols*.

[7] Jung, *Archetypes and the Collective Unconscious*, 29, par. 61.

[8] In *Mysterium Coniunctionis*, Jung writes: "The *nigredo* corresponds to the darkness of the unconscious, which contains in the first place the inferior personality, the shadow. This changes into the feminine figure that stands immediately behind it, as it were, and controls it: the anima" (452, par. 646).

[9] Jung, *Mysterium Coniunctionis*, 178, par. 221.

[10] Jung, *Mysterium Coniunctionis*, 452, par. 646.

[11] Jung, *Archetypes and the Collective Unconscious*, 30, par. 59.

[12] Zimmer, *Philosophies of India*, 38.

[13] Zimmer, *Myths and Symbols in Indian Art and Civilization*, 163–164.

[14] Jung, *Archetypes and the Collective Unconscious*, 30, par. 62.

[15] Jung, *Aion*, 13, par. 26.

[16] Jung, *Aion*, 13, par. 24.

[17] Jung, *Archetypes and the Collective Unconscious*, 26, par. 56.

[18] Jung, *Archetypes and the Collective Unconscious*, 30, par. 64.

Chapter 12

Fantasy, Enchantment, and the Spirit

In an encounter with the unconscious during individuation, Jung places the archetypes in a sequence of emergence: the initial facing of the shadow leads next to the anima-animus phase, which in turn brings one into contact with the archetypal figure of the mana-personality.

The Mana-Personality

The mastery of the challenge posed by the anima and animus can give one deep insight into the nature of life. These archetypes in different ways give us access to the inner knowledge of the unconscious, an occult knowledge of the hidden laws of life. One sees and knows things most other people do not—an experience that inevitably brings with it the danger of inflation. "Knowledge puffeth up," as the old biblical dictum) has it.[1] Identification with this archetype brings, Jung notes, an "uncomfortable kinship with the gods."[2] One is elevated, seemingly, to a position of superhuman knowledge and power.

Each instance of self-overcoming, of becoming free of unconscious identification with a particular impulse or feeling, and overcoming the compulsion associated with it, brings a sense of triumphant mastery or of what Goethe called "godlikeness." As one progressively overcomes the compulsion of the anima, one grows in power and insight, and one is thus elevated in stature. At that point, out of the background of the psyche the archetypal figure of the mana-personality is called forth, and one is faced with the subtle and alluring prospect of believing oneself to be some kind of superior spiritual being, perhaps a savior or a prophet or a spiritual master or magician, or a person of "superior wisdom" and "superior will"—Jung suggests as examples Goethe's Faust and Nietzsche's *Übermensch* in the person of Zarathustra, the magician and the god-man, which convey well the power, will, and mastery associated with the mana-personality.[3] After the encounter with the anima, he explains, "it is the figure of the magician, as I will call it for short, who attracts the mana to himself, i.e., the unconscious valency of the anima."[4] The mana-personality is a figure imbued with magical power and insight resulting from the ego's encounter with the unconscious. In women especially, Jung contends, the figure of the magician finds its equivalent in that of "the Great Mother, the All-Merciful, who understands everything, forgives everything, who always acts for the best, living only for others, never seeking her own interests, the discoverer of the great love just as the magician is the mouthpiece of the ultimate truth."[5] Identifying with either figure, magician or Great Mother, deprives one, in spite of the steps one has already taken on the road to individuation, of a true relationship with the Self.

We can recognize something of the character of the mana-personality in the power and influence wielded by spiritual gurus or the authority often imbued upon mediums, psychics, psychotherapists, and religious leaders, who inhabit the sphere of the archetypal "high priest" or "high priestess," possessing special access to the inner workings of the mind, the lines of fate, and the biddings of the divine. Such figures are imbued with a kind of magical power because of the role they perform and the unconscious expectations the role elicits in those seeking help. A field is constellated in which one may become overly receptive, as if one is receiving a pronouncement of ultimate truth from a higher source. The unwitting populace is therefore susceptible to fall under the sway of these figures, especially in times of desperate need or moral weakness, granting them an authority to instruct and guide that is not always justified or legitimate. Today, such magical-religious power is also wielded, ironically, by the scientific "expert," typically revered by politicians as the arbiter of indisputable objective facts, in spite of the sometimes transient nature of scientific theories, which can shift from year to year, and in spite of the political and ideological influences that always influence interpretation. With a little critical reflection we can see through the allure and sometimes dubious authority of such figures, but when we ourselves enter into the territory of unexplored knowledge and untapped power, how much more readily we can be blinded and seduced by the insights we have stumbled across. "The enormous prestige" of the mana-personality, Jung observes, "casts a spell over the ego."[6]

In the mana-personality we see a combination of at least three astrological archetypes: Jupiter, Pluto, and Neptune. While the susceptibility to grandiose inflation and possession by a power complex are themes associated with Jupiter and Pluto, respectively, the figures of savior, prophet, magician, and spiritual guru are primarily Neptunian. These principles act in concert to produce the intoxicating combination of mystery, triumphant mastery, and spiritual power associated with these figures. Naturally, it is difficult to put aside and relinquish one's identification with such feelings and qualities, especially as it is an identification that can often be reinforced by the prestige and admiration bestowed upon one by others, who wait in desperate need of a spiritual savior or charismatic hero to lead them out of the wilderness or to offer conviction and surety in an uncertain world. The tendency to identify with the numinous power of the mana-personality, in these circumstances, is almost unavoidable, as Jung stresses.

> But in so far as the ego apparently draws to itself the power belonging to the anima, the ego does become a mana-personality. This development is almost a regular phenomenon. I have never yet seen a fairly advanced development of this kind where at least a temporary identification with the archetype of the mana-personality did not take place. . . . One can scarcely help admiring oneself a little for having seen more deeply into things than others, and the others have such an urge to find a tangible hero somewhere, or a superior wise man, a leader and a father, some undisputed authority, that they build temples to little tin gods with the greatest promptitude and burn incense upon the altars.[7]

The necessary response to the inflationary consequences of such an identification is to come to recognize within oneself the traits of the mana-personality, in order to differentiate the archetypal figure from one's conscious identity and one's all-too-human personality. Holding one's shadow weaknesses before one's consciousness—reminding oneself of one's faults and failures—can puncture the inflation. Or simply seeing it for what it is—as a fantasy, an image, that is not intrinsic to one's authentic experience—can be enough to enable one to step outside of this archetypal figure. Liberated from this identification with the mana-personality, one can then come into a relationship with the Self, which is the true source of the mana, the magical power.

The Archetype of the Spirit
The mana-personality arises from an unconscious identification with the "archetype of the spirit"—the failure, that is, to recognize this archetype as an autonomous principle and pattern existing outside of one's conscious identity. As we have seen, the "archetype of the spirit,"

which Jung also describes as the "archetype of meaning," is often personified as a wise old man or crone or animal spirit guide that may appear as numinous presences in "big dreams," with their characteristic sense of mystery and the uncanny. We considered the Saturnian dimension of these figures above, but the spiritual essence of this figure, and its supernatural and prescient qualities, are most obviously related to the Neptune archetype in astrology. Similar qualities are present in the savior archetype, too, which is called forth in situations of dire necessity. Only the savior can liberate us from the ego's entrapment in the tangled web of its machinations or from the overwhelming claustrophobic darkness and pain of an encounter with the shadow. The danger and difficulty themselves call forth the saving grace: "Where there is danger some, Salvation grows there too," as the poet Hölderlin observed.[8]

In astrology, the Neptune archetype incorporates in its meaning all manner of spiritual and numinous experiences, as well as faith, devotion, prayer, compassion, empathy, sacrifice, redemption, and salvation. It pertains to the realm of myth and dream, and to the imagination and the imaginal figures that populate it. It manifests as the urge to transcendent the usual limits of personal identity, perhaps through meditation or spiritual revelation, or perhaps through intoxication and medication, giving rise to non-ordinary states of consciousness—we have already met Neptune in the god of the vine, Dionysus. The Neptune archetype possesses a dissolving power and mesmerizing allure that inspires in us the highest and subtlest feelings or pulls us into disintegration and self-loss. It manifests as the impulse to find enchantment and mystery, and in the yearning for a more ideal life. Yet it also manifests in the longing to escape and withdraw from that which is limiting, crude, or painful in our experience.

Neptune in Depth Psychology

Given these many associations, themes associated with Neptune have a significant place in the canon of depth psychology, especially Jungian and archetypal psychology with their prominent focus on myth. We see it most immediately in depth psychology's concern with psychopathology, with Neptune evident in the personality dissolution and detachment from reality of schizophrenia, in the escapism and flight from reality in neurosis, and the loss of self in psychosis and other conditions.

We see Neptune also in Freud's description of religion as arising from an experience of "oceanic" consciousness in which, by Freud's account, the ego's boundaries are temporarily dissolved and consciousness is opened to the fullness of the id, reconstituting for a short while the absorption in the id that characterizes the magical experience of childhood.[9] The description "oceanic" calls to mind the mythic god Neptune (the Greek Poseidon), who rules over the sea, and it reflects too the Neptune archetype's association with the dissolution and unity that are often prominent in religious experience. Aptly, then, Freud also notes that religious experience is often accompanied by the feeling "of being one with the external world as a whole" and a "sensation of eternity," both of which capture essential elements of Neptune: the eternal and oneness.[10] Yet Freud, as is well known, was skeptical of spiritual realities, seeing religion as an "illusion," albeit one with a crucial sociological function. These views, as we will later consider, reflect Freud's own experience of the archetypal Neptune, conditioned, in his case, by Saturn. Also related to Neptune is the Freudian understanding of the process of sublimation, by which crude instinctual desires find higher or subtler forms of expression in art and culture, for instance. It has been noted by astrologers that Neptune serves to spiritualize and sensitize the expression of the other planetary archetypes when it is in significant relationship to them, as indicated by major aspect alignments.

In alchemy, the dissolving power of Neptune is evident in the alchemical operation *solutio*, by which solid matter is reduced to a liquid state, implying, in psychological terms, that coagulated energies and fantasies bound up in psychological complexes are released and then flow, or perhaps flood, into consciousness, or that the hard shell of the ego is dissolved, opening consciousness to an influx of fantasies. Alchemical images of the king drowning in the watery depths of his own desirousness are Neptunian. This archetype can pull us under water, as in the mythic "night-sea journey," utterly incapacitating the human will, dissipating our energy and clouding our attention, and rendering us in a state of suspended animation, like the Hanged Man of the Rider-Waite Tarot, who, as one commentary declares, "appears to be sacrificed by those on earth but is displaying his allegiance with higher powers."[11]

Neptune is also present in the alchemical symbol of the *aqua permanens*, the "wonderful waters of transformation," which perform the *solutio* operation, described above, and constitute the spiritual essence within matter, "extracted" through the various operations performed by the alchemist.[12] As in a traditional religious context, water is associated with absolution and purification, as one is baptized in water and in spirit. The Neptunian principle, associated with the symbolism of water, can act to baptize one into the reality of the spirit.

The tendency towards illusion and self-loss, and escapism and delusion, is Neptunian, for identification with the archetypes of the collective unconscious provides an escape from the often painful and uncertain experience of being one's self. Under the influence of Neptune, one is inclined to take a fantasy as reality and thus lose sight of objective facts. Neptune can be recognized in the mirage on the horizon or the chimerical oasis in the desert. Similarly, the depth psychological phenomenon of projection, the distortion of the clear perception of reality under the spell of an archetypal image, is a further instance of the *maya*-like property of the Neptune archetype, blurring the lines between external fact and inner fantasy, between truth and illusion. As we have seen, the way of individuation demands that we withdraw projections, and thus counter the Neptunian tendency to fall victim to the spellbinding power of archetypal images in the collective unconscious.

The archetypal Neptune can be recognized in the adopting of a persona, the donning of a mask. It is the Neptunian capacity for imagination and empathy that allows one to take on a particular role. Neptune is therefore a blessing for the actor or impersonator, yet in ordinary life such acting can easily become pretense, and a gift for imitation can preclude the realization of one's own truth and character. For all these reasons, the developed capacities for discernment and brutal honesty are invariably essential to cultivate a healthy relationship with Neptune.

Participation Mystique and the Porous Self

Individuation promotes a departure from the condition of *participation mystique*, so named by French anthropologist Claude Lévy-Bruhl to describe an experience of preconscious non-differentiation of the self from the environment evident in premodern cultures. This state is characterized by the existence of a "porous self," to use Charles Taylor's term—that is, by an undeveloped self-sense or weakened ego boundaries and personal will. This condition is devoid of the fortified boundaries between self and world that so define the modern sense of individual ego selfhood. Taylor calls this modern ego the "buffered self." The experience of the world as enchanted, mostly lost to us today, arose from the fluid and permeable relationship between the porous self and the environment, as Taylor explains:

Almost everyone can agree that one of the big differences between us and our ancestors of five hundred years ago is that they lived in an "enchanted" world, and we do not; at the very least, we live in a *much less* "enchanted" world. We might think of this as our having "lost" a number of beliefs and the practices which they made possible. But more, the enchanted world was one in which these forces could cross a porous boundary and shape our lives, psychic and physical. One of the big differences between us and them is that we live with a much firmer sense of the boundary between self and other. We are "buffered" selves. We have changed.[13]

He continues:

> . . . the boundary between agents and forces is fuzzy in the enchanted world; and the boundary between mind and world is porous. . . . The porousness of the boundary emerges here in various kinds of "possession"—all the way from a full taking over of the person, as with a medium, to various kinds of domination by or partial fusion with a spirit or God. Here again, the boundary between self and other is fuzzy, porous. And this has to be seen as a fact of *experience*, not a matter of "theory" or "belief."[14]

The experience of porousness, in the manner Taylor defines it, is still available to us periodically today, under certain psychological conditions. Jung noted, for example, that when the unconscious is powerfully activated, such as in cases of synchronicity, there is typically an *abaissement du niveau mental*—a lowering of the threshold of consciousness, in which we effectively dip into the *participation mystique* and experience again, for a brief time, the dark mysterious unity of the magical world more readily available to our ancestors. The experience of the Neptune archetype makes us more porous, our ego boundaries more permeable, permitting an entry into an enchanted reality ordinarily excluded from conscious awareness.

Of course, such experiences are not without their dangers. As we have seen, both experiences of dissolution, disintegration, and self-loss, on the one hand, and experiences of unity, spiritual identity, and enchantment, on the other, fall under the jurisdiction of Neptune, and both classes of experience are present in the condition of *participation mystique*. This state is that of a dim twilight or diffused consciousness, in which there is a less acute sense of individual selfhood, and one can experience a partial merger with the environment or a sense of oneness, of union with the world and with nature. The Neptunian experience of identity with nature and with spirit can restore to our existence a magical glow, as one comes to experience the sense of brooding mystery of the *participation mystique*, as if one has fallen into a dream or entered again the enchanted forest of childhood fairytales. When the Neptune archetype is activated, the ordinary everydayness of life can be transcended in a greater mystical, mythical, or magical awareness. The recovery of the state of *participation mystique* can be thought of as a kind of "horizontal" identity with the *anima mundi*, the soul of the world.

Mystical and Psychedelic Experiences

In addition to the experience of *participation mystique*, a litany of themes and traits associated with the Neptune archetype are also evident in experiences of the immanent and transcendent divine, extensively documented in mystical literature and the psychology of religious experience. Mysticism was defined by Rufus Jones as "the type of religion which puts the emphasis on immediate awareness of relation with God, on direct and intimate consciousness of the Divine Presence."[15] Mystical experiences of the immanence of the divine lead to an apprehension and experience of God or spirit as infusing the world around us, with nature and all of Creation as the revealed glory of God. The alchemical *unio mystica*—the mystical union with God and the world—is the condition of the realization of one's absolute identity with the divine; it is a union of human consciousness with "the Eternal ground of all empirical being," as Jung put it.[16] The transcendent form of mystical experience discloses the reality of the Divine as existing outside of the phenomenal world, outside of Creation, as in the Christian idea of God's kingdom as "not of this world." In one or other form, the mystic penetrates to the eternal silence within which our busy lives of relentless activity are ever contained. Alongside "horizontal" identification, then, we might also experience Neptune as a "vertical" ascent of consciousness towards God reaching outside of the bounds of space and time, or a descent of spirit from a transcendent realm.

In a number of classic studies dating from the early twentieth century, Richard Bucke, William James, Evelyn Underhill, Roberto Assagioli, Aldous Huxley, and others have described mystical experience in terms of the perennial philosophy, comprising the spiritual truths common to all religions and revealed in mystical experiences from all traditions. These experiences are of unity and transcendence, possessing an ineffable quality that cannot be put into words, but only immediately apprehended in rare moments of revelation or approached through the language of the poet and the artist. Mystical experience often elicits surrender and sacrifice, infusing us with the rapture of divine presence and love, inspiring devotion and selfless service—all defining attributes of the experience of the archetypal Neptune. Yet, if not successfully integrated into the reality of one's life, mystical experiences can have a disintegrating effect on the personality, giving rise to delusions and a flight from reality, and as likely therefore to result in insanity as enlightenment. For those without a sufficiently stable ego and grounding in the world, absorption in the spiritual dimension of reality can be acutely problematic, giving rise to a weakened self-sense, inadequate ego boundaries, and an impotence of personal will.

The effects of mystical experience, as discussed by Assagioli in his *Transpersonal Development*, are manifest through intuition, imagination, illumination, revelation, inspiration, creation, and understanding, all of which bear strong connections to the archetypal Neptune.[17] Similar qualities to those reported by mystics are evident in the "non-ordinary states of consciousness" instigated by psychedelic drugs or "sacred medicines," as they are known, which also fall into the category of experiences associated with the Neptune, with the plant or chemical compound opening the "doors of perception" to the subtle worlds and spiritual realities beyond the ordinary confines of limited ego-consciousness. Today, native plant medicines, such as ayahuasca, have for growing numbers of people become a portal to non-ordinary states of consciousness and the hidden dimensions of the unconscious.

Used judiciously, with appropriate attention given to "set and setting" and then afterwards to "integration" of the experience, such substances can initiate profound transformation and afford us revelatory insights into the nature of reality. On the other hand, dependence on drugs and alcohol, as many therapists have stressed, is often an unconscious substitute for spiritual experience and, more broadly, for the Neptunian experience of "flow." To smoke a cigarette or drink a glass of wine, for instance, serves to liberate one from a felt sense of entrapment in the world and to experience being back in the flow, temporarily transcending the inherent constrictions and discomforts of the moment. The thirsting for the Neptunian experience of flow might be seen as a displaced yearning for transcendence. Recovering alcoholics and drug users have often passed through some kind of "conversion" experience, possessing a religious quality, in which they come into relationship with what is construed as a "higher power." Neptune pertains to the experiences of sacrifice, surrender, and service to such a power.

Ideals and Illusions

More generally, even for those people not expressly religious or spiritual, Neptune makes itself known in the experience of the exquisite, the search for the ideal and for perfection, or in the quest for the spotless and the pure. Neptune manifests in the yearning for paradise. We have already noted the relationship in Grofian perinatal psychology between the Neptune archetype and the paradisiacal experience of non-differentiated unity of the fetus in the womb. The manifestation of the Neptune principle in human experience throughout the life course serves to put one in touch with this lost paradise or moves one to try to return to it. Visions of future bliss and fulfillment, the fairytale imagination of the pot of gold at the end of the rainbow, or simply the dream and hope of a better future—these are forms of idealism evoked by politicians of every persuasion. Such idealism is also a primary motivation behind prophecy and divination, which fall under the dominion of Neptune too: invariably, we want to know that the future will bring the fulfillment of our wishes; or if pain and problems lie ahead, that we might transmute these into meaningful experiences or pathways to the divine, by coming to understand their deeper spiritual significance. This latter function is also served by myth, enabling us to connect our own worldly experiences to their spiritual purpose and archetypal background.

In a secular guise Neptunian idealism can find an outlet in the allure of glamour and celebrity, with the stars of stage and screen worshipped and revered in our own time almost as the gods were in ages past. The promise of fame and the idealization of the celebrity is an instance of the Neptunian phenomenon of projection, reflecting the need to be in relationship with the kind of ideal and magical reality cultivated by Hollywood, with the movie theater the place of worship that permits us entry into a vivid alternate reality and thus provides an escape from the mundane, as we bathe in the inspiration and enchantment that film and other media can provide.

Bliss and enchantment, magic and mystery, illusion and madness, intoxication and transcendence, dissolution and flow—the archetypal Neptune pertains to those experiences, motivations, and qualities that seek to put us in touch with the infinite and to live in the flow of the Tao, as we play our parts within the great universal dream.

Notes

1. I Corinthians 8:1.
2. Jung, *Two Essays on Analytical Psychology*, 237, par. 396.
3. Jung, *Two Essays on Analytical Psychology*, 237, par. 397.
4. Jung, *Two Essays on Analytical Psychology*, 228, par. 378.
5. Jung, *Two Essays on Analytical Psychology*, 228, par. 379.
6. Jung, *Two Essays on Analytical Psychology*, 234, par. 391.
7. Jung, *Two Essays on Analytical Psychology*, 233, par. 389.
8. "Wo aber Gefahr ist, wächst das Rettende auch." Hölderlin, "Patmos," in *Selected Poems*, 54.
9. Freud, *Civilization and Its Discontents,* 11–12.
10. Freud, *Civilization and Its Discontents*, 11–12.
11. Mann, *Elements of Tarot*, 50–51.
12. Jung, *Mysterium Coniunctionis*, 277, par. 372.
13. Taylor, "Buffered and Porous Selves," accessed September 13, 2016, http://blogs .ssrc.org/tif/2008/09 /02/buffered-and-porous-selves.
14. Taylor, *Secular Age*, 39.
15. Jones, "Studies in Mystical Religion," quoted in Scholem, *Major Trends in Jewish Mysticism*, 4.
16. Jung, *Mysterium Coniunctionis*, 534, par. 760.
17. Assagioli, "Part One: The Study of the Superconscious," in *Transpersonal Development*, 19–104.

Chapter 13

Growth, Inflation, and the Journey to Wholeness

In traditional astrological literature, Jupiter is described as the "great beneficent," which says much about how phenomena and experiences characteristic of this archetypal principle are usually viewed.[1] We invariably welcome the growth, optimism, and plenitude that the archetypal Jupiter brings, in contrast to the guarded or negative manner in which Saturn is often perceived and experienced. Such responses tell us more about human nature, however, than they do about the objective positive or negative status of Jupiter and Saturn, for both growth and limitation, optimism and pessimism, abundance and scarcity, have their place in life—indeed, each is a necessary counterpart and complement to the other.

Growth and Improvement

Jupiter, then, engenders a complex of qualities and types of experience that we ordinarily consider positive and therefore desirable: faith, optimism, confidence, expansion, success, and a buoyant or trusting psychological mood. Astrologers connect Jupiter to a sense of perspective, the capacity to see the big picture, and to see life as a whole. The very notion of wholeness is Jupiterian, in the sense of the fullness of a good life, a life well lived, or a life rich in cultural experiences, blessed with good fortune and opportunity. Jupiter is therefore prominent in notions of human flourishing and the aspiration towards self-actualization.

In humanistic psychology and certain transpersonal psychologies, the necessity of an aspiration towards growth is often taken as axiomatic. The fantasy of growth tacitly informs approaches to human wellbeing and understandings of the *raison d'être* of human existence. To grow, to become more, to improve, to make progress—these are fundamental ideals of the modern West especially, and are thus integral to its psychology. Indeed, I would imagine that we all subscribe, one way or another, to the hope that tomorrow things will get better, our own form of the "myth of progress," which might well be delusional, but its capacity to motivate us to all manner of human activity and ambition is beyond question. Indeed, I have given the Jupiterian motif of the way or the journey prominence in this book because the aspiration to move to a condition of more, of better, of higher, of fuller, is so universally applicable. To reach for the stars and strive for a path to the glories of heaven is a motivation that perhaps never leaves us, even if our notions of what constitutes improvement and what is actually better evolve over time.

We must acknowledge too, however, that despite the positive dimension of this aspiration, much of the pathology of the modern world can be attributed to Jupiterian traits and themes: indulgence without restraint, growth without limit, immoral opportunism and speculation, excess and extravagance, waste and profligacy, exaggeration and pomposity. In the consumerist age, within free-market capitalist society, the Jupiter impulse often manifests as the striving for affluence and material prosperity, to make good in an age of plenty (while half the planet's population suffers with scarcity or starves). Yet Jupiter need not be expressed in materialistic terms or selfishly, for the feeling of abundance and good will associated with Jupiter naturally translates into generosity, sharing one's good fortune or one's talents or wealth with others. Jupiterian trust and faith enable one to let go of egocentric self-concern and the tendency to grab after things.

Traditionally, Jupiter is associated with the religious impulse to connect to a larger order. We see this dimension of the archetype in the beneficence and blessings of life, bestowing upon us the riches of the earth. Jupiter is divine providence or simply what seems to be good luck. It is the experience of ease and that which comes to us without effort—thus grace, in religious terms, as opposed to (or in conjunction with), the labor and exertions associated with Saturn.

The archetype's jurisdiction also includes the impulse to reach out to the wider world, as in publishing and promotion, and in philosophies, worldviews, and religions connecting peoples. This principle promotes cultural advancement and social betterment, for it blesses us with the positive expectation that all things can improve and that we can become more than we are, and can reach higher and raise ourselves up. Jupiter imbues the confidence and assured conviction to open ourselves to the world and to spread the Gospel, to preach the truth. It promotes the enlargement of personality and grants a sense of psychological spaciousness. It fills us with the readiness and faith to walk through the open door and embrace the opportunity when it arises—in this respect it has resonances with the beneficent aspect of the Hindu deity Ganesha, the remover of obstacles, as described by Zimmer: "In his left hand he here carries a bowl, full either of rice, on which he feeds, or of jewels, pearls, and corals, which he showers on his devotees. Paunchy and well-off, he is the bestower of earthly posterity and well-being."[2]

The Archetypal Wanderer and the Journey Motif

The Jupiterian spirit of adventure and of enterprise is paramount in commerce or in great voyages of discovery to distant lands and faraway places. Jupiter represents the boon and the bounty of the successful voyage or undertaking. Its themes are writ large in many of the banners describing the modern era: the Age of Exploration or Discovery, the Age of Opportunity, and the pursuit of happiness. For it was a Jupiterian motivation that impelled expansion across the globe from the time of the voyages of Columbus to the New World, and the same aspiration, technologically empowered, that is evident still in space exploration and in globalization. Under the influence of this archetypal energy, we look to the distant horizon and yonder shores, or to the mountaintop and even beyond—traditionally, Jupiter is associated in astrology with travel and foreign affairs. The panoramic vista, elevated viewpoint, and global perspective are in keeping with the breadth and expanse of a Jupiterian vision of life. Jupiter spurs us on to greatness and victory. It is the crowning glory of success, the ascent to the throne, like the Roman god Jupiter and the Greek Zeus—the king of the gods.

In terms of the archetypal patterns and personages of the collective unconscious, Jupiter is personified in the form of the wanderer archetype, which is closely connected to the motif of the journey.[3] Although Jung does not explicitly focus on the wanderer as a distinct principle in the archetypal pantheon of the collective unconscious, it is, of course, implicitly present in the motif of the journey and in the circling process by which the ego draws ever closer to the Self. The fate of the hero is realized in a journey of restless wandering, in an unconscious yearning for a return to the source, and for this reason the myth of the hero is envisaged as a journey, as enshrined in Joseph Campbell's work. The literary forms of the hero as wanderer are as ubiquitous as the mythic. Thomas Hampson describes well the numerous guises of this figure, giving a sense of its prominence in the artistic imagination of the West:

Throughout the cultural history of the Western world from Antiquity to the late 19th century, the figure of the Wanderer appears in several distinct manifestations. In the epic vein he is a hero with superhuman traits (Achilles, Odysseus, Siegfried, Parzival, or Dante) or a god with anthropomorphic ones (Nordic myth's Wotan turned Wanderer, the transmigratory Zeus, or the peripatetic Finn and Oisin of Anglo-Celtic legend). In the picaresque genre the voyager appears as pilgrim (Chaucer's Canterbury travelers), Crusader (Rodrigo of La Poema del Cid or Roland of Le Roman de Roland and Orlando Furioso, and Scott's Ivanhoe), rogue (the highwayman MacHeath or the amorous bastard Tom Jones), or the questing idealist (Voltaire's Candide, Cervantes' Don Quixote). In travel literature he surfaces as the impressionable protagonist of the Bildungsroman—the traveler experiencing the Wanderjahr as an educational voyage (Wilhelm Meister, Gulliver, Fanny Burney or Tristram Shandy). And finally he debuts as Romantic Wanderer, who synthesizes the properties of his prototypes, while grafting onto them those quintessential 19th century emotions of *Sehnsucht* (longing), *Heimweh* (homesickness), and *Weltschmerz* (world weariness). Infusing the journey with a new psychological dimension, the 19th century Wanderer marches into [the] 20th with the epic journeys of Joyce's Ulysses, Hemingway's rootless heroes, or Salinger's adolescent outsider in *Catcher in the Rye*.[4]

The specific qualities and inflections of the voyages undertaken by each of these wanderers might be understood in terms of combinations of many different planetary archetypes, but the motif of the wanderer itself is principally Jupiterian.

The experience of wandering and journeying is reflected in Jupiter's described meaning in traditional astrological texts, most especially in its connection with travel, "long journeys," and dealings with foreign countries. Where the expansion of horizons comes instead through the mind rather than travel, Jupiter manifests in the "higher learning" of the philosophically attuned vision or the study of the life, literature, and languages of foreign cultures. Jupiter elevates and expands, uplifts and amplifies, often for the better, and occasionally for the worse.

Inflation and Excess

For as with all archetypes what is at one time and in one circumstance a blessing becomes at another time and place a curse. Jupiterian plenty and abundance can very easily become over-extension, greed, and extravagance. Growth unchecked and unrestrained can lead to inflation and hubris—an insight not lost on the ancient Greeks, for whom hubris was a significant focus of their myths and teachings. Jupiter is evident in the alchemical *sublimatio*—the capacity to rise above something and thus to gain a sense of perspective, but also the flight or elevation dangerously out of touch with the grounding reality of the earth. The great height then precipitates the crashing fall.

We have already encountered the archetypal Jupiter in the grandiose inflation of the mana-personality. This tendency towards inflation following an encounter with the unconscious is an undesirable and sometimes acutely problematic mode of expression of the principle of growth and expansion in life. The cultural elevation afforded by Jupiter can become superiority, invariably as a compensation for some unacknowledged weakness. It can make one vainglorious, boastful, and overconfident. High moments of success can spill over into mania and grandiosity. Jupiter today is "worshipped" in the form of what Lewis Mumford termed giantism.[5] We see Jupiter towering on the horizon in the immensity of the metropolis skyscraper. It is behind the drive for always faster, better, more dramatic, more popular, more successful, more famous, more celebrated. Having too much of a good thing, taking on too much too soon, over-confidence and over-reliance on faith and good fortune—we recognize among these Jupiterian themes perennial human missteps from which our moral instruction and childhood fables try to protect us.

Yet, essentially, the experience of Jupiter is invariably welcomed, for it pertains to the positive dimension of life—those experiences that we wish for, and that make life flow and flourish as we feel it should if only we were unhindered by problems and restraints, pathologies and resistances, such that trust, faith, and optimism could prevail.

Notes

[1] For a rich survey of the meanings of Jupiter in astrology, see Stephen Arroyo, *Exploring Jupiter: Astrological Key to Progress, Prosperity & Potential* (Sebastopol, CA: CRCS Publications, 1996).

[2] Zimmer, *Myths and Symbols in Indian Art and Civilization*, 183–184.

[3] See, for example, Jung's discussion of Michael Maier's journey to four continents in his "mystic peregrination," in *Mysterium Coniunctionis*, 210–235, par. 276–314.

⁴ Hampson, "Winterreise," accessed April 5, 2017, http://www.thomashamp son.com/ category/winterreise/. Quotation reformatted from internet source for presentation within the text.
⁵ See Figure 20 in Mumford, *Myth of the Machine*.

Chapter 14

The Self: The Archetype of Center and Totality

A midst this multiplicity of archetypes, how are we to find center? Which god are we to serve? One answer is that there is no center, or whatever center there is shall not hold. James Hillman advocates such a view, as we have seen, in his belief that we should allow ourselves to fall apart into our multiplicity, honoring all the gods as they live through us and press their claims for our attention. For some people, however, the reality of existence in a state of such multiplicity might be impractical when faced with pressing life decisions and responsibilities, or outright painful if the multiplicity becomes a raging war between the various instincts and archetypes. In a state of neurosis one is painfully divided against oneself. In psychosis or schizophrenia archetypal fantasies might sweep over us, obliterating or drowning consciousness. Serving more than one master and riding more than one horse might be unsustainable and catastrophically injurious in the long term.

The compensatory nature of the psyche, as Jung understood it, means that multiplicity is naturally counterbalanced by a center and unity, just as (to use a fitting celestial analogy) the multiplicity of planets is centered on a single star. The final archetype for us to consider here, and the most fundamental of them all, is the principle of center that Jung called the Self. It might be envisaged as the central archetype in the pantheon of figures described above.

Jung describes the Self as a "living something" and the "God within us" that is "strange to us and yet so near, wholly ourselves and yet unknowable, a virtual centre of so mysterious a constitution that it can claim anything—kinship with beasts and gods, with crystals and the stars."[1] In this respect, the Self embraces the opposites, and its realization brings us into creative communion with the whole of life. This wholeness, and the dynamic reconciliation of the opposites, is depicted, Jung believes, in mandala drawings—images of a "sacred circle" often enclosing a quaternity structure of some sort, such as a cross. In this respect, an astrological chart is a mandala, for it partakes in this very form, and it may thus be considered an image of the Self as it finds expression through us in a particular incarnation in space and time. Circumscribed by the zodiac, all the planets fall within the bounds of the chart mandala, just as all the archetypes are, in the final analysis, functions of and expressions of the Self.

As center and totality of the psyche, the Self pertains to the Sun, the center of the solar system and the resplendent light that circumscribes the entire zodiac, through which all the planets move in their orbits. The Self is the primary "dominant" of the psyche around which all other archetypes orbit, like the planets around the Sun.

As the matrix of consciousness, from which the ego progressively emerges and from which consciousness is born daily, the Self pertains to the Moon, symbolizing the maternal ground of existence, the mythic Great Mother that births and nourishes the hero. The emergence of the Self is heralded and symbolized in dreams and fantasies by the child archetype, which is also associated with the Moon. The Self, Jung observed, is the "child of the pregnant anima" and the anima and child, we noted, are both related to the astrological Moon.[2]

As the incarnate "God-image," the Self is connected to *logos* and thus to the astrological Mercury. And as Mercury pertains to the Truth, intellectually apprehended, Venus pertains to Beauty, in the Platonic sense, and to cosmic harmony and balance. In the Christian vision, it relates to God as Love. In Mars we find God or the Self expressed in act and deed, for the Self can only be realized through the exertions of the ego, willing to act courageously and take risks.

As wholeness, and the movement towards fulfillment, the Self pertains to Jupiter, for, as Jung notes of the Self, "all our highest and ultimate purposes seem to be striving towards it"[3] and it represents "the full flowering not only of the single individual, but of the group, in which each adds his portion to the whole."[4] As the king of the gods, Jupiter conveys, too, the Self's superior position in the pantheon of archetypes.

As the ruling authority of the psyche, and the circumscribed limits of the individual's experience, the Self pertains to Saturn and to the father-senex archetype—manifest as God the Father with imperatives and commandments that we are obliged to reckon with and often obey. The Self is in some sense the Saturnian boundary of our experience, outside of which we cannot stray. It imposes upon the ego a pressure to actualize and to individuate, the fruit of which is the realized *lapis*, the Philosopher's Stone, also envisaged as the polished "diamond body"— the hard-earned fulfillment of Saturnian labor through a lifetime or perhaps more.

As the principle of individual uniqueness, realized through going one's own way in life and undertaking the process of individuation, the Self pertains to the astrological Uranus and its associations with freedom, individualism, and the spark of creative genius. The manifestations of Uranus as the trickster reflect the idiosyncratic nature of the Self as unique and original, never to be repeated, and also pertain to the capacity of the Self, as the "God within us" to cross our path unexpectedly and throw us, in spite of ourselves, in a direction we did not anticipate.[5]

The numinosity of the Self, as the incarnate God-image, is related to Neptune as the principle of oceanic unity and the oneness of the experience of the world as an undivided whole. In its connections with the divine, the Self partakes in the yearning for transcendence, heaven, and the recovery of the state of lost paradise. And as the God principle, the Self elicits from the ego sacrifice and service—Neptunian themes both—as it dissolves boundaries between ego and world, purifying and redeeming the state of fallen human nature.

The fateful and fated nature of the experience of the Self pertains to Pluto, that creative-destructive evolutionary principle and power that inexorably compels us, often half blindly, to fulfill some calling or vocation. Pluto is especially related to the dark half of the Self, the unconscious spirit within nature, buried within the instinctual underworld of the psyche, to be realized through our own transformation and death-rebirth.

Finally, following the directives of the Self entails moving beyond prevailing human standards of justice and fairness in the acceptance of a greater principle of cosmic justice, affirming strife and discord and counterbalancing reactions as inevitable and essential manifestations of the movement of life energy between opposites, even as we try to heal and reconcile these opposites. In these respects, the Self incorporates the dynamics and themes of the archetypal principle associated with Eris.[6]

In symbolically portraying the Self, the astrological birth chart depicts the positions of the planets associated with each of these archetypal principles and helps us understand how they are related to each other.

Figure 1: Astrological Planetary Archetypes Mapped to Principles of Depth Psychology and Jungian Archetypes

PLANETARY ARCHETYPE	PRINCIPLES AND ARCHETYPES IN DEPTH PSYCHOLOGY, AND RELATED MEANINGS
The Sun ☉	consciousness, ego, hero, king, alchemical *Sol*, the *yang* principle, dominant, ruler, spirit, libido (as life energy), self-esteem, self-expression, identity, identification, intentionality
The Moon ☽	unconscious as matrix, mother, child, anima, alchemical *Luna* and queen, the *yin* principle, feelings, personal relationality, the soul, nurturing and care, habits, the past, the home and family
Mercury ☿	*logos*, *nous*, Hermes, trickster, reason, thinking, rational ego, understanding, the animus
Venus ♀	anima, Eros, pleasure principle, love, beauty, harmony, aesthetic sense, attraction, evaluation, social urge
Mars ♂	animus, warrior, will, courage, fight or flight, aggression, assertion, force, dominance, selfishness
Jupiter ♃	growth, amplification, inflation, mania, hubris, holism, wholeness, alchemical *sublimatio*, affirmation, optimism, the journey, the wanderer
Saturn ♄	senex, wise old man, shadow, super-ego, reality principle, father, death, *Chronos*, resistance, repression, censorship, fear, judgment, guilt, ego structures and boundaries, defenses, alchemical *mortificatio, coagulatio, separatio*, negation, pessimism, depression, Grofian BPM II (no-exit entrapment)

Uranus ⛢	trickster, shadow, awakening, individualism and individuation, liberation, alchemical *albedo,* birthing, breakthroughs, the promethean urge, freedom, rebel, revolution, creativity, genius, *enantiodromia,* Grofian BPM IV (birth moment, liberation)
Neptune ♆	archetype of the spirit, the religious instinct, the oceanic sense, the numinous, spiritual experience, prophet, savior, "supernatural aid," image, projection, illusion, dreams, myths, fantasies, imitation, disintegration, dissolution, unity, oneness, Dionysus, enchantment, self-loss, *solutio,* Grofian BPM I (preconscious unity in the womb)
Pluto ♇	instincts, the id, shadow, rebirth, Dionysus, Wotan, Hades, alchemical Mercurius, Devil, daimon, the will and the will-to-power, archetypal compulsion, possession, uroboros, pyrocatharsis, fate, depth and the underworld, creative-destructive power of Shiva, *kundalini* energy, alchemical *calcinatio,* dismemberment, Grofian BPM III (instinctual empowerment, life-and-death struggle)
Eris ⚸	strife and discord, homeostasis, tension of opposites, violations and counterbalancing reactions fuelled by resentment, fairness and cosmic justice, turning points

Figure 2: Jungian Archetypes Mapped to Astrological Planetary Archetypes

JUNGIAN ARCHETYPE	PLANETARY ARCHETYPES
Hero	Sun: intentional will, the ego, the light of consciousness, becoming an individual Mars: courage, strength, the warrior
Shadow	Saturn: moral judgment, inferiority, embarrassment, guilt, suffering, sin, constriction of the "narrow passageway" Pluto: primitive instincts and drives, the underworld, the abyss, compulsion, evil, power, the taboo Uranus: unconscious slips and accidents, disruptive neurotic symptoms, shadow as trickster
Anima	Moon: anima as soul, wife/mother Venus: anima as *Eros*, femme fatale, siren, inner female image Neptune: anima as *maya*, enchantment, projection
Animus	Mars: strength, independence, assertion, inner masculine image Mercury: ideas, opinions, *logos* Saturn: critical judgment
Child	Moon: innocence, dependency, gentleness, emotionality, the past Sun: authentic creative expression, spontaneous life energy
Mother	Moon: matrix of being, maternal care Pluto: the "maternal abyss" Jupiter: the bounty of the Great Mother

Father	Sun: father as "representative of the spirit," conscious dominant Saturn: authority, ruler, disciplinarian
Trickster	Uranus: accidents, slips, breaks, disruption, reversals, awakenings Mercury: excessive cleverness, duality
Dionysus	Neptune: dissolution, self-loss, god of wine, intoxication Pluto: orgiastic annihilation, wild passions, dismemberment, elemental power of nature
Spirit	Sun: the light of consciousness, spirit as life energy Neptune: spirituality, religion, the numinous, enchantment, the urge to oneness and unity
Wise Old Man/Senex	Neptune: as a form of the archetype of the spirit, supernatural aid Saturn: as wise guide, tester of moral qualities, learned authority, Satan/Lucifer
Rebirth	Pluto: as the cycle of birth-death-rebirth, as self-overcoming, power of evolution Uranus: as the moment of birth or rebirth, the breaking dawn

Notes

[1] Jung, *Two Essays on Analytical Psychology*, 237, par. 398.

[2] Jung, *Mysterium Coniunctionis*, 176, par. 217.

[3] Jung, *Two Essays on Analytical Psychology*, 238, par. 399.

[4] Jung, *Two Essays on Analytical Psychology*, 240, par. 404.

[5] Jung, *Two Essays on Analytical Psychology*, 238, par. 399.

[6] An analysis of archetypal themes associated with Eris does not form part of this book, but may be found in my earlier publication, *Discovering Eris*.

PART FOUR

Principles of Archetypal Astrology

Chapter 15

The Geometry of the Gods

The changing patterns of expression of the planetary archetypes in human experience can be examined by tracking the movements of the planets relative to each other, as viewed from positions on Earth. As the planets move along their courses, so the archetypes within the unconscious "move" into different relationships with each other. This supposition forms the basis of the astrological understanding of a correspondence between inner and outer, psyche and cosmos, archetype and planet—a correspondence conveyed by the Hermetic maxim, "As Above, so Below." In this chapter, we will explore the nature of these relationships and introduce the basic method used in astrology to study archetypal patterns.

The Planets and the Zodiac

The study of the significance of the planetary archetypes in human experience is based on the precise observation of and calculation of planetary movements in the heavens, including the Sun, the Moon, and the planets.[1] Archetypal astrology focuses primarily on the positions and cycles of these ten "planets," each of which is associated with a corresponding planetary archetype whose meanings we considered in the previous chapter. To this primary list, we might add the planetoid Chiron, discovered in 1977, positioned between Saturn and Uranus in the solar system, and now used by many astrologers in association with the mythic motif of the wounded healer after the eponymous figure of Greek myth; and Eris, the dwarf planet discovered in 2005, which I considered in an earlier publication (*Discovering Eris*), in connection with the archetypal themes of strife, discord, counterbalancing reactions, violations, injustice, and more. The meaning of these two planetary bodies, which is less well substantiated than the primary ten planets, is not, however, a central focus of this book. A case could be made for the inclusion of other astronomical bodies and astrological variables, such as Ceres and various asteroids, but evidence for their meaning is scant, and I myself have only very limited experience of them and do not therefore feel well placed to offer informed comments or analysis. Focusing on the ten primary planetary archetypes provides a comprehensive, if not complete, basis for the archetypal analysis of human experience.

Figure 3: The Orbital Periods of the Planets[2]

PLANET	DURATION OF ORBIT AROUND THE SUN
Sun	365 days
Moon	28 days
Mercury	88 days
Venus	227.4 days
Mars	687 days
Jupiter	11.86 years
Saturn	29.45 years
Chiron	50.76 years
Uranus	84.02 years
Neptune	164.79 years
Pluto	248.09 years
Eris	557 years

Each planet has a different duration of orbit, depending on its position within the solar system, and its proximity to the Sun and the Earth. The distant planets, such as Neptune and Pluto, obviously take far longer to fulfill their orbits than do the planets closer to the Sun, such as Venus and Mercury.

The orbits of the planets are measured against the zodiac, the primary frame of reference in astrology. The zodiac is itself based on the ecliptic, a line that traces the apparent passage of the Sun around the Earth over the course of a year, as seen by an observer on Earth. Covering an eight-to-nine degree region either side of the ecliptic, the zodiac forms a great band across the sky, within which all the planets appear to move.[3] The band is divided into twelve thirty-degree segments, which comprise the well-known signs of the zodiac from Aries to Pisces. At any given time, each planet in its orbit appears to occupy a position within one of the signs. The positions of the planets are stated in the form "20 degrees Scorpio," or "16 degrees Libra," and so forth, as recorded in an ephemeris, and they are plotted using glyphs or symbols within astrological birth charts. Minutes of degrees are typically used for greater precision.

Astrological charts, then, are based on the positions of the planets as seen from particular locations on Earth. From this viewpoint, over the course of time the planets appear to move counterclockwise from sign to sign according to their individual orbits and velocities. For example, from viewpoints on Earth, the Sun appears to move around the Earth, along the line of the ecliptic, over the course of a single year, moving from one sign to another every month. Saturn moves around the zodiac in approximately 29 years, whereas Uranus takes 84 years. In this manner, all the planets appear to move at various speeds through the signs of the zodiac and therefore are seen to occupy a particular sign at any given time.

Aspects or Alignments

In addition to their placement in signs, as the planets continue along their orbits their positions relative to the other planets on the ecliptic change and they form different geometric alignments or aspects with each other. It is this changing pattern of planetary relationships that is studied in astrology in order to understand the changing relationships between the archetypal principles associated with the planets. The major aspects recognized in the astrological tradition are the *conjunction* (planets approximately 0 degrees apart), the *sextile* (60 degrees), the *square* (90 degrees), the *trine* (120 degrees), and the *opposition* (180 degrees).[4] When two or more planets are placed in the birth chart such that they form one of these geometric relationships they are said to be "in aspect" or "in alignment," indicating a blending and mutual activation of the meaning of the corresponding planetary archetypes.[5]

Every aspect is considered to be operative, i.e., in effect, within a range or *orb*. For example, if two planets are positioned 170 degrees apart, they are still considered to be "in orb"—i.e., within the permitted range for an opposition. For the major aspects the orbs in astrological birth charts and world transits are generally between 6 and 12 degrees. All alignments are considered to be more powerful the closer they are to the exact angle.[6] Orbs vary according to whether one is working with birth charts, world transits, or personal transits. For personal transits, orbs are generally much smaller than for birth chart analysis and world transit analysis. Typically, orbs are around 4–5 degrees for personal transits (for major aspects) as the planets move into alignment and about 3 degrees after the exact alignment has passed.

Figure 4: The Movement of the Planets through the Zodiac

The charts below, for January and June 1990, January 2002, and January 2030, give an indication of the relative movements of the planets and their shifting configurations.

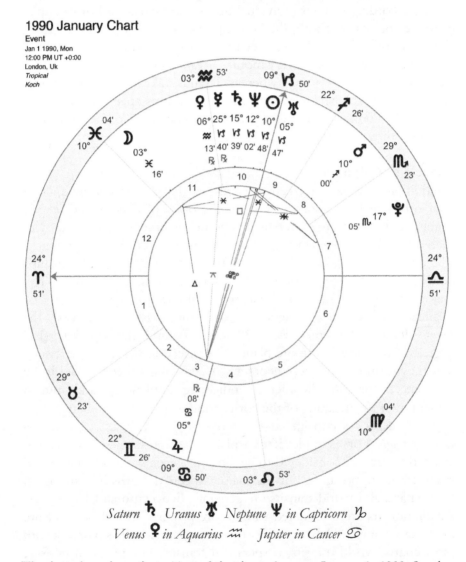

Saturn ♄ Uranus ♅ Neptune ♆ in Capricorn ♑
Venus ♀ in Aquarius ♒ Jupiter in Cancer ♋

The chart above shows the positions of the planets for noon, January 1, 1990, London. Note the grouping of five planets in the sign Capricorn. Together with the nearby Venus in

Aquarius, these planets form an unusual six-planet conjunction, centered on the triple conjunction of Saturn, Uranus, and Neptune. Each of these three planets moves relatively slowly around the zodiac (Saturn 29 years, Uranus 84 years, Neptune 165 years)—hence a conjunction between them is a rare occurrence. All three planets are opposite Jupiter (circa 180 degrees), positioned in Cancer, with Jupiter almost exactly opposite Uranus.

1990 June Chart
Event
Jun 1 1990, Fri
12:00 AM BST -1:00
London, Uk
Tropical
Koch

Six months later, in June 1990, the same conjunction of Saturn, Uranus, and Neptune can be observed on the left side of the chart, with these planets having moved (in a counterclockwise direction in the chart) only a few degrees within Capricorn from their January 1990 position. All three remain in an opposition to Jupiter, in Cancer, on the right side of the chart. Jupiter has moved from 5 degrees Cancer in January to 12 degrees. The closest opposition is now between Jupiter and Neptune (at 14 degrees Capricorn). Note in this chart that many of the other planets have moved significantly since January. The Sun, the Moon, Mercury, Venus, and Mars move fairly quickly in their orbits so change position more rapidly within the space of a six-month period. The outer planets, furthest away from the Sun, move very slowly. It therefore takes years, rather than months, for these planets (especially Neptune and Pluto) to significantly change position.

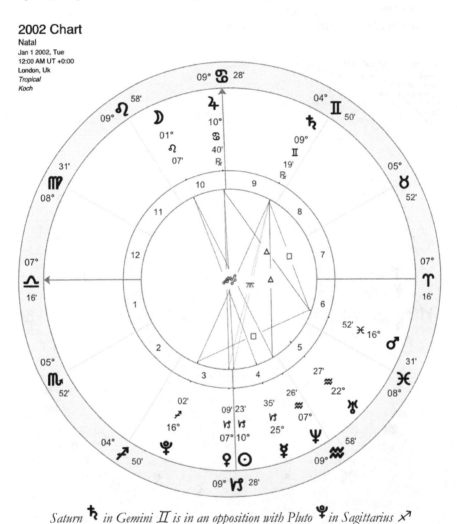

Saturn ♄ *in Gemini* ♊ *is in an opposition with Pluto* ♇ *in Sagittarius* ♐

By 2002, shown above, Saturn, Uranus, and Neptune are no longer in a conjunction (the Uranus-Neptune conjunction lasted through the entire 1990s but is now out of range as the two planets are 15 degrees apart). Note here that both Uranus and Neptune have moved from the sign Capricorn into Aquarius. Meanwhile, Saturn (shown in the top right section) is now positioned in Gemini in an opposition alignment with Pluto in Sagittarius—the major planetary configuration of the period 2001–2004. Everyone who was born during this time will have the Saturn-Pluto opposition in their birth charts, and express in recognizable ways the archetypal meanings associated with this combination.

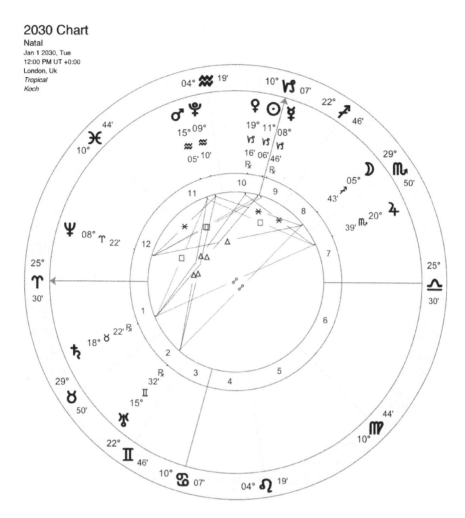

2030 Chart

Natal
Jan 1 2030, Tue
12:00 PM UT +0:00
London, Uk
Tropical
Koch

The final example chart shows the positions of the planets on January 1, 2030, 40 years after the date of the first chart. Compared to chart 3, notice now that Pluto has moved from its position in Sagittarius counterclockwise into the sign Aquarius, passing en route through Capricorn. Pluto is now in a relatively fleeting conjunction with Mars, while Jupiter is opposite Saturn. One can see, comparing the four charts, that as the planets move over time they enter into different configurations with each other. These aspects indicate relationships between the corresponding planetary archetypes. Interpreting the meaning of the aspects is a key dimension of archetypal astrology, and our central focus in volumes II and III.

Number Archetypes and the Meaning of Aspects

In order to understand the particular meaning or quality of the relationships between these astrological principles, we need to consider another class of archetypes discussed by Jung: those based on number.

Jung first noticed that numerical arrangements seem to be prominent in fantasies that arise during the course of individuation— one dreams of pairs of opposites, for instance (such as light and dark, young and old, male and female), or of being in an elevator ascending and descending to particular floors of a building, or of geometric structures of labyrinths or city squares. Jung had also posited that the psyche is comprised of four psychological functions—intuition, sensation, thinking, and feeling—which some astrologers have mapped onto the four elements in astrology: fire, earth, air, and water, respectively. As we have already seen, number, as geometric form, is also especially evident in mandala drawings, produced spontaneously in times of psychological confusion and turbulence, suggesting to Jung that the unconscious psyche uses number as an "ordering principle." He concluded that numbers are themselves archetypes—they are "archetypes of order" existing as a priori organizing factors in the unconscious.[7] He reasoned that numbers—specifically the small whole numbers—are not merely instruments for counting quantities, as we tend to assume, for they also possess specific qualities. For example, the number *one* has to do with the qualities of oneness and beginning, *two* with duality and oppositions, and *three* with bridging relationships and harmonies between opposite poles.

Jung's position was not dissimilar to the philosophical perspectives of Pythagoras and Plato, who envisaged numbers as numinous metaphysical principles upon which all of reality is ordered. Indeed, Jung's view of number as archetypal, and his recognition that archetypes have a *psychoid* dimension, led him, in his later reflections, to adopt a broadly Pythagorean position, as he moved towards a recognition that numbers are ordering factors evident throughout reality, in the cosmos as much as in the psyche. His most compelling explanation of astrology, as I have argued elsewhere, rests upon these concepts, although he did not fully develop it himself.[8]

In astrology, the meaning of every alignment or aspect depends upon the particular angle of relationship between the planets. The meaning of the primary set of aspects is based on these archetypal principles of number, for each significant aspect is produced by the division of the 360° of the astrological chart by small whole numbers. A conjunction is based on the meaning of the number one (360° ÷ 1) indicating beginning, the urge to initiate, and a unified or conflated expression of the planetary archetypes. The opposition (180 degrees) is based on number two (360° ÷ 2), associated with duality and the tension of opposites. The trine (120 degrees) is based on the meaning of number three (360° ÷ 3), and is considered to represent a supportive and stable expression of archetypal energy, resulting from a balancing of opposites through a third factor. And a square aspect of 90 degrees (360° ÷ 4) is related to the meaning of four and is therefore interpreted as a tension or conflict between the planetary archetypes involved—a conflict that is felt as a pressure to actualize and to release inner pressure through action and growth. The specific meanings of each of the "major aspects" are summarized below in Figure 5.

Figure 5: Illustrations of the Major Aspects

Conjunction (0 degrees)

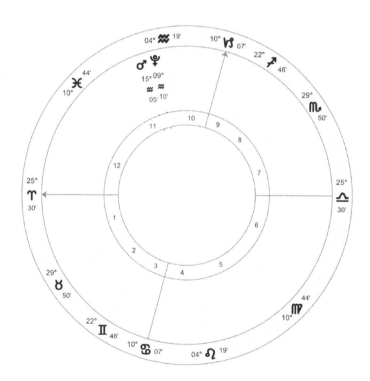

Conjunctions indicate potent, dynamic relationships between planetary archetypes, characterized by a release of initiatory energy, and the synthesized or conflated combinations of the archetypes' meanings. Because the archetypal principles act in unison, although not necessarily harmoniously, the principles might not be differentiated from each other, and might thus manifest instinctively and unconsciously.

Square (90 degrees)

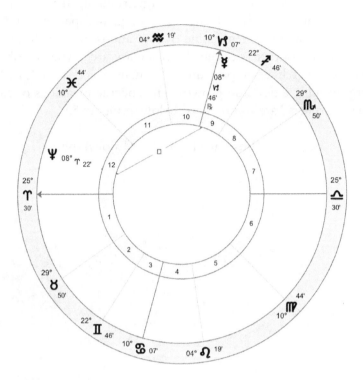

Square alignments also indicate dynamic, energized relationships between the planetary archetypes. However, unlike the conjunction, the square suggests a greater degree of inherent conflict between the principles, and therefore elicits one's conscious participation in the expression of the principles to manage or resolve the conflict and tension between them. We tend to find that those parts of our experience associated with square alignments challenge us. They tend to push us towards action, and to promote increasing consciousness and self-awareness.

Opposition (180 degrees)

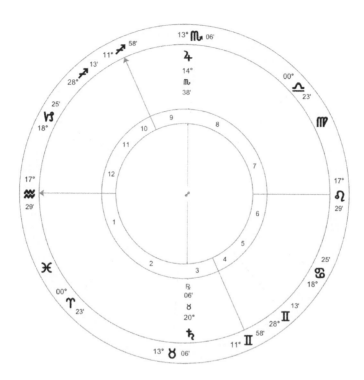

Like the conjunction and the square, oppositions symbolize dynamic, creative, and often conflicting relationships between the archetypal principles. However, with oppositions one tends to encounter experiences associated with the archetypes involved through relationship or to experience the planetary archetypes as pulling one in opposite directions, often see-sawing back and forth between the pull of one archetype and the other. Whereas the square tends to promote action to seek to resolve the inherent conflict between archetypal principles, the opposition tends to manifest as an unresolved tension of opposites that one is forced to endure until one can move towards a creative balance of the principles involved. Like the square, the opposition alignment tends to promote the development of conscious awareness.

Together, the conjunction, square, and opposition are considered to be "hard aspects" in that they indicate relationships between the planetary archetypes that are invariably challenging, marked by creative tension. The trine and sextile (described below) are referred to as "soft aspects."

Trine (120 degrees)

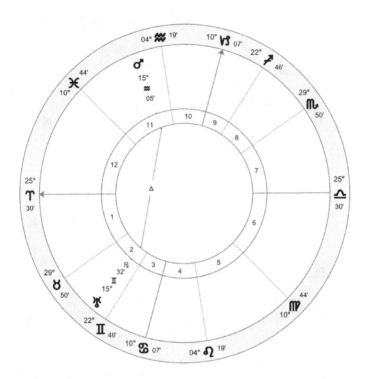

Trines symbolize supportive, well-established, and stable relationships between the archetypal principles involved. They tend to indicate "soft," harmonious, and confluent relationships, although that does not mean they are uniformly positive, and it can still require some effort to assimilate and express the combined energies of the planetary archetypes. Trines might be construed as indicative of abilities and talents that come fairly easily and naturally to us, and that we tend to find comfortable and rely on for support, but that we might therefore take for granted.

Sextile (60 degrees)

The sextile is also a harmonious, "soft" or confluent aspect, and can be construed as a slightly less powerful version of the trine—geometrically it is half a trine (120° ÷ 2). The sextile tends to indicate talents and potentials that we can draw on, develop, and express if we choose to. We have the opportunity to do this, but there is no compulsion or external pressure to do it. Again, like the trine, we might take such talents for granted or fail to see them or to seize the opportunity to express them. But, generally speaking, these aspects indicate supportive, helpful combinations of the planetary archetypes.

This set of the primary aspects can also form more complex "aspect patterns" when they fall in combination with other aspects. These larger configurations include the T-square (two planets in opposition to each other with another planet in a 90-degree square to both), a grand cross (two sets of oppositions and four squares), a grand trine (three trines—i.e., three or more planets each 120 degrees from each other), and a stellium (four or more planets in a conjunction) These configurations reflect the meaning of the individual aspects involved but indicate especially complex and powerful relationships between the corresponding archetypal principles correlating with major themes and dynamics in a person's life.

A number of so-called "minor aspects" might also be considered in the interpretation of astrological charts. Chief among these is the 150-degree alignment known as the *inconjunct* or *quincunx*.

Figure 6: Illustration of the Quincunx

Quincunx (150 degrees)

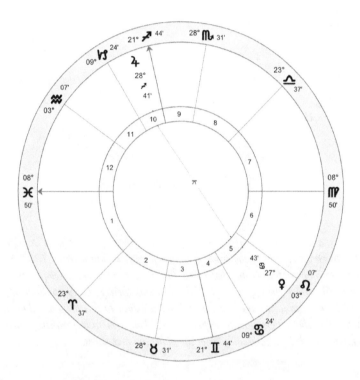

The quincunx indicates relationships of awkward dissonance and incompatibility between the archetypal principles associated with the planets in alignment. The aspect often accompanies situations of irresolution and tension that one cannot act to resolve and so therefore has to adapt to and endure. The incongruence requires perseverance and a flexible adjustment if it is to be handled skillfully. Although somewhat uncomfortable to experience, the incongruence can be creative in promoting growth through adaptation, requiring flexible self-awareness to reconcile the expression of the planetary archetypes.

All these aspects feature in birth-chart analysis and transit analysis. That is, one can study the geometric relationships between the planets at the moment of an individual's birth to understand the archetypal themes and patterns of that person's life and character; and one can also study the changing alignments between the planets over time, as the planets fulfill their orbits. The study of these changing planetary alignments—transits—can be used to illuminate the qualities of particular periods of time, both retrospectively, if one is studying historical periods or earlier episodes of a biography, and prospectively, if one is seeking insight into emerging themes and patterns at future times. Examples of alignments in birth charts, world transits, and personal transits—the three "forms of correspondence," as Tarnas called them—are given below, in Figure 7.[9]

As shown in the examples in Figure 7, personal transits are derived by comparing the positions of the planets in the sky on a given date with the positions of the planets in an individual's birth chart. If a transiting planet enters a significant geometric alignment with a planet in the birth chart—say, for instance, the position of Pluto in the sky is the same degree as the position of Venus in the birth chart—then this indicates a personal transit is in effect. In this case, transiting Pluto is conjunct natal Venus. For a period of four or five years, the archetypal themes and qualities of Pluto (power, intensity, Dionysian passion, compulsion, transformation, and so forth) would manifest in the domain of life pertaining to Venus (love, beauty, pleasure, romantic relationships, friendships, social life, and more). In Volumes II and III, we will consider examples of natal alignments, world transits, and personal transits.

The combination of two or more planetary archetypes, as symbolized by these alignments between the planets, produces a coherent array or complex of themes and meanings—an archetypal complex, as Tarnas called it, adapting the language of Jungian psychology. Thus, in the analysis to follow, we will encounter terms such as the *Saturn-Neptune complex* or the *Venus-Pluto complex*, which refers to the cluster of meanings and themes created by the combination of the Saturn and Neptune archetypes or the Venus and Pluto archetypes, respectively. Each archetypal complex serves as a window into a person's life, revealing major themes of one's biography, and thus contributing to the revelation of the deeper meaning and pattern of one's life, perhaps taking form in a personal myth.

An additional method of understanding the relationship between planetary archetypes is midpoint analysis. Three planets are considered to be in significant relationship if one planet is positioned at the midpoint of two other planets, within a range of 1–2 degrees. If, for instance, the Sun were positioned at 15 degrees Libra, Pluto positioned at 0 degrees Libra, and Uranus at 29 degrees Libra, then the Sun is at the midpoint of the two other planets. In astrological notation, this is often indicated as follows: Sun=Uranus/Pluto. Like aspects, such midpoint alignments indicate that the corresponding archetypes are in significant relationship, indicating the capacity for a progressive working through and integration of the energies and themes associated with the planetary archetypes involved.

Figure 7: Birth Chart, World Transits, and Personal Transits

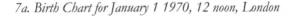

7a. Birth Chart for January 1 1970, 12 noon, London

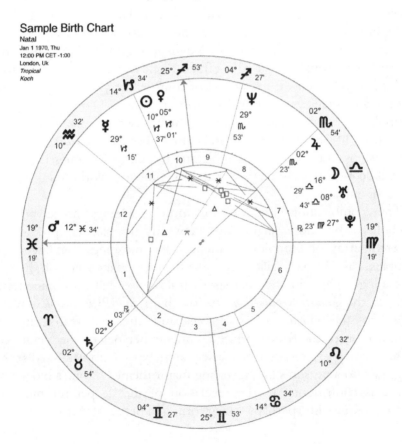

The second chart (below) shows the position of the planets on June 1 1981, centered on London, England. These are the world transits for that date.

7b. World Transits, June 1 1981, London

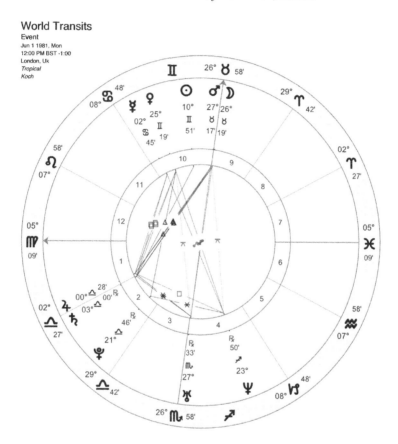

The third chart showing personal transits (overleaf) combines the planetary positions in chart 7a (the birth chart), in the inner circle, and 7b (the world transit chart for June 1, 1981) in the outer circle. Alignments between planets in the two circles might then be calculated. In this example, Chart 7c shows that transiting Uranus (27 degrees Scorpio) is conjunct the natal position of Neptune (29 degrees Scorpio) on that date—that is, there is a Uranus personal transit to Neptune. Transiting Saturn (3 degrees Libra) is also square to the natal position of Venus (5 degrees Capricorn). This means that the position of Saturn on June 1 1981 is square (roughly 90 degrees) from the position of Venus in the birth chart for January 1 1970—a personal transit of Saturn to Venus.

Uranus ♅ *Neptune* ♆ *Saturn* ♄ *Venus* ♀

7c. Personal Transits, June 1 1981, London

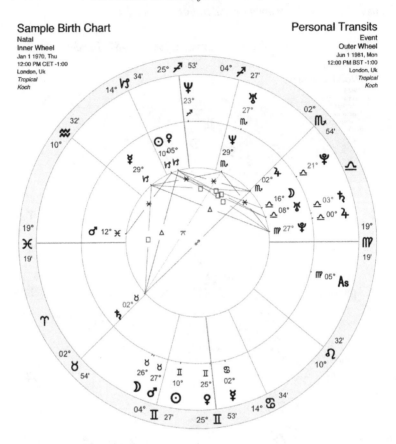

From the Universal to the Particular

Tarnas's conceptualization of the archetypal basis of astrology emphasized that, properly understood, astrology is concerned with universal themes, which take on specific form only when they manifest in individual experience or in collective historical events. Without studying the particular context in which it is used, astrology is wholly abstract. Charts, Tarnas stressed, do not indicate a person's gender, cultural context, or socioeconomic status, for instance, which can obviously dramatically impact the life possibilities and experiences available to us. Thus he emphasized above all the archetypal character of astrology. For it is this recognition of astrological factors as archetypes, as the name implies, that distinguishes archetypal astrology from the many other forms of astrological practice concerned with studying the correlations between the planets and human affairs.[10] The planetary archetypes, and indeed all astrological symbols, possess the same general set of thematic meanings for all people, but they manifest differently in the concrete details of every human life. This can be the cause of considerable misunderstanding for those appraising astrology's truth claims. For instance, the case of so-called "time twins"—two people born at approximately the same time and the same location—has given rise to the question as to why two such individuals often appear to be vastly different from each other, perhaps, for example, having completely different interests or careers. If astrology is valid, the argument goes, then "astrological twins" must be very similar on all counts due to the fact that their birth charts will be identical. But having the same birth charts indicates only that the two lives are defined by the same archetypal pattern, which can manifest in a wide diversity of ways while still remaining consistent with the accepted astrological meanings of the planetary relationships within the chart. How each person expresses this pattern cannot be determined from the information in the astrological birth chart by itself. We need only think of all the people born on the same day at a similar time and in nearby locations—perhaps numbering in the hundreds or thousands. These people will have very similar birth charts but express the pattern of the chart in ways unique to them and their circumstance.

The archetypal nature of astrology also helps to account for why astrologers might give different, yet equally valid, interpretations of the same charts. As Tarnas, discussing the meaning of aspects between two planets, puts it:

> That a given natal aspect can express itself in a virtually limitless variety of ways and yet consistently reflect the underlying nature of the relevant archetypes is of course not only characteristic of all astrological correspondence but essential to it. Astrology is not concretely predictive. It is archetypally predictive.[11]

Astrological factors, then, do not reveal the specific details of life, but the universal archetypal themes and patterns of our experience. The themes associated with the archetypes do not change, but the manifestation of these universal themes in an individual life or a particular historical moment is widely varying. Such variation or multivalence has long been recognized in astrology, but often only implicitly. Thus Charles Carter was able to write in 1930:

> While we can understand the abstract significance of the planets and so form a conception of the theoretical meaning of each

aspect, it still remains true that when we descend from these abstractions to the effects of the aspects in actual life we find ourselves confronted with a very intricate task. That which is unitary above becomes many below; the trend of manifestation is always towards increased diversity. Thus, even in terms of character, the same aspect exhibits great differences in manifestation according to the almost innumerable possible concurrent circumstances that may arise. When we seek to determine the probable external form of the aspects in the affairs of life, we meet yet greater variation.[12]

This "greater variation" can be understood in terms of the inherent multivalence of each principle, as Tarnas has described. Each archetypal complex can assume many forms while remaining consistent with an unchanging core meaning.

Causality, Participation, and Fatalism

A related consideration when exploring and appraising astrology is the question of causality. Contrary to the prevailing assumptions of some outside the field, it is not that the planets are causal agents influencing human beings through an emitted force of some kind. Supposed astrological influences of this kind cannot be accounted for in terms of any of the four known forces recognized in science. Rather, the planets are to be understood, I believe, as synchronistically related to the expression of the corresponding archetypes. That is, there is an underlying correspondence between the planets in space and the archetypes in the psyche, and it is the archetypes that are the active powers, exerting an influence on us from the depths of the human unconscious.[13]

Because astrology symbolizes the activity of archetypes in the collective unconscious, we have the opportunity, in becoming more conscious of archetypes through astrology, of influencing the way they are expressed in our lives. Astrology has been helpfully described by Tarnas and others as *participatory* in nature. If the astrological meanings symbolized in a chart are not set in stone, but rather are open to a wide degree of variance as to how they manifest and are expressed, then our consciousness and free will can become involved, shaping how the archetypes find expression. Rather than being unconsciously moved, as if we were puppets of unrecognized archetypal forces, we can become informed participants engaging with the archetypes, just as in times past humans might have negotiated their fates with the gods.

While this participatory view has proved influential in modern understandings of astrology, and supports the popular idea of the individual as a "co-creator" with the universe and therefore able to work with the archetypal powers to determine how they are expressed, we would be wise to recognize the limits of our capacities in this regard. We can participate in the expression of archetypes, it is true, but it is important to keep in mind that human consciousness does not stand apart from the rest of the psyche, in a detached neutral position from which to choose how it interacts with archetypes. Rather, consciousness is itself always being conditioned by archetypes. Our creative input, the form of our participation, is itself inextricably bound up with the archetypes, which goes against the simplistic idea that we might engage with the universe as equal "co-creative" partners. Put differently, human creativity and individual freedom also arise from archetypes—in astrology they are especially related to the Sun and Uranus. Furthermore, as Jung stressed, archetypes possess an inherent aim, *telos*, or directionality. We cannot simply redirect archetypal energies where we want them to go. Nor can we survey a range of expressions of archetypes and implement a choice as to what is most beneficial to us or that will bring us the most satisfaction and the least amount of pain. Much of the work of individuation is coming to terms with the pre-given aims and purposes that are working through us, and coming to recognize the quite limited capacity of the conscious ego to forge its own reality or make its own meaning. We should not lose sight of the fact that archetypes are *unconscious* factors and therefore unpredictable and beyond our control to a significant degree.

It might be taken as axiomatic that one would and should work with the archetypal powers in order to promote the most life-fulfilling, creative, and constructive modes of expression. But at a certain point of the individuation process, what is most life-fulfilling might well entail engaging with and falling into the "negative" and undesirable expressions of the archetypes. For it is only in the experience of the full range of the psyche that it can be transformed. One needs to stir up all that remains untouched and unredeemed in human nature if one is to become whole. In short, astrology is not always to be used to promote categorically "positive" outcomes that support and enhance one's sense of selfhood or that bring happy and pleasurable experiences. During individuation, the ego personality that is involved in the participatory co-creation of life is deconstructed and unraveled, as one's very sense of identity is radically transformed. This obviously makes the simple enactment of co-creation impossible.

The recognition of the determining power of the Self or the unconscious in our experience flies in the face of the humanistic idea that astrology merely shows our potentials and patterns that we can choose to enact if we wish and in the way we wish. In moving away from any association with fatalism—the inborn compulsion of the stars—and in keeping with the modern emphasis on the autonomy of the individual human will, psychological astrology, in some forms, has tended to champion freedom of choice in how we express the dynamics of our charts. In so doing, psychological astrology has moved from a description of one's seemingly inexorable fate into a concern with tendencies, possibilities, and potentials, yet in the process it runs the risk of losing the awareness that the archetypal powers can often blind us, grip us, possess us, leaving us little if any room for maneuver. It is a delusion to look at one's birth chart and imagine that one can realize its archetypal pattern as one sees fit. For it is a "humanistic fallacy," as Hillman stressed, to assume that the unconscious can be controlled, or, to state this differently, that the gods and goddesses can be brought into the sphere of human psychology, and subjugated to human ends and values.

Astrology has long since been linked with the belief in fate, but we should be clear that astrological charts do not reveal one's fate in the sense this is normally understood, as a future that is preordained. One cannot rely upon astrology to determine or reveal the specific course of one's life—where one will end up, what one will become, who one will marry, or when one will die. However, astrology does give us information into the ways we meet limitation or encounter the experience of feeling fated or of binding compulsion. The various archetypes can give rise to different perceptions of the degree of freedom we might possess. When Uranus is activated, in relationship to the Sun or Mars, for instance, we are often attuned to our individual uniqueness and freedom to express ourselves or to act as we wish, pioneering new paths and creatively willing our future. By contrast, when Pluto and Saturn are activated in a personal transit, we might experience being in the grip of inexorable forces of binding power that command and compel, giving little if any room for free choice. These variations in our experiences of freedom and fatality will become apparent in the chapters to follow.

While astrology does not reveal the workings of an immutable fate, it remains possible of course that life itself is indeed fated in some way. In a serious exploration of astrology and depth psychology one is compelled to examine this question. We considered earlier, for instance,

Hillman's idea of the soul's code, of being drawn forward by the innate form within us to fulfill a particular vocation, to live a particular life. This perspective casts a different light on the belief that life is to be forged through acts of free will. The psychological experience of free will is very real; indeed, it is often a weighty existential burden. But in retrospect, as Arthur Schopenhauer noted, despite the innumerable free choices and decisions we must make, it can often seem that our lives have been directed by an unseen hand, and that our choices could not really have been different. While we are naturally inclined to affirm the Western ideal of the freedom of the individual will, for this fits the reality of our experience, it might be observed that even decisions of seemingly free choice effectively come over us. Deepening psychological reflection and the affirmation of whatever life brings can lead us, as Nietzsche put it, to a "joyful and trusting fatalism" in which free will takes its place within the workings of a "transcendent fatality."[14] The complexity of this question is obvious, and in the final analysis reaching a determination of the extent to which our life is fated is a personal philosophical matter.

Sources of Data and Interpretation

The origins of astrology appear to have been in primitive agriculture, perhaps as long as 20,000 years ago, in correlating the movements of the sun and the moon with observed changes in crop cycles. The first recognizable form of horoscopic astrology (that is, planets plotted in a horoscope or chart) began in Mesopotamia, around 3400 BCE, and passed from there into ancient Egypt, Greece, and Rome, where the planets took on the names of the Roman gods and goddesses that we still use today. From the astrology of monarchs and empires in the Middle Ages, by the early twentieth century in the West astrology was applied to individuals across society. The Theosophical movement was especially influential in birthing this modern form of individual astrology, which rose to unexpected heights of popularity in the twentieth century, in spite of its seeming irrationalism and its incongruence with the scientific worldview.

In its modern form, the field of astrology as a whole has developed according to a kind of loose intuitive empiricism, with astrologers, decade by decade, liberally drawing on the work of their predecessors and contemporaries, while adding their own interpretations of astrological factors based on their experiences and insights. Through this process, there has been a gradual incremental accretion and evolution in the understanding of the meanings of the different factors examined in astrology, with a broad consensus today as to how these factors are to be interpreted. The discovery of the outer planets— Uranus in 1781, Neptune in 1846, and Pluto in 1930—led to the incorporation of an additional three archetypal principles into the astrological canon, permitting the recognition of the deeper transformative or transpersonal powers shaping human experience and a more precise differentiation of the meanings of the traditional planets. As several astrologers have noted, the archetypal qualities and themes associated with these newly discovered planets were manifest in collective synchronicities, with the planetary meanings suggested by the historical events of the time and even by the mythic deities after which they were named. For example, astrologers came to associate Uranus with principles of revolution and invention, themes vividly reflected in the revolutions in America and France in the late nineteenth century, and in the birth of the Industrial Age close to the time of the planet's discovery. And Pluto's meaning, which was subsequently corroborated in astrological practice, is reflected in the mythic god Pluto or Hades, the Greco-Roman ruler of the underworld, as well as in historical synchronicities, not least the splitting of the atom and the unleashing of nuclear power in 1931.[15]

In addition to the assimilation of the body of existing knowledge in astrological reference books, astrological data might be derived from four main sources.

1. Studying the lives and creative works of prominent cultural figures.
2. Studying the changing themes and patterns of world history.
3. Client data from astrological consultations.
4. Personal insight into and experience of the workings of astrology.

First, one can study the life and work of prominent cultural figures—an approach which offers a range of examples of how particular archetypal complexes might find expression. This type of archetypal biographical analysis allows one to illuminate the underlying universal themes of an individual's personality and life experiences. Today, with instant online access to artists' work and with many biographical resources available, the study of well-known figures provides insights into the archetypes that are both widely accessible and publicly verifiable. Films, books, and music offer shared cultural reference points and vivid examples that we can readily call to mind. Themes evident in a piece of art (such as a film or work of literature), which might be related to Jungian archetypal images, psychodynamic factors, or biographical experiences from the artist's life, are also connected in archetypal astrology to themes associated with the various sets of planetary alignments in the artist's birth chart. These alignments are symbolically representative of the inherent qualities—or archetypal dynamics—of that moment in time, which continue to define individual personality and biographical experiences throughout a person's lifetime.

In all forms of creative expression, themes associated with the archetypal patterns of an artist's birth chart are often magnified and dramatized, writ large on the artistic canvas, finding particularly striking forms of expression. The same archetypal complexes shaping an artist's own experiences, which are evident in the various conflicting impulses and motivations of character, provide the *prima materia*, as it were, of the artist's work. This holds true even in those cases in which the individual is the performer rather than the creator of a piece of art—as in the case of an actor cast by a film director in a particular role or a singer recording and performing song lyrics and music created by others. In these cases, as Tarnas has remarked, there seems to be something like a synchronistic factor at work that brings people to the film parts they were born to play or to the songs they were supposed to sing—or so it often seems. Obviously, choice is a factor here (although, as discussed above, this too is archetypally conditioned), but often we read of the peculiar circumstances behind the casting of a particular actor, who later becomes synonymous with the role, such that we could not imagine it being played by anyone else. Similarly, there are a great many examples of musical performers and singers working with songs composed by other artists and making the songs their own in the creative act of recording and performance, when the themes of the song powerfully resonate with something in their own nature.

In most cases we can safely assume that in the act of creation or performance the artists had no awareness of archetypes or astrology, but nevertheless came into close proximity with the unconscious through the creative process. The artist, not unlike a person in the throes of an encounter with the unconscious during individuation, is subject to an upsurge of fantasies, energies, and inspirations that demand to be given expression in concrete form. Thus art is a primary vehicle for the expression of archetypes. In Part V, in turning to the arts for examples, we are able to benefit from artists' particular experience of and insight into the archetypal powers and themes manifesting through them. Artists enable us to gain deeper access to the archetypal factors shaping human experience and then we might apply this understanding to help illuminate the individuation process.

A second source of astrological data is the study of world history: one can apply astrology to the study of historical events using world-transit analysis and thus augment one's understanding of the collective expression of archetypes. This method, exemplified by Richard Tarnas's research in *Cosmos and Psyche*, illuminates the underlying archetypal themes and patterns evident in cultural history or in particular cultural movements.[16] Although historians ordinarily restrict their attention to causal factors when analyzing world events by looking for prior conditions and sequences in history that cause events to happen, archetypal astrology complements such linear-historical analysis by providing insight into the archetypal dynamics within which causal chains of events seem to occur. For example, the events of the French Revolution might be explained entirely as a direct consequence of a combination of contributory causal factors—such as the economic hardship of the proletariat in the late eighteenth century in France, the weak character of the reigning monarch Louis XVI, the ostentatious lifestyles of the French aristocracy, the political ambitions of Robespierre and Napoleon, the philosophical ideas of Montesquieu and Rousseau, and so on. But, from an archetypal astrological perspective, it is also illuminating to see this period of history as an expression of the Uranus-Pluto world transit of that time with its characteristic themes of violent revolution, emancipatory movements, the overthrow of the established order, political radicalism, mass societal changes, the release of powerful instinctual energies, and more. These themes all reflect the combination of energies and qualities associated with the Uranus and Pluto archetypes. From one perspective, we might say that the combination of the prior events and conditions in history or the personalities of the main protagonists caused the storming of the Bastille and the overthrow of the *ancien régime* in Paris in 1789, and led to the subsequent rise of Napoleon. However, what is remarkable is that the various chains of causal events should come together to bring about the French Revolution at the very time that the planets Uranus and Pluto were in major geometric alignment, that the events of this period should conform to the established archetypal meanings associated with these planets, and that other major Uranus-Pluto alignments have consistently coincided with periods of history characterized by extraordinarily similar events and qualities. Clearly, the geometric relationship between the two planets did not *cause* the French

Revolution in any kind of linear, deterministic sense. Yet, as Tarnas's research suggests, it seems to be the case that again and again the events of world history unfold in close accordance with the framework of thematic meanings associated with the planetary alignments formed during those times. Naturally, this does not invalidate linear causal analyses of history; it just suggests one might also take into account the deeper archetypal and cosmic picture framing such analyses. Taking an archetypal view, then, can draw our attention to a background order or formal cause in which the chains of historical events unfold, and enable us to "see through" the events of history to their mythic background and archetypal reasons. James Hillman describes this perspective well. "Outer historical facts," he notes, "are archetypally colored, so as to disclose essential psychological meanings. Historical facts disclose the eternally recurring mythemes of history and of our individual souls. History is but the stage on which we enact mythemes of the soul."[17]

Third, practicing astrologers are able to draw on their experience working with clients as the source of their interpretations, through the study of clients' birth charts and personal transits. Needless to say, to explore these correlations one needs access to the personal, often private, details of an individual's life during particular time periods. Obviously, such data is usually not publicly verifiable or collectively visible, but the archetypal themes are evident all the same, even if sometimes in less conspicuous ways than in those individuals who have risen to cultural prominence.

A key consideration guiding astrologers in their work with clients is how the information disclosed in the chart in being used. Astrologers such as Dane Rudhyar and Stephen Arroyo have framed this in terms of the "level of consciousness" at which the pattern of the chart is being expressed, which determines the purpose of the astrological reading. Rudhyar identified and described biological, sociocultural, individual, and transpersonal levels, with the kind of astrology practiced tailored to these levels.[18] Astrology can be used to try to facilitate a good life within the usual parameters and expectations of life in society, such that the individual can satisfy biological urges and live a happy and fulfilling life measured by conventional standards. Or it can be used to help people individualize, realize their potentials, and go their own way in life, beyond the bounds of tradition and societal pressure. Or, again, it can be applied to guide people on a path of spiritual realization, as they seek to transcend the limits of ordinary ego-consciousness and come into relationship with the divine, embarking on a way of radical transformation.

In working with astrology, then, one is faced with a range of related questions: What kind of guidance or insight is being conveyed? What, more broadly, are the aims of astrology and the aims of the individual's life? What moral assumptions are shaping the astrological guidance? Often, one finds, astrology is used to help individuals navigate a safe path through the turbulence of life, with guidance offered as to how to avoid suffering and problems, and to maximize potentials and opportunities. One might read, for instance, of different classes of positive and negative expressions of particular astrological factors. Generally speaking, the implicit assumption in such cases is that compassionate, controlled, considerate, and harmonious expressions of archetypes are good and desirable. Expressions that lead to suffering and conflict, or expressions of anger and desire, are bad and to be avoided (if indeed that is possible). But this morality is not, or should not be, a given. The Nietzschean philosophy of self-overcoming, Jung's call to face the shadow, or the Hillmanian emphasis on "falling apart" suggest different ends and values that could guide the use of astrology, in which destructive, painful, perhaps even evil expressions of the archetypal complexes might in the larger picture prove to be "good." Clearly, much depends on one's moral assessment of what constitutes good and what evil.

I mention these considerations because, first, they are often overlooked in the presentation of astrological interpretations and in the practice of astrology more broadly, and, second, I hope to make my own aims and guiding assumptions more explicit. In Part V, the interpretations I discuss, although drawing on well-known examples from society and culture, are intended to serve as a guide to the individuation process. Recalling astrology's connection with the Greek vision of an ordered cosmos of goodness, truth, and beauty, one guiding aim in this book is to indicate how one might come into a more conscious, more fulfilling relationship with the creative powers of the universe. But equally, recalling the Gnostic vision of a universe under the oppressive rule of *heimarmene*, understood as instinctual-archetypal compulsion, an emphasis on individuation is concerned with revealing how one might overcome the grip of such powers through self-knowledge and suffering as the ego is restructured in service of the Self.

The fourth source of astrological data is one's own life experience. An understanding of astrology can, and perhaps must, be derived from personal application and insight. For a deep comprehension of archetypal astrology there is no substitute for working with one's own birth chart and studying one's transits, year by year over a significant period of time. It is only through the firsthand experience of the archetypes, mapped by planetary transits, that one comes to understand astrological archetypes in one's life not only intellectually, but at an immediate feeling level, as living realities. Depth of insight into the archetypes comes from one's own inner life, from living one's transformative journey and seeing archetypes at work as the agents of the individuation process. The experience of non-ordinary states of consciousness, through spiritual emergencies or psychedelic exploration or Grofian breathwork, also delivers insights and revelations into the archetypal patterns of one's life. In non-ordinary states of consciousness, these patterns are powerfully activated and immediately experienced, often accompanied by biographical and sometimes historical memories, somatic symptoms, and mythic fantasies.

I will be drawing on each of these four sources in the analysis to follow in Volumes II and III, using an understanding of archetypes gleaned both from my own life experience and from working with astrological clients over twenty years to provide an interpretative commentary and analysis of examples drawn from biographies, works of art, and cultural history.

*　　*　　*　　*　　*

Looking Ahead

In Part Five, then, which opens Volume II, I will present a range of examples of the expression of combinations of the different planetary archetypes, mostly considered as pairs. For instance, in the first chapter of Volume II, we will explore the themes and experiences associated with aspects involving Saturn—such as Sun-Saturn and Moon-Saturn. The examples throughout draw on the lives and works of philosophers and scientists, political figures and sports people, but chiefly they are sourced from the arts—actors, writers, and musicians—and from within depth psychology itself.[19]

Among the possible ways the material could be presented, I decided to focus first on Saturn for that archetype has much to do with the fundamental context, themes, and experiences of human life— incarnation and mortality, work and suffering, aging and limitation, maturity and responsibility, hard facts and concrete reality. In many respects our experience of the reality of Saturn is the basis from which we might understand the transpersonal and transformative themes associated with the outer planets: Uranus, Neptune, and Pluto. As Saturn pertains to material reality, with its practical problems and struggles, so Neptune pertains to the realm of dreams, ideals, and spiritual experience. The two planetary archetypes are therefore contrasting, even as they form a pair of dialectically linked opposites. For this reason, after Saturn, we will turn our attention to alignments involving Neptune. Volume III will then consider the archetypal worlds of Pluto and Uranus, in the perinatal rebirth sequence set forth by Stanislav Grof—from the life-and-death struggle of BPM III associated with Pluto, to the birthing experiences of BPM IV associated with Uranus. Throughout, the focus will be on the role of these formative archetypal principles within the individuation process. If we are to realize the Self, as the unique universal center of our being, we must come to terms with the transformative trajectories of each of the transpersonal powers associated with the outer planets.

Notes

[1] Although Pluto has been re-categorized as a dwarf planet in astronomy, this change of status has no bearing on the significance of the associated planetary archetype in astrology. See my discussion of this topic in Le Grice, *Discovering Eris*.

[2] Data derived from NASA, "The Planets," accessed July 1, 2011, http:// solarsystem.nasa.gov/planets/index.cfm.

[3] The exceptions are Pluto, which has an eccentric orbit of 17° inclination to the ecliptic, and Eris, which has a 44° inclination.

[4] Known as the *major aspects*, the conjunction, sextile, square, trine, and opposition are the most significant angles of relationship studied in astrology, along with the quincunx. In addition to these, there are also a number of other *minor aspects*, including the semi-square (45 degrees), the semi-sextile (30 degrees), and the quintile (72 degrees).

[5] For a helpful explanation of aspects in astrology, see Robert Hand, *Horoscope Symbols*. Hand also discusses midpoint theory in the same book. See also Sue Tompkins, *Aspects in Astrology*, for a reference book offering interpretations of sets of aspects between different planets.

[6] In the analysis in Part V, one will read descriptions of an aspect as "exact" or "close-to-exact," referring to the degree of exactitude of the alignments. For instance, an 89-degree angle between two planets is obviously closer to an exact 90-degree square than an 87-degree angle. Generally, the closer an alignment is to exact the more powerful and significant it is.

[7] Jung, "Synchronicity: An Acausal Connecting Principle," in *Structure and Dynamics of the Psyche* (CW8), 517, par. 870.

[8] See my introduction to Part IV of *Jung on Astrology*.

[9] There are numerous other significant factors that might be studied in astrology. Most notably, the signs of the zodiac and the astrological houses are highly significant in interpreting the meaning of birth charts, affording us incredibly rich and nuanced understandings of human nature. These have been emphasized above all else in modern astrology. To give a brief explanation of their place in astrology, signs indicate qualities and modes of being, and are therefore especially significant for characterological analysis and understanding personality types in natal astrology. Houses—the numbered sectors in the chart—pertain to areas of life or fields of experience. For instance, the first house pertains to the body, movement, energy, and action; the second to money and resources; the seventh to relationships; the tenth to career and public life, and so forth. They have much to do with understanding the fundamental pattern and purpose of one's life.

What is important to keep in mind here is that each sign and house is thematically associated with one or more planet. Thus, for example, Mars is said to "rule" Aries in that this sign is associated with qualities such as forcefulness, ardor, the quick release of energy, decisiveness, independence, and such like. Mars also rules the first house, associated with the natural expression of the personality in the body and action. The Moon rules Cancer, associated with qualities such as nurturing, care, emotional sensitivity, and so forth; and it also rules the fourth house, the area of the chart pertaining to the home, the past, and the family.

Although I mention signs and houses here and there in the analysis to follow in volumes in volumes II and III, our focus will be primarily on the richness and multi-faceted complexity of the planetary archetypes in relationship to each other. It is this component of astrology that has been the major focus of research in archetypal cosmology to date and for which there is a growing body of documented empirical evidence. I hope to be able to consider signs and houses in a separate study.

[10] The basis of the archetypal approach to astrology was developed by Richard Tarnas, set forth especially in his 2006 publication, *Cosmos and Psyche*. After introducing an expanded theoretical framework for astrology, drawing on Jung's later research into synchronicity, Tarnas then presents a detailed body of evidence pointing to a consistent and coherent correlation between the planetary cycles and the archetypal patterns of world history, from the Axial Age in the first millennium BCE to the present day, encompassing many spheres of human endeavor and dimensions of life—social, political, cultural, artistic, philosophical, scientific, and spiritual. Tarnas's research suggests the events of world history unfold in close accordance with the framework of meanings associated with the planetary alignments formed during those times.

Archetypal astrology is part of the academic field of archetypal cosmology, which is concerned not only with empirical research into astrological correlations and the application of astrology to human experience, but also with articulating a new world view or cosmology that can support and account for these correlations. In many ways, archetypal cosmology represents a continuation of developments that began with psychological astrology—the recognition of the archetypal significance of the outer planets for understanding the deeper dynamics of the unconscious psyche, the recognition of the participatory role of the modern self in shaping the expression of the archetypal patterns studied in astrology, the use of astrology for providing psychospiritual insight and to develop self-knowledge. However, archetypal cosmology aspires towards a greater empirical and philosophical rigor, drawing on Pythagorean and Platonic philosophy, mythic perspectives, depth psychology (Jung, Hillman, Grof), process philosophy (Alfred North Whitehead), and the new-paradigm sciences (including the work of Bohm, Capra, Sheldrake) to seek to better understand and explain astrological correlations.

Crucially, archetypal cosmology situates psychological astrology's emphasis on the individual psyche within a larger cosmological and metaphysical context. Like earlier forms of astrology, archetypal cosmology explicitly recognizes the existence of something like an *anima mundi*—the interiority of the universe at large. From this perspective, planetary archetypes are seen not as wholly psychological factors merely reflected in, or projected onto, the planetary order of the solar system, but as cosmological and metaphysical principles shaping and informing both the inner and outer worlds. Psyche and cosmos are seen as intimately interconnected, as related expressions of a deeper underlying ground. Archetypal cosmology thus directly addresses, and seeks to overcome, the modern dichotomy between inner and outer, between the subjective human self and the objective cosmos. It seeks to make explicit the deeper unity between psyche and cosmos, microcosm and macrocosm, that has been the concern of astrological practitioners through the ages.

[11] Tarnas, *Prometheus the Awakener*, 20.

[12] Carter, *Astrological Aspects*, 7.

[13] The causes studied in astrology are therefore archetypal causes, but even these are not to be understood in terms of a simple linear chain of cause and effect. It is not that the archetypes are triggering agents causing things to happen in the way that one ball striking another would cause it to move. Rather, as we have seen, archetypes pertain to formal causation, to the thematic patterns and framework of meanings within which life unfolds. The meanings and patterns manifest through the events of our lives and can be recognized in our states of consciousness and how we act.

[14] In a comment on Goethe, and in reference to his principle of *amor fati*, Nietzsche remarked: "A spirit thus emancipated stands in the midst of the universe with a joyful and trusting fatalism, in the faith that only what is separate and individual may be rejected, that in the totality everything is redeemed and affirmed—he no longer denies" (*Twilight of the Idols*, 114).

[15] I have discussed in detail elsewhere the primary factors involved in the determination of the archetypal meaning of a newly discovered planetary body. See Le Grice, *Discovering Eris*.

[16] Rod O'Neal, co-founder of *Archai: The Journal of Archetypal Cosmology*, has called this methodology "archetypal historiography."

[17] James Hillman, *Senex & Puer*, ed. Glen Slater (Putnam, CT: Spring, 2013), 29.

[18] See Rudhyar, *Astrology of Transformation*.

[19] Although the examples covered in volumes II and III are fairly extensive in their range, the choices are inevitably a reflection of my own interests and biases. To engage in archetypal astrological analysis one needs to have a feeling for, and sufficient understanding of, the examples under discussion. I have therefore selected well-known figures whose lives, ideas, and creative works have, for the most part, entered my life in a significant way.

BIBLIOGRAPHY

Abrams, M. H. *Natural Supernaturalism: Tradition and Revolution in Romantic Literature.*1971. Reprint. New York: W.W. Norton & Co, 1973.

Addey, John. *Harmonic Anthology.* 1976. Reprint. Tempe, AZ: American Federation of Astrologers, 2004.

Aristotle. *De Anima.* Cited in Christopher Shields, "Aristotle's Psychology." *The Stanford Encyclopedia of Philosophy* (Winter 2020 Edition). Edited by Edward N. Zalta. Accessed October 20, 2021. https://plato.stanford.edu/archives/win2020/entries/aristotle-psychology.

———. *Metaphysics.* Cited in Christopher Shields, "Aristotle's Psychology." *The Stanford Encyclopedia of Philosophy.* Edited by Edward N. Zalta. Accessed October 20, 2021. https://plato.stanford.edu/archives/win2020/entries/aristotle-psychology.

Arroyo, Stephen. *Astrology, Karma, & Transformation: The Inner Dimensions of the Birth Chart.* Sebastopol, CA: CRCS Publications, 1978.

———. *Astrology, Psychology, and the Four Elements: An Energy Approach to Astrology and Its Use in the Counseling Arts.* Sebastopol, CA: CRCS Publications, 1975.

———. *Exploring Jupiter: Astrological Key to Progress, Prosperity & Potential.* Sebastopol, CA: CRCS Publications, 1996.

Assagioli, Roberto. *Transpersonal Development: The Dimension Beyond Psychosynthesis.* London: The Aquarian Press, 1991.

Becker, Ernest. *The Denial of Death.* New York: The Free Press, 1973.

Bellah, Robert. *Religion in Human Evolution: From the Paleolithic to the Axial Age.* Cambridge, MA: The Belknap Press of Harvard University, 2011.

Brooke, Roger. *Jung and Phenomenology.* 1991. Reprint. London: Routledge, 1993.

Bryant, Christopher. *Jung and the Christian Way.* London, UK: Darton, Longman and Todd, 1983.

Butler, Renn. *The Archetypal Universe: Astrological Patterns in Human Culture, Thought, Emotion and Dreams.* Kindle Direct Publishing, 2017.

———. *Pathways to Wholeness: Archetypal Astrology and the Transpersonal Journey.* London: Muswell Hill Press, 2014.

Campbell, Joseph. *The Hero with a Thousand Faces.* 1949. Reprint. London: Fontana, 1993.

———. *The Masks of God, Volume IV: Creative Mythology.* 1968. Reprint. New York and London: Penguin Arkana, 1991.

———. "Joseph Campbell—The Mythology of the Trickster." Joseph Campbell Foundation. Accessed November 27, 2020. https://www.youtube.com/watch?v=JM10 AvJ3bsM.

———. *A Joseph Campbell Companion: Reflections on the Art of Living*. Selected and edited by Diane K. Osbon. New York: HarperCollins, 1991.

Campbell, Joseph, and Bill Moyers. *Joseph Campbell and the Power of Myth with Bill Moyers*. New York: Mystic Fire Video, 1988.

Carter, Charles. *The Astrological Aspects*. Revised and enlarged edition. 1951. Repr. Tempe, AZ: The American Federation of Astrologers, 1992.

Clarke, John J. *Jung and Eastern Thought: A Dialogue with the Orient*. London: Routledge, 1994.

Cunningham, Donna. *An Astrological Guide to Self-Awareness*. Sebastopol, CA: CRCS, 1978.

Descartes, René. "Discourse on Method." In *Descartes: Selected Philosophical Writings*, translated by John Cottingham, Robert Stoothoff, and Dugald Murdoch, 20–56. Cambridge: Cambridge University Press, 1988.

———. *Meditations on First Philosophy With Selections From the Objections and Replies*. 1986. Edited by John Cottingham. Repr. Cambridge: Cambridge University Press, 2003.

Diamond, Jared. *The World until Yesterday*. New York: Viking, 2012.

Edinger, Edward. *Anatomy of the Psyche: Alchemical Symbolism in Psychotherapy*. Peru, IL: Open Court, 1994.

———. *Ego and Archetype: Individuation and the Religious Function of the Psyche* Boston, MA: Shambhala, 1972.

Eliade, Mircea. *The Forge and the Crucible: Origins and Structures of Alchemy*. New Edition. 1978. Repr. Chicago: University of Chicago Press, 1979.

Ellenberger, Henri. *The Discovery of the Unconscious: The History and Evolution of Dynamic Psychiatry*. New York: Basic Books, 1970.

Freud, Sigmund. *Civilization and Its Discontents*. 1929–1930. The Standard Edition. Translated by James Strachey. New York: W. W. Norton & Company, 1989.

———. *New Introductory Lectures on Psycho-Analysis*. 1933. Standard Edition. Translated by James Strachey. New York: Norton & Company, 1965.

Grof, Stanislav. "Holotropic Research and Archetypal Astrology." *The Birth of a New Discipline. Archai: The Journal of Archetypal Cosmology, Issue I*. San Francisco, CA: Archai Press, 2009: 50–66.

———. *Psychology of the Future: Lessons from Modern Consciousness Research*. Albany, NY: State University of New York Press, 2000.

Grof, Stanislav, and Hal Z. Bennett. *The Holotropic Mind*. San Francisco, CA: Harper Publications, 1992.

Hamilton, Edith. *Mythology: Timeless Tales of Gods and Heroes*. 1942. New York: Bay Back Books, 1998.

Hampson, Thomas. "Winterreise." Accessed April 5, 2017. http://www.thomashampson.com/category/winterreise.

Hand, Robert. *Horoscope Symbols*. West Chester, PA: Whitford Press, 1981.

Harding, Michael, and Charles Harvey. *Working With Astrology: The Psychology of Harmonics, Midpoints, and Astro-Cartography*. London: Arkana, 1990.

Harvey, Charles. *Anima Mundi: The Astrology of the Individual and the Collective*. London: CPA Press, 2002.

Heidegger, Martin. *Being and Time*. 1927. Translated by J. Macquarrie and E. Robinson. Oxford: Basil Blackwell, 1962.

Hillman, James. "Anima Mundi: The Return of the Soul to the World." 1982. In *The Thought of the Heart and the Soul of the World*. Dallas: Spring, 1992.

———. *Archetypal Psychology: A Brief Account*. Dallas, TX: Spring Publications, 1983.

———. *The Myth of Analysis: Three Essays in Archetypal Psychology*. New York: HarperPerennial, 1992.

———. *Re-Visioning Psychology*. 1975. Reprint. New York: HarperPerennial, 1992.

———. *Senex & Puer*. Edited by Glen Slater. Putnam, CT: Spring Publications, 2013.

———. *The Soul's Code: In Search of Character and Calling*. New York: Warner Books, 1996.

Hölderlin, Friedrich. *Selected Poems*. Second edition. Translated by David Constantine. Highgreen, UK: Bloodaxe Books, 1996.

Hone, Margaret. *The Modern Text-Book of Astrology*. Revised Edition. 1955. Reprint. London, UK: L. N. Fowler & Co., 1972.

Huxley, Aldous. *The Perennial Philosophy*. 1946. Reprint. London: Fontana Books, 1959.

Jaffé, Aniela. *The Myth of Meaning in the Work of C. G. Jung*. Translated by R. F. C. Hull. Zürich: Daimon Verlag, 1984.

Jones, Rufus, "Studies in Mystical Religion." In Gershom Scholem, *Major Trends in Jewish Mysticism*. 1941. Reprint. New York: Schocken Books, 1961.

Jung, Carl Gustav. *Aion: Researches into the Phenomenology of the Self*. Second edition. Volume 9, part II, of *The Collected Works of C. G. Jung*. Translated by R. F. C. Hull. Princeton, NJ: Princeton University Press, 1969.

———. *Alchemical Studies*. Volume 13 of *The Collected Works of C. G. Jung*. Translated by R. F. C. Hull. Princeton: Princeton University Press, 1968.

———. *Answer to Job. The Problem of Evil: Its Psychological and Religious Origins*. 1960. Translated by R. F. C. Hull. Reprint. Cleveland, OH: Meridian Books, 1970.

———. "Archetypes of the Collective Unconscious." 1934/1954. In *The Archetypes and the Collective Unconscious*. Second edition. Volume 9, part I of *The Collected Works of C. G. Jung*. Translated by R. F. C. Hull. Princeton: Princeton University Press, 1968.

————. *The Archetypes and the Collective Unconscious*. Second edition. Volume 9, part I of *The Collected Works of C. G. Jung*, Translated by R. F. C. Hull. Princeton: Princeton University Press, 1968.

————. *C. G. Jung Letters II: 1951–1961*. Edited by Gerald Adler and Aniela Jaffé. Translated by R.F.C. Hull. London: Routledge & Kegan Paul, 1973.

————. *Civilization in Transition*. Second edition. Volume 10 of *The Collected Works of C. G. Jung*. Translated by R. F. C. Hull. Princeton: Princeton University Press, 1970.

————. "Commentary on 'The Secret of the Golden Flower'." In *Alchemical Studies*. Volume 13 of *The Collected Works of C. G. Jung*. Translated by R. F. C. Hull. Princeton: Princeton University Press, 1968.

————. *Jung on Astrology*. Edited by Safron Rossi and Keiron Le Grice. Abingdon, UK: Routledge, 2017.

————. *Man and His Symbols*. Edited by C . G. Jung and Marie-Louise von Franz. 1964. Reprint. London: Aldus Books Ltd., 1979.

————. *Memories, Dreams, Reflections*. 1963. Edited by Aniela Jaffé. Translated by Richard Wilson and Clara Wilson. Reprint. London: Flamingo, 1983.

————. *Mysterium Coniunctionis*. Second edition. 1955–1956. Volume 14 of *The Collected Works of C. G. Jung*. Translated by R. F. C. Hull. Reprint. Princeton: Princeton University Press, 1989.

————. *Nietzsche's Zarathustra: Notes on the Seminar Given in 1934–9*. Edited by James Jarrett. 2 Vols. Princeton, Princeton University Press, 1988.

————. "On the Nature of the Psyche." 1947/1954. In *The Structure and Dynamics of the Psyche*. Volume 8 of *The Collected Works of C. G. Jung*. Translated by R.F.C. Hull. London: Routledge & Kegan Paul, 1960.

————. "On the Psychology of the Unconscious." 1917/1926/1943. In *Two Essays on Analytical Psychology*. Volume 7 of *The Collected Works of C. G. Jung*. Second edition. Translated by R. F. C. Hull. London: Routledge, 1966.

————. "The Phenomenology of the Spirit in Fairytales." 1945/1948. In *The Archetypes and the Collective Unconscious*. Second edition. Volume 9, part I of *The Collected Works of C. G. Jung*. Translated by R. F. C. Hull. Princeton: Princeton University Press, 1968.

————. *Psychology and Alchemy*. Second edition. Volume 12 of *The Collected Works of C. G. Jung*. Translated by R. F. C. Hull. Princeton: Princeton University Press, 1968.

————. *Psychology and Religion: West and East*. Volume 11 of *The Collected Works of C. G. Jung*. Translated by R. F. C. Hull. London: Routledge & Kegan Paul, 1958.

————. "The Psychology of the Child Archetype." 1940. In *The Archetypes and the Collective Unconscious*. Second edition. Volume 9, part I *of The Collected Works of C. G. Jung*, Translated by R. F. C. Hull. Princeton: Princeton University Press, 1968.

———. *The Red Book*. Edited and Introduced by Sonu Shamdasani. Translated by Mark Kyburz, John Peck, and Sonu Shamdasani. New York: W. W. Norton & Co., 2009.

———. "The Relations between the Ego and the Unconscious." 1928. In *Two Essays on Analytical Psychology*. Second Edition. Volume 7 of *The Collected Works of C. G. Jung*. Translated by R.F.C. Hull. London: Routledge & Kegan Paul, 1966.

———. "Richard Wilhelm: In Memoriam." 1957. In *The Spirit in Man, Art, and Literature*. 1966. Vol. 15 of *The Collected Works of C. G. Jung*. Translated by R. F. C. Hull. Reprint. Princeton: Princeton University Press, 1971.

———. *The Solar Myths and Opicinus de Canistris*. Edited by Riccardo Bernardini, Gian Piero Quaglino, and Augusto Romano. Zürich: Daimon Verlag, 2016.

———. *The Spirit in Man, Art, and Literature*. 1966. Volume 15 of *The Collected Works of C. G. Jung*. Translated by R. F. C. Hull. Reprint. Princeton: Princeton University Press, 1971.

———. "The Spiritual Problem of Modern Man." 1928/1931. In *Civilization in Transition*. 2nd edition. Volume 10 of *The Collected Works of C. G. Jung*. Translated by R. F. C. Hull. Princeton: Princeton University Press, 1989.

———. *The Structure and Dynamics of the Psyche*. Vol. 8 of *The Collected Works of C. G. Jung*. Translated by R. F. C. Hull. London: Routledge & Kegan Paul, 1960.

———. *Symbols of Transformation*. 2nd ed. 1967. Vol. 5 of *The Collected Works of C. G. Jung*. Translated by R. F. C. Hull. Reprint. Princeton: Princeton University Press, 1976.

———. "Synchronicity: An Acausal Connecting Principle." 1955. In *The Structure and Dynamics of the Psyche*. Vol. 8 of *The Collected Works of C. G. Jung*. Translated by R. F. C. Hull. London: Routledge & Kegan Paul, 1960.

———. "Transformation Symbolism in the Mass." 1954. In *Psychology and Religion: West and East*. Volume 11 of *The Collected Works of C. G. Jung*. Second edition. Translated by R. F. C. Hull. Princeton: Princeton University Press, 1969.

———. *Two Essays on Analytical Psychology*. Second edition. 1966. Volume 7 of *The Collected Works of C. G. Jung*. Translated by R. F. C. Hull. Reprint. London: Routledge, 1990.

———. "The Undiscovered Self." 1957/1958. In *Civilization in Transition*. Second edition. Volume 10 of *The Collected Works of C. G. Jung*. Translated by R. F. C. Hull. Princeton, NJ: Princeton University Press, 1970.

———. "Wotan." 1936. In *Civilization in Transition*. Second edition. Volume 10 of *The Collected Works of C. G. Jung*. Translated by R. F. C. Hull. Princeton, NJ: Princeton University Press, 1970.

Koestler, Arthur. *The Roots of Coincidence*. New York: Random House, 1972.

Le Grice, Keiron. *Archetypal Cosmology and Depth Psychology: Selected Essays*. Ojai, CA: ITAS Publications, 2021.

———. *The Archetypal Cosmos: Rediscovering the Gods in Myth, Science and Astrology*. Edinburgh, UK: Floris Books, 2010.

———. "Astrology and the Modern Western World View." In *Archetypal Cosmology and Depth Psychology: Selected Essays*. Ojai, CA: ITAS Publications, 2021.

———. "The Birth of a New Discipline: Archetypal Cosmology in Historical Perspective." In *Archetypal Cosmology and Depth Psychology: Selected Essays*. Ojai, CA: ITAS Publications, 2021.

———. *Discovering Eris: The Symbolism and Significance of a New Planetary Archetype*. Edinburgh: Floris Books, 2012.

———. *The Lion Will Become Man: Alchemy and the Dark Spirit in Nature—A Personal Encounter*. Asheville, NC: Chiron Publications, 2023.

Levellers, The. "One Way." On *Levelling the Land*. London, UK: China Records, 1991.

Mann, A. T. *The Elements of Tarot*. Shaftesbury, Dorset: Element Books, 1993.

Mumford, Lewis. *The Myth of the Machine: The Pentagon of Power*. New York: Harcourt Brace Jovanovich, Inc. 1970.

Neumann, Erich. *The Great Mother: An Analysis of the Archetype*. 1955/1963. Second edition. Translated by Ralph Manheim. Princeton: Princeton University Press, 1991.

———. *The Origins and History of Consciousness*. 1954. Translated by R. F. C. Hull. Princeton: Princeton University Press, 1995.

Nietzsche, Friedrich. *Basic Writings of Nietzsche*. Translated by Walter Kaufmann. New York: The Modern Library, 2000.

———. "Beyond Good and Evil." In *Basic Writings of Nietzsche*. Translated by Walter Kaufmann. New York: The Modern Library, 2000.

———. *The Birth of Tragedy: Out of the Spirit of Music*. Translated by Shaun Whiteside. Edited by Michael Tanner. London: Penguin Books, 1993.

———. *The Gay Science: With a Prelude in Rhymes and an Appendix of Songs*. Translated by Walter Kaufmann. New York: Vintage Books, 1974.

———. "On the Genealogy of Morals." In *Basic Writings of Nietzsche*. Translated by Walter Kaufmann. New York: The Modern Library, 2000.

———. *Thus Spoke Zarathustra*. Translated by Richard J. Hollingdale. New York: Penguin, 1968.

———. *The Twilight of the Idols and The Anti-Christ*. 1990. Translated by Michael Tanner. Reprint. London: Penguin, 2003.

O'Neal, Rod. "Archetypal Historiography: A New Historical Approach." In *The Birth of a New Discipline, Archai: The Journal of Archetypal Cosmology*, Issue 1 (2009). Reprint. San Francisco: Archai Press, 2011.

Otto, Rudolf. *The Idea of the Holy*. 1923. Reprint. London: Oxford University Press, 1958.

Ross, Hugh McGregor, trans. *The Gospel of Thomas*. London: Watkins Publishing, 2002.

Rudhyar, Dane. *The Astrology of Personality*. Santa Fe, NM: Aurora Press, 1936.

———. *The Astrology of Transformation: A Multilevel Approach*. Wheaton, IL: Quest Books, 1984.

Schopenhauer, Arthur. *The World as Will and as Representation*. Translated by F. J. Payne. Mineola, NY: Dover Publications, 1966.

Shields, Christopher. "Aristotle's Psychology." Accessed October 20, 2021. In *The Stanford Encyclopedia of Philosophy* (Winter 2020 Edition). Edited by Edward N. Zalta. https://plato.stanford.edu/archives/win2020/entries/aristotle-psychology.

Solomon, Robert C. and Kathleen M. Higgins. *A Short History of Philosophy*. New York: Oxford University Press, 1996.

Swami, Sridhare,. "Commentary on the Rudra Vaisnava Sampradaya." Accessed October 20, 2021. http://www.bhagavad-gita.org/Gita/verse-13-12.html.

Tarnas, Richard. *Cosmos and Psyche: Intimations of a New World View*. New York: Viking, 2006.

———. "An Introduction to Archetypal Astrology." Accessed August 4, 2009. www.cosmosandpsyche.com/pdf/IntroductiontoAstrology.pdf.

———.*The Passion of the Western Mind: Understanding the Ideas That Have Shaped Our World View*. Reprint, London: Pimlico, 1991.

———. *Prometheus the Awakener: An Essay on the Archetypal Meaning of the Planet Uranus*. Woodstock, CT: Spring Publications, 1995.

Taylor, Charles. "Buffered and Porous Selves." *The Immanent Frame*. 2008. Accessed September 13, 2016. http://blogs.ssrc.org/tif/2008/09/02/buffered-and-porous-selves.

———. *A Secular Age*. Cambridge, MA: The Belknap Press of Harvard University Press, 2007.

———. *Sources of the Self: The Making of the Modern Identity*. Cambridge, MA: Harvard University Press, 1989.

Tompkins, Sue. *Aspects in Astrology: A Comprehensive Guide to Interpretation*. Shaftsbury, Dorset: Element Books, 1989.

Underhill, Evelyn. *Mysticism*. 1911. Reprint. New York: Image Books, 1990.

von Franz, Marie-Louise. *Psyche and Matter*. 1988. Reprint, Boston, MA: Shambhala Publications, 1992.

Washburn, Michael. *The Ego and the Dynamic Ground: A Transpersonal Theory of Human Development*. Second edition. Albany, NY: State University of New York Press, 1995.

Wordsworth, William. "Ode," In *Intimations of Immortality*. London: Phoenix, 1996.

Zimmer, Heinrich. *Myths and Symbols in Indian Art and Civilization*. Edited by Joseph Campbell. Princeton, NJ: Princeton University Press, 1972.

————. *The Philosophies of India.* 1951. Edited by Joseph Campbell. Reprint. Princeton, NJ: Princeton University Press, 1989

INDEX

abaissement du niveau mental
165

accidents
75, 89, 127, 181

Achilles heel
113, 173

acorn theory
22f

active imagination
64

Adam (biblical)
76

Adler, Alfred
4, 42, 78f, 117

adventure (heroic, life)
49, 73, 75, 119f, 172

aggression (drive)
16f, 80, 133, 137, 148f, 179

aging
89, 213

aha moment
128

albedo
76, 180

alchemy
39, 72, 75–78, 80, 100, 102, 107, 115,
122, 141f, 155, 163, 166, 174, 179f

alcohol
167

alienation
54, 67f, 70, 80, 86, 107, 114f

alignments (planetary)
(*see* aspects)

altruism
58, 141

amor fati
139, 143, 216

amplification
173, 179

analytic philosophy
2

analytical psychology
29–34

Anaximander
22

ancestors
31, 67, 86, 165

ancien régime
210

angels
25, 154

anima
38, 108, 144f, 150–161, 177, 179, 181

anima mundi (world soul)
35, 94, 97, 121, 155, 166, 216,

animus
30, 39, 144–153, 157, 159, 179, 181

Anthropos
57

Aphrodite
18, 34, 152

Apollo
134f

appetites
24, 132f, 138, 141, 154f

aqua permanens
76, 163

archai
22

archetypal astrological analysis
10f, 186, 208, 210, 217

archetypal astrology
4f, 8–12, 19f, 26, 36, 40f, 45, 75, 78,
83, 89f, 93, 97, 104, 183, 185, 191, 202,
209f, 212, 215

archetypal cause
136, 216
archetypal complexes
93, 124, 199, 204, 208f, 212
archetypal compulsion
180
archetypal cosmology
4, 8, 11f, 36, 38, 45, 215f
archetypal eye
34f, 88, 93
archetypal figures
33, 38, 91, 105, 120, 126, 146, 148, 159, 161
archetypal historiography
217
archetypal images
33, 44, 59, 121, 164, 209
archetypal matrix
34
archetypal patterns
5, 8, 23, 40, 59, 62f, 65, 87, 92, 137, 172, 185, 203, 206, 209, 213, 215f
archetypal powers/principles
17, 21–23, 35, 38, 63, 75, 78, 93, 99, 104, 119, 129, 133, 149, 170, 178, 187, 192f, 195f, 198, 205f, 208, 210, 214
archetypal psychology
23, 34f, 37, 78, 83, 94, 121, 162
archetypal themes
10, 77, 89, 93, 111, 182, 185, 199, 203, 210f
archetypes
1, 4–6, 8f, 15–45
archetype per se
33
(see also planetary archetypes, entries for specific archetypes, psychoid)
archons
23f
Ariadne
156
Aristotle/Aristotelian philosophy
22f, 25, 65, 104
Arroyo, Stephen
36, 45, 211
art
8, 30, 35, 92f, 163, 209, 213

As Above, So Below (Hermetic maxim)
185
asceticism
63–65
aspects (alignments)
6, 12, 16–19, 22, 32, 34, 37, 39f, 42, 44f, 53, 55, 57–63, 72f, 84, 89f, 92, 100, 107f, 111–114, 116f, 119, 121, 124f, 127, 134, 138–140, 149, 151, 153, 163, 172, 187, 191–193, 197–200, 203f, 213f, 216
(see also hard aspects, major aspects, minor aspects, soft aspects)
Assagioli, Roberto
78, 166f
astrologers
36f, 40, 45, 192, 203, 207f, 211
astrology
3f, 6–11, 21, 23, 26, 33, 36–38, 40f, 75, 77, 185–187, 192, 202–208, 211–216
astronomy
185, 214
Atman
66, 98, 103
atomism
7, 26
Augustine of Hippo
25, 99
authenticity
2, 35, 55, 62, 79, 81, 111–113, 118f, 121, 123, 126, 129, 155, 161, 181
Axial Age
215
ayahuasca
167

Babylonia
23
barbarism
68, 132
Basic Perinatal Matrices (BPMs)
80–83, 127, 130, 179f, 214
Basilides
24
Bastian, Adolf
30, 227
Batman
112

Beatrice (*The Divine Comedy*)
156
Becker, Ernest
105f
Bellah, Robert
98
beneficence
170–172
Bhagavad-Gita
98
biblical
70, 114, 159
biography
1, 8, 12, 40, 59, 82, 113, 199, 208f, 213
biology
29, 42
birth charts
40, 75, 124, 178, 187, 199–203, 206, 209, 213
birthday
100
birthing
79, 82, 130, 180, 182, 214
blackening/blackness
76, 122
Blavatsky, Helena
26
Bleuler, Eugen
42
blueprint (developmental)
22
blunders
113, 125, 127
Bohm, David
8, 216
Bollingen
24
boon
73, 87, 128, 172
Brahman
18, 98
breathing/breathwork
78, 80, 213
Brooke, Roger
94, 109
Bryant, Christopher
70
Bucke, Richard
166

Buddha, the
39, 49, 56f, 99
Buddhism
16, 49, 99, 114, 137, 147
buffered self
164f
Butler, Renn
83

calcinatio
77, 142, 180
calculation (of chart positions)
4, 185, 201
call/calling
17, 21, 51f, 55, 58–60, 73, 75, 106, 140, 178
Campbell, Joseph
2, 7, 11–12, 49f, 52, 65, 70, 72f, 75, 82, 92, 124, 126, 130, 172
capitalism
171
Capra, Fritjof
8, 216
cardinal directions
4, 16
carnivals
136
Carter, Charles
203f
Cartesian-Newtonian worldview
6, 26, 104
Carus, C. G.
42
categories (Kantian, archetypal)
1, 4, 8, 16, 25, 27, 117, 126, 129, 152, 167
catharsis
133, 136
causation
23, 25f, 33, 204, 210, 211, 216
celebrity
168
censorship
61, 115, 117, 119, 133, 179
centralizing principle
38
centration
102

centroversion
102
Ceres
186
chaos
2, 6, 112, 127, 133
characterological analysis
215
characters
55, 64
chart readings
40, 211
child archetype
1, 30, 38, 59–63, 107f, 177, 179, 181
childhood/children
23, 44, 60, 68, 81, 91, 107, 116, 138,
145, 153f, 163, 166, 174
Chinese philosophy
49, 100, 107
Chiron (planetary archetype)
185f
Chomsky, Noam
43
Christ
2, 39, 56f, 99, 103, 137, 141
Christianity
2, 16, 21–23, 25, 26, 29, 34f, 49, 56, 70,
84f, 92, 97–99, 101, 103, 117, 135, 137,
139 141f, 147, 166, 177
Chronos
39, 120, 122, 179
chthonic
39, 141, 151
church
16, 21, 122
Cicero
102
Clarke, John
41
coagulatio
77, 122, 163, 179
co-creation
24, 205f
coincidence
28, 33, 88, 128, 210
collective unconscious
5, 29f, 32, 61–63, 108, 112, 156, 164,
172, 204

commandments
119, 177
compensation (in the psyche)
37, 117, 138, 141, 144, 154, 174, 176
complexes
4, 19, 29f, 38, 55, 59, 62, 113, 117, 153,
160, 163
(*see also* archetypal complexes, ego-
consciousness/ego-complex)
complexio oppositorum
69
configurations (of planets in charts)
4, 8, 10, 37, 93, 188, 190f, 197
Confucianism
16
coniunctio
77
conjunction aspect
157, 187–195, 197, 199, 201, 214
conscience
25, 59, 116–118
consciousness
17, 19, 29, 31, 43–45, 56–66, 74, 90, 94,
98–109, 114f, 117, 127, 130, 133, 135,
137f, 149f, 154, 157, 163, 165–167,
176f, 179–181, 194, 204f, 216
(*see also*, ego-consciousness, levels of
consciousness, non-ordinary states of
consciousness)
Constantine (Roman Emperor)
21
corn spirit
137
correlations
4, 36, 38, 198, 202, 207, 211, 215f
correspondences
8, 11, 37, 76, 79, 185, 199, 203f
cosmological powers (Swimme's theory)
109, 130
cosmology
4–6, 8
crises
2, 19, 55, 57, 59, 73, 78, 84, 113
critic (inner)
147, 149
crone
162

crows
33
Cunningham, Donna
45, 130
cycles
5, 31, 40, 75f, 100, 137, 182, 185, 207,
215

daemons
5
daimon
23, 139f, 180
Dante (Alighieri)
16, 49, 173
Dasein
103
dawn
11, 76, 81, 100, 130, 182
death-rebirth process/experience
38, 67, 73f, 77f, 81f, 84, 105, 127, 136f,
142, 178
defenses
25, 81, 103, 179
defensiveness
58, 79, 115, 119
dehumanizing (Hillman's concept)
92
deities
3, 16, 18, 22, 28, 39, 98, 126, 152, 172,
208
delusions
42, 44, 164, 167, 171
demiurge
23
demon/demonic
61, 132, 141, 146
departure (theme in hero's adventure)
50, 73, 164
depression
35, 53, 76, 87, 114, 118, 179
depth psychology
1, 4, 19, 21, 28f, 36, 42, 60, 79, 87, 139,
149, 153, 162, 164, 179
Descartes, René
26, 102
descent (theme, experience of)
39, 73f, 76, 105, 109, 137, 139

desires/desirousness
3, 17f, 30, 59f, 64, 69, 84, 87, 117,
127, 133f, 138f, 141f, 150–155, 157,
163, 212
despair
53, 57, 67
desperation
138
destiny
23, 50, 54, 59, 73, 90, 140, 156
destruction
112, 132, 134, 139, 141, 152, 155
determinism
23, 203, 211
development (psychological)
9, 19, 22, 25, 27f, 30, 42f, 50, 56, 66–
70, 72, 100–103, 113, 119, 130, 146–
148, 153, 192, 194f, 197
Devil
16, 39, 61, 139, 141, 180
dialectic
64, 130, 214
dialogue
64
diamond body
178
Diamond, Jared
86
differentiation
64, 69, 100, 103, 108, 135, 147, 149,
154–156, 193, 208
Dionysus/Dionysian
38f, 60, 63, 65, 87, 132–139, 141, 154,
162, 180f, 199
discord
178, 180, 185
discoveries (of planets)
128, 185, 208
disenchantment
6, 26f
disidentification
63, 69
dismemberment
39, 76f, 87, 102, 137, 180f
dissolution
58, 68, 77, 80, 82, 108, 113, 122, 134f,
162f, 165, 168, 178, 180f
divination
168

divine/divinity
16, 18, 22, 24, 34, 39, 56f, 70, 81, 101–
103, 105, 108, 122, 126, 134f, 140f,
166–168, 178, 211
doors of perception
167
dragon
74, 76, 141
dramatis personae
64
dread
114
dreams
5, 30, 33, 35, 44, 89, 91, 100, 111, 120,
125, 146f, 162, 166, 177, 192, 214
drives
16f, 21, 28, 30, 38, 65, 69, 92, 111f, 117,
129, 132f, 136–139, 149, 151, 174, 181
drowning
102, 163, 176
drugs
167
dualism/duality
101f, 181, 192
dwarf planets
112, 185, 214

earth (element)
77, 141, 192
earth (ground)
3, 21, 174
Earth (planet)
4, 6, 23, 98, 185–187
Eastern religion/philosophy
11, 16, 36f, 41
eccentric orbit
75, 214
Eckhart, Meister
122, 124
ecliptic
186f, 214
ecological crisis
2
ecstasy
65, 81, 134, 136, 142
Eden (biblical)
70, 80

Edinger, Edward
77, 82
egocentricity
171
ego-consciousness/ego-complex
29, 65, 67–69, 81, 86, 90, 100, 102,
104f, 107f, 114f 127, 129, 135, 151,
154, 160, 162f, 167, 211
ego-ideal
118
ego-strength
149
Egypt
24, 84, 98, 207
Eidos
43
Eightfold Path (Buddhism)
49
Electra complex
30, 153
electricity
130
elements
21, 77, 142, 192
elementary ideas (Bastian's concept)
30
Eleusis
137
Eliade, Mircea
6, 85
elves
25
emergencies
(*see* spiritual emergencies)
empirical evidence/empiricism
4, 22, 28, 36–38, 43, 79, 207, 215f
enantiodromia
130, 180
enchantment
88, 151, 159, 162, 164–166, 168, 180f
Enlightenment, the
26, 37, 99, 135
enlightenment (spiritual)
49, 56, 99, 167
epiphenomenalism
26, 42
equinoxes
4

Eranos Foundation/Conference
100
Erikson, Erik
43
Eris (planetary archetype)
178, 180, 185f, 214
Eros
30, 150, 152, 179, 181
Esalen Institute
81
escapism
162, 164
esoteric
7, 16, 39, 139
estrangement
53, 66, 68
ethics
16, 53, 66, 68, 92, 117, 133, 156
ethnic ideas (Bastian's concept)
30
evil
16, 44, 53, 55, 69, 111f, 117, 132f, 181,
212
evolution
27, 31, 67f, 82, 86f, 130, 139, 142, 155,
178, 182
exile
80f, 121
existentialism
2f, 41, 67, 80, 103, 123, 207
extraversion
73, 105

fairies
25, 152
fantasy
5, 53, 55, 63f, 91, 148, 150, 154, 159,
161, 164, 170
fatalism
101, 204, 206f, 216
fate
6, 10, 23f, 38–40, 55, 59, 74, 77, 92,
102, 112, 121, 126, 139, 142, 160, 172,
178, 180, 205–207
father principle/archetype
38f, 52, 57, 103, 117, 119, 121f, 145,
148f, 153, 161, 177, 179, 181

Father Time
39, 122
Faust
159
Faustian drive
87
female
38, 144, 148, 150, 154, 192
feminine principle
38, 74, 100, 105, 144, 150, 153–155
femme fatale
154, 181
fetus
79–81, 168
Fight Club, the (motion picture)
111
fire (element)
21, 77, 85, 87, 128, 142, 192
fisherman (biblical parable)
66
folk psychology
25, 145, 153
forgetting (as expression of the
unconscious)
125
Forms (Platonic)
25, 27, 36, 43, 99, 150, 177
freedom/free will
10, 15, 17, 23, 36, 38, 45, 50, 58, 62, 65,
67, 69, 77, 101f, 118, 127–129, 142,
178, 180, 204–207
French Revolution
128, 210f
Freud, Sigmund
4, 27–30, 78f, 115, 118, 124, 127, 133,
138, 153, 162f
Freudian psychology
29, 42, 116, 117, 119–121, 125, 133,
138, 149, 154, 163
Frodo (*The Lord of the Rings*)
31

Gandalf (*The Lord of the Rings*)
33, 120
Ganesha
172
gender
144f, 148, 202

Genesis, Book of
98
genetics
19, 27
genius
128, 178, 180
geometry/geometric relationships
30, 40, 185, 187f, 192, 197 199, 210f
Gestalt psychology
118
giantism
174
Gilgamesh
49
globalization
172
glyphs
187
gnosis
25, 101
Gnosticism
23–25, 41, 57, 63, 108, 141, 212
goblins
25
God
2, 23, 25, 34, 56f, 70, 84, 97–99, 101,
103, 122, 126f, 139–141, 165f, 176–178
(*see also* divine, sacred, spirit)
godhead
102, 106
God-image
56, 177f
"God is dead" (Nietzsche)
28
god-man
39, 56f, 76, 141, 159
gods and goddesses
1, 3, 5, 11, 18, 21–23, 25, 28f, 34–37,
39, 84f, 87, 92–94, 101, 104, 106f, 121,
128, 152f, 159, 161, 168, 172, 176f,
185, 205–207
Goethe, Johann Wolfgang von
159, 216
gold
75, 77, 168
golden age
70, 80
golden mean
65

good/goodness (moral category)
16, 22, 25, 44, 55, 69, 98f, 111f, 117,
141, 150, 212
Gospels
51, 57, 63, 70, 99, 101, 103, 109, 171
grandiosity
160, 174
gratification
30, 63, 154
Greek myth
2, 18, 21f, 30, 60, 104, 107, 120, 128,
134f, 152, 156, 163, 172, 185, 208
Greek philosophy
2, 16, 22, 25f, 45, 99, 103f, 207
Greene, Liz
36, 45
Grof, Stanislav
45, 72, 78–83, 115, 127, 130, 142, 168,
179f, 213f, 216
Grofian psychology
72, 79f, 115, 127, 130, 168, 179f, 213
growth
7, 10, 19, 22, 35, 58, 170f, 174, 179,
193, 198
guardian of the threshold
23, 75
guilt
112–114, 117–119, 179f
gurus
39, 148, 160f

Hades
39, 87, 139, 180, 208
Hamilton, Edith
133f, 137, 142
Hampson, Thomas
172, 174
Hanged Man, The (tarot)
163
Heaven
28, 49, 68, 70, 98, 171, 178
heavens
37, 185
hedonism
19, 65
Heidegger, Martin
103, 109, 146

heimarmene
23f, 77, 101, 212
Helen of Troy
154
Hell
39, 49, 74
Hephaestus
85
Hera
18
Heraclitus
144
Hermes
34, 104, 179,
Hermeticism
185
hero archetype/mythic pattern
1, 9f 12, 30–32, 38f, 49, 59–61, 63, 65,
72–75, 77, 82, 91, 105f, 107, 109, 120,
124, 137, 146, 148, 161, 172f, 177, 179f
heroic attitude
73
heroism
2, 31f, 38, 58–61, 63, 73f, 90, 105f, 146,
149
Hestia
107
hierophany
6
hieros gamos
74, 77, 108, 155
Higgins, Kathleen
41
Hillman, James
23, 32, 34f, 41, 45, 78, 90–94, 97, 121–
124, 176, 206f, 211f
hindrances
16
Hinduism
18, 108, 137, 139, 152, 172
history/historical events
5f, 11–12, 15, 21, 25, 27, 35, 38, 40, 43–
45, 56, 86f, 135, 173, 199, 202f, 208,
210f, 213, 215
historiography
217
Hölderlin, Friedrich
162, 169

holism
179
Hollywood
168
holotropic breathwork
82f
holy power
18, 20
homeostasis
180
Homer
49
hominoids
86
horizon
3, 105, 164, 172, 174
horizontal spirituality
166
horoscope
40, 207, 214
houses (in astrology)
40, 214f
hubris
87, 174, 179
Hulk, The
111
human nature
5f, 9f, 17, 19f, 30, 132, 170, 178, 205
humanistic fallacy
34, 92, 206
humanistic psychology
34, 70, 92, 170, 206
Huxley, Aldous
124, 140, 143, 166
Hyde, Maggie
111

"I Am" experience
102f
idealism
143, 168
idealization
67, 168
ideals
6, 15, 17, 22, 36, 51, 59, 64–66, 90, 92,
64, 97, 118, 128, 139, 144, 148–151,
153, 155, 168, 170, 207, 214

identification
　　50, 53, 61f, 64f, 82, 115, 127–129, 137,
　　157, 159, 161, 164, 166, 179
　　(*see also* disidentification)
identity
　　19, 38, 53f, 56–58, 61, 63, 65, 69, 73,
　　100, 102, 104, 106–108, 137, 145, 147,
　　149, 161f, 165f, 179, 205
idiosyncrasies
　　92, 178
id, the (Freudian concept)
　　30, 117f, 133, 138, 154, 163, 180
illness
　　42, 90f, 115
illusions
　　63, 151, 155, 163f, 168, 180
imitation
　　67, 164, 180
immanent spirit
　　22, 139, 140, 166
immorality
　　126
imperatives
　　117–119, 177
inauthenticity
　　52f
incarnation
　　56f, 79, 97, 103, 114, 177f
inclination (to the ecliptic)
　　214
inconjunct aspect
　　198
independence
　　56, 101, 103, 108, 146f, 149, 181, 215
Indian religion
　　18, 49, 140, 152
individualism
　　50, 128f, 178, 180
individuality
　　100, 106, 134
individuation
　　9, 11, 17, 24, 30–32, 35, 41, 52, 54f,
　　57f, 61–65, 67–70, 72–74, 76f, 80, 84,
　　89–91, 102, 108, 111, 113, 117, 119,
　　123, 129, 132, 136–138, 141, 144–146,
　　148–151, 155, 157, 159f, 164, 178, 180,
　　192, 205, 209f, 212–214
infancy
　　56, 63, 68

initiation
　　73, 113, 117, 167, 192f
injustice
　　185
innocence
　　59, 107, 114, 181
instinctive
　　31, 69, 153, 193
instincts
　　1, 3f, 16f, 21, 24, 27f, 30f, 36, 38, 42f,
　　58, 64, 66–69, 76, 81, 105, 108, 112,
　　117, 119, 124, 133f, 138, 141f, 149, 151,
　　154f, 176, 180f, 212
　　(*see also* id)
integration
　　19, 64f, 67, 114, 121, 126, 129, 137f,
　　167, 200
intellect
　　97, 104, 148
intelligence
　　103f, 120
intelligible character
　　22, 54
intentionality/intentional consciousness
　　56, 100, 104f, 108, 179f
intoxication
　　18f, 24, 60, 63, 74, 134f, 161f, 168, 181
introjection
　　116f, 149
intuition
　　25, 97, 107, 155f, 167, 192, 207
irrationality/irrationalism
　　7, 28, 37, 42, 66, 94, 130, 145, 149, 151,
　　156f, 207

Jaffé, Aniela
　　31
James, William
　　105, 166
Janet, Pierre
　　4, 42
Jekyll and Hyde
　　111
Jesus
　　16, 51, 56f, 99, 103, 141
Job (biblical)
　　57, 103, 140
Johnson, Robert
　　135f, 142

John's Gospel
51, 99, 101
Joker (Batman character)
112
jokes
125
Jonas, Hans
23, 41, 108
Jones, Rufus
166
journey (mythic model, motif)
7, 9, 11, 12, 39, 49–51, 58, 72–75, 77,
82, 105, 109, 163, 170–174, 179, 213
Joyce, James
173
Judaism
21
Jung, Carl Gustav
4f, 8f, 11, 17f, 19–21, 23–25, 28–33,
35–39, 41, 43–45, 52–54, 56f, 59, 61,
64, 66–72, 74–79, 82, 84–92, 94, 97,
100–103, 105–113, 115, 117, 119–
127, 130, 135–138, 141–147, 149–162,
165f, 169, 172, 174, 176f, 182, 191f,
205, 212, 214–216
Jungian psychology
5, 7–10, 19–21, 24–26, 36–39, 41–45,
53–72, 80, 82, 91, 93, 102, 107, 111,
117, 119f, 135, 144f, 148, 162, 180, 199,
209
(see also analytical psychology, depth
psychology)
Jupiter (planetary archetype)
10, 160, 170–174, 177, 179, 181, 186,
189, 191
justice
16, 77, 145, 178, 180

Kali
39, 108, 140, 231
Kāma
152
Kant, Immanuel
25
karma
82
king (mythic, alchemical symbol)
76, 102, 115, 121f, 155, 163, 172, 177,
179

Krishna
98
kundalini
39, 180

labyrinths
192
lapis philosophurm
77, 121, 178
Lebenswelt
103
leopard
65
Levellers, The
51f
levels of consciousness
73, 79, 129f, 211
Leviathan
140
Lévi-Bruhl, Claude
30, 164
Lewi, Grant
45
liberation
24, 38, 56, 76, 81f, 98, 125, 127, 134,
180
liberty
15, 50, 129
libido
31, 86, 104f, 134, 138, 179
life-and-death struggle
80, 137, 180, 214
light (symbol)
38, 69, 74, 81, 97–99, 101–103, 105–
107, 111, 117, 122, 130, 141, 144, 150,
177, 180, 182, 192
lightning
114, 130
literal interpretation/literalism
34f, 37, 51, 87, 91, 93, 122
Locke, John
26
logic
2, 6, 66, 103, 125, 127, 157
logia
63, 70, 103, 109
logos
101, 103f, 177, 179, 181

love
2, 15f, 18, 27, 34, 39, 62, 105, 140f,
150–153, 160, 167, 177, 179, 199
Lucifer
182
Luna
155, 179
lust
16, 34, 132f, 135, 154

macrocosm
24, 216
madness
78, 82, 134, 168
Maenads
134
magical (quality of experience)
20, 25, 80, 85, 120, 151f, 154, 160f, 163,
165f, 168
magician (archetypal figure)
120, 159–161
Maier, Michael
77, 82, 174
major aspects
163, 187, 193–197, 214
mana-personality
159–161, 174
mandala
176f, 192
mania
81, 127, 132, 174, 179
Manicheans
25
Mann, A. T.
45, 169
Mara
39
Mardi Gras
136
mārga
49
Mars (planetary archetype)
10, 38, 144, 148f, 157, 177, 179–181,
186, 189, 191, 206, 215
martial arts
148
masculine principle
73f, 100, 144, 148f, 155, 181

mask
54, 117, 164
Maslow, Abraham
70, 78
materialism
3, 6f, 30
maternal instinct
105–108, 135, 177, 181
maturation/maturity
42, 68, 116, 119f, 137, 148, 213
maya
155, 164, 181
meaning (archetype of)
121, 162
meaninglessness
3, 86
melancholia
76, 118, 122f
memories
43, 59, 76–79, 97, 113, 117, 123, 213
Mercurius
39, 76, 141, 180
Mercury (planetary archetype)
10, 103f, 148f, 157, 177, 179, 181, 186,
189
Merlin
33
Mesopotamia
49, 207
metamorphosis
49
metaphors
34, 49–51, 76f, 91f, 109
metaphysics
1, 3, 6, 22, 25, 28, 103, 109, 139, 150,
155, 192, 216
microcosm
24, 216
midlife
109
midpoints
200, 214
minor aspects
198, 214
Mithraism
98, 141
modalities
42, 78

moksa
98
monarchs
207
monomyth
73, 75
monotheism
21f, 34f, 102, 106
Montesquieu
210
moods
8f, 19, 59, 107, 151, 156f, 170
Moon (planetary archetype)
21, 38, 76, 97, 100, 106–109, 111, 144, 150, 154, 177, 179, 181, 185f, 189, 207, 215
morals/morality
2f, 5, 16, 22, 25, 30, 43, 53, 57, 65, 92, 111–114, 116–121, 126, 132f, 135, 140f, 149, 152, 156, 160, 174, 180, 182, 212
mortality
79, 89, 123, 213
mortificatio
77, 122, 179
mother (archetype)
30f, 38, 60f, 65, 79, 81, 106–110, 135, 150, 153f, 160, 177, 179, 181
Mother Earth
106
Mother Nature
106
Moyers, Bill
70
multidimensionality
39, 73
multiplicity
19, 176
multivalence
203f
Mumford, Lewis
175
muse
154
music
18, 93, 209, 213
mysterium tremendum et fascinans
18

mysticism
37, 50–52, 78, 134, 137, 166f, 169, 174
myth/mythology
1f, 5f, 8, 10–12, 16, 18, 21f, 25, 28–30, 33, 35, 37–39, 44, 49f, 52, 70, 72–75, 82. 84, 87–89, 91–93,, 96, 100f, 104f, 107, 119–121, 125, 128, 137, 139, 151f, 155f, 162, 168, 172, 174, 180, 185, 199, 208, 211, 213
mythemes
211
mythmakers
92
mythospeculation
98

Nag Hammadi Gnostic texts
24
Napoleon Bonaparte
210
natal charts
40, 157, 199, 201, 203, 215
Nazism
44, 136
negation (principle of)
115, 179
Neoplatonism
34, 97
Neptune (planetary archetype)
10, 39, 81–83, 120, 124, 129, 133f, 151f, 154, 160–168, 178, 180–182, 186, 188–190, 199, 201, 208, 213f
Neumann, Erich
102, 109f
neuroscience
19, 26, 43
neurosis
29, 35, 42, 44, 54, 68, 128, 162, 176
new-paradigm science
7f, 45, 216
Newton, Isaac
26
Nietzsche, Friedrich
28, 43, 57, 67, 118f, 123, 134, 137–139, 141, 143, 159, 207, 212, 216
night
3, 50, 76, 81, 98f, 105–107, 111, 147
night-sea journey
163

nigredo
 76, 122, 158
nihilism
 28
nixies
 25, 152
no-exit situation
 179
non-ordinary states of consciousness
 78f, 82–84, 162, 167, 213
noon
 105, 109, 188, 200
nous
 104, 179
nuclear energy
 139, 208
number (archetype, symbolism)
 18, 22, 30, 32, 36–39, 43, 52, 76f,
 87, 112, 132f, 165–167, 191–193, 198,
 214
numina
 18
numinous/numinosity
 18, 20, 22, 32f, 36, 42, 57, 75, 85, 140,
 161f, 178, 180, 182, 192
nymphs
 152

occult
 26, 159
ocean
 55, 74, 80, 100
oceanic feeling/consciousness
 80, 162f, 178, 180
Odysseus
 49, 173
Odyssey, The
 49
Oedipus complex
 30, 153
ogre
 115, 121f
Olympians/Olympus
 21, 28f, 104
O'Neal, Rod
 217
oneness
 39, 163, 165, 178, 180, 182, 192

opposites
 16, 64, 67, 69, 77, 111, 144, 176, 178,
 180, 192f, 195, 214
opposition aspect
 187, 189f, 192, 195–197, 214
orbits/orbital periods
 4, 177, 186f, 189, 199, 214
orbs
 187
orgasm
 138
orgiastic
 60, 141, 181
otherness
 129
Otto, Rudolf
 18, 78f
outsider
 129, 173
overcoming
 42, 69, 77, 120, 138, 142, 159

paganism
 25, 37
pain
 58f, 68, 79–81, 84, 112–116, 126, 132,
 162, 164, 168, 205, 212
parable
 66
Parabrahma
 98
paradigm
 6, 26
paradise
 39, 70, 80f, 152, 168, 178
participation mystique
 80, 101, 164–166
participatory theory
 105, 204f, 216
passions
 3, 8, 24, 28, 38, 60, 63f, 76, 81, 124,
 131, 133–135, 138–141, 155, 181, 199
pathologizing
 94
pathology
 19, 29, 34, 41, 43, 65f, 90–92, 123, 135,
 171, 174
patriarchy
 39

pearl of great price
73
perception
25, 78, 88, 104, 152, 164, 167, 206
peregrination (mystic)
174
perinatal psychology
78–82, 116, 130, 137, 168, 214
Perls, Fritz
118
Perry, John Weir
78, 82
Persephone
87, 137
persona
53f, 58, 62, 113, 115f, 129, 164
personalities
19, 36, 55, 59f, 111, 210
personality
1, 5, 8f, 17–19, 22f, 40f, 53–55, 57f,
60–62, 65, 68, 111–116, 119, 133, 137f,
144, 146f, 150, 154, 158, 161f, 167, 171,
205, 208f, 215
personification
16, 18, 25, 39, 76, 105f, 112, 115, 118–
122, 136, 140, 144, 146, 148, 150, 154,
157, 162, 172
pessimism
170, 179
phallus
44
phenomenal world
25, 166
phenomenology
80f
Philosopher's Stone
77, 178
philosophy
2f, 5, 10, 20, 22, 25f, 28, 35, 41, 43,
101–104, 158, 171, 173, 192, 210, 212,
215f
phobias
29
physics
12, 27
Piaget, Jean
43
pilgrimage
50

planet
40, 104, 107, 109, 128, 185f, 197, 199f,
214f
planetoid
185
Plato/Platonism
22, 25, 27, 36, 38, 43, 97, 99, 109, 150,
177, 192, 216
pleasure
16, 30, 57f, 65, 84, 124, 133f, 138, 150,
154, 179, 199, 205
pluralism/plurality (of the psyche)
19, 34f, 41, 58–60, 66, 69, 73, 91, 106,
156
Pluto (planetary archetype)
36, 38–40, 75, 81–83, 105, 112, 132–
142, 151f, 154, 157, 160, 178, 180–182,
186, 190f, 199, 206, 208, 210, 214
pneuma
24
polarity
141
polytheism
22, 34, 106, 138
pornography
154
porous self
164f, 169
possession
18f, 28, 44, 65, 68, 133–135, 138, 142,
152, 160, 165, 180, 206
postmodern era
3
preconsciousness
81, 108, 164, 180
predestination
23
prediction
203
premodern era/cultures
12, 137, 164
Presocratic philosophy
22
pride
16, 100
prima materia
77, 209
primal human
24

primates
27
primordial images
1, 30, 110, 137
(*see also* archetypal images)
principium individuationis
134
projection
28, 37, 62, 68, 76, 144, 148f, 153f, 157,
164, 168, 180f, 216
Prometheus
87, 128, 130, 180, 216
prophecy
168
prophet
159, 161, 180
prototypes
22, 173
psyche
17, 19, 24, 28–35, 38, 41–44, 53–69
(*see also* collective unconscious, personal
unconscious, consciousness, ego, Self)
psyche-body relationship
42
psyche-matter relationship
42
psychedelics
83, 166f, 213
psychiatry
92, 123
psychics
160
psychoactive substances
78
psychoanalysis
29f, 42, 78, 125, 133, 142
(*see also* Freud)
psychodynamics
10, 78, 80, 130, 132, 138f, 209
psychoid (basis of archetypes)
33, 192
psychological functioning
41, 58, 88, 146, 150, 156
psychological functions (Jungian)
192
psychopathology
5, 29, 35, 61, 125, 162
psychosis
42, 44, 61, 68, 82, 162, 176

psychospiritual development/
transformation
49, 70, 73, 76, 78, 81, 216
psychotherapy
35, 78, 82, 123
punishment
30, 118
purgatory
39, 49, 80, 142
purification
142, 163, 178
purity
141, 154
pyrocatharsis
142, 180
Pythagoras
22, 192, 216

quadrature alignments
233
quaternity symbolism
177
queen (alchemy)
76, 155, 179
quincunx aspect
198, 214
quintile aspect
214

Rank, Otto
42, 78f
rationality
2, 26, 29, 37, 42, 56f, 61, 64, 67f, 81, 85,
92, 97, 99, 104, 126, 129f, 135, 145,
151, 155–157, 179
rationalization
154
reality principle
30, 120f, 124, 179
rebel archetype
38, 60–63, 127, 180
rebellion
36, 63, 65, 127, 147
rebirth archetype/experience
1, 12, 30, 36, 38, 52, 58, 70, 73, 76, 78–
82, 87, 91, 102, 105, 127, 132, 136–138,
142, 180, 182, 214
reductionism
7, 26

regression (developmental)
68, 153
reincarnation
137
religion
2–7, 11, 16, 18, 22f, 30, 37, 41f, 44, 50,
75, 98, 100, 108f, 162f, 166, 169, 171,
182
religious experience
163, 166f
religious instinct
3, 16, 171, 180
religious practice
1
religious traditions
2, 5, 16, 39, 50
Renaissance, the
34f, 101
repression
35, 38, 42, 59, 61, 67f, 111–115, 117,
119, 125, 128, 133, 136, 138, 154, 179
resistances
42, 59, 69, 81, 114f, 119, 122, 138, 174,
179
reunion (with the unconscious)
69, 107, 138, 155
Revelation (New Testament)
70
revolution
19, 36, 38, 128, 180, 208, 210f
rites of passage
137
rituals
84f, 136
Roman myth/civilization
2, 16, 21, 98, 122, 149, 172f, 207
romantic urge/feeling/experience
28, 42, 70, 144, 150–155, 157, 173, 199
Romanticism
21, 65
rootlessness
86, 107, 173
rubedo
76
Rudhyar, Dane
36f, 45, 211
rulerships
107, 215

sacred
15, 27, 84–86, 135
sacred medicine
167
sacrifice
31, 59, 61, 73, 87, 90, 140f, 162, 167f,
178
saints
16, 25
salvation
2, 162
samsara
114
Satan
182
Saturn (planetary archetype)
10, 38f, 75, 81–83, 89f, 112–124, 129f,
148f, 157, 162f, 170f, 177–182, 185–
191, 199, 201, 206, 213f
satyr
134
savior archetype
126, 159, 161f, 180
Schelling, Friedrich Wilhelm Joseph
42
schizophrenia
44, 61, 68, 162, 176
Scholastics
101
Scholem, Gerschom
169
Schopenhauer, Arthur
22, 105, 109, 207
science
2–4, 6–8, 26–28, 30, 36f, 43, 45, 78f,
87, 128, 160, 204, 207, 215f
scintillae
107
secularism
2, 27, 52, 74, 84, 108, 168
self-actualization
70, 170
self-annihilation
135
self-assertion
146, 149
self-awareness
38, 130, 146, 194, 198

self-consciousness
117, 126
self-destruction
140
self-discipline
63
self-esteem
100, 179
self-expression
100, 179
self-knowledge
17, 25, 31, 42, 54f, 116, 147, 212, 216
selflessness
16, 167
self-loss
53, 162, 164f, 180f
self-mastery
65
self-organization
45
self-overcoming
65, 90, 138, 159, 182, 212
self-preservation instinct
16, 17, 115, 119
self-protection
126
self-realization
70
Self, the (Jungian archetype)
35, 38, 56–58, 63–66, 69f, 73, 75, 89, 91
102f, 105, 114, 116f, 127, 129, 137,
140f, 150, 155f, 160f, 172, 176–178,
205, 212, 214
semi-sextile aspect
214
semi-square aspect
214
senex
34, 38, 91, 94, 111, 119, 121f, 124, 179,
182
sensations
41
separatio
77, 179
sextile aspect
187, 197, 214
sexual urge/drive
16f, 80, 133, 138, 144, 154
spirit (defined)

shadow (Jungian archetype)
30, 38, 61, 69, 108, 111–125f, 132f,
150, 156, 158f, 161f, 179–181, 212
shamanism
10, 41, 51
Sheldrake, Rupert
216
Shiva
39, 139, 180,
signs of the zodiac
37, 40, 88f, 186f, 214f
Sinatra, Frank
51
sins
16
siren motif/call
152, 181
skin-encapsulated ego
79, 82
slips of the tongue
125
smith (metalworker)
85
Sol Invictus
98
solar myth/motif
44, 100–105
solar system
4, 21, 36, 38, 45, 99, 102, 107, 130,
177, 185f, 216
Solomon, Robert
41
solutio
77, 163, 180
soul
23f, 34f, 37, 41f, 50, 53, 60, 76, 85, 91f,
94, 97–110, 135, 144, 150, 152–155,
166, 179, 181, 207, 211
soullessness
35, 97
soul-making
84, 90–94, 97, 123
soul-vestments
24
spells
63, 152, 160, 164
spirit (archetype of)
1, 30, 117, 157, 161f, 180, 182
(see also wise old man)

97–100, 140f, 165
spirit and nature
  23f, 64, 74, 141, 155, 166, 178
spirits
  5, 25, 97
spiritual experience
  5, 10f, 15, 17f, 20, 25, 27–29, 39, 41,
  49–52, 64, 69, 72, 74, 76–79, 84, 87, 98,
  101, 137, 141, 148f, 154f, 159–163,
  165–168, 180, 211, 213–215
spiritualism
  37
spirituality
  5–7, 11, 37, 51, 72, 182
spiritualizing (function of Neptune)
  163
spiritus vegetavius
  141
square aspect
  187, 192–195, 197, 201, 214
stars
  6, 28, 77, 98f, 102, 107, 130, 176, 206
stellium aspect pattern
  197
strife
  178, 180, 185
subhuman
  112, 126, 132
sublimatio
  77, 174, 179
sublimation
  138, 140, 148, 163
sub-personalities
  19, 36, 55, 59f, 147
sulphur
  142
Sun (planetary archetype)
  21, 97–107, 148f, 177, 185–187, 205–
  207
Sun/Sol (alchemical symbol)
  76
sunrise/sunset
  106
superconscious
  169
super-ego
  30, 111, 116–119, 121, 124, 133, 149,
  179

superhuman
  18, 90, 126, 140, 159, 173
supernatural
  120, 162, 180, 182
superstitions
  7, 99, 101
suppression
  19, 25, 61, 68, 73, 135
Sutich, Anthony
  78
Swimme, Brian
  8, 102, 109, 130
Switzerland
  24
symbols
  2, 28, 55, 57, 85, 100, 102, 119, 141f,
  155, 163, 202f
symbolic attitude
  88–90
symbolic life
  84–88
symptoms
  5, 29, 35, 54, 80, 92, 135, 213
synchronicities
  33, 45, 76, 88f, 156, 165, 204, 208f, 215

taboos
  111, 132, 135, 181
Tao
  49, 127, 156, 168
Tarnas, Richard
  8, 10, 36, 38f, 45, 78, 81, 83, 108, 115,
  128, 130f, 139, 143, 199, 202–204, 209–
  211, 215f
tarot cards
  16, 163, 169
Taylor, Charles
  50, 52, 99, 108, 164f, 169
technology
  2, 26, 128, 172
Teilhard de Chardin, Pierre
  8
telos/teleology
  75, 139, 205
tension of opposites
  64, 68f, 180, 193–195, 198
Terrible Mother (mythic motif)
  108, 135

Thanatos
30
theology
16, 25, 101
theosophy
26, 36f, 207
theou (gnosis)
101, 108
thou shalt (Nietzsche's concept)
118f
thresholds
34, 73, 75, 78, , 127, 165
threshold-guardian
119
time (principle)
120, 122
timelessness
63, 80, 85, 87
Tolkien, J. R. R.
51
Tompkins, Sue
214
top dog
118f
totality
35, 41, 60, 64, 92, 177, 216
tower (symbol)
24, 114, 126
traditional societies
86
traditionalism
122
transcendence
5, 39, 162, 166–168, 178
transcendent function
64
transcendent meaning
3, 50, 207
transcendent/transcendental realm,
5, 22, 25, 27f, 32f, 98, 155, 166f
transfiguration
52, 99
transgression
53, 117
transits
40, 45, 77, 83, 89, 93, 187, 199–202,
206, 210f, 213

transpersonal powers/principles
45, 57, 82, 88, 132, 169, 208, 213f
transpersonal psychology
72, 78, 167, 170, 211
transrationality
66
trauma
42, 74, 78f, 82
trials
73, 82, 120
trickster archetype
30, 38, 61, 75, 127, 113, 125–130, 178–
181
trine aspect
187, 193, 196f, 214
Trinity (of God)
57
T-square aspect configuration
197
twins
203
types (psychological, character)
40, 215
tyrant/tyrannical ego
23, 61, 115

Übermensch
57, 159
unconscious
(see collective unconscious, personal
unconscious, depth psychology)
Underhill, Evelyn
50, 166
underworld
39, 58, 73–76, 87, 105, 112f, 132f, 136,
139, 142, 151, 154, 178, 180f, 208
unio mystica
166
union
77, 79, 108, 134, 138, 153, 165f
unity
7, 58, 61, 65f, 68–70, 80, 82, 102, 138,
163, 165f, 168, 176, 178, 180, 182, 216
universal (nature of archetypes, myth)
1, 4–6, 9, 13, 15, 17, 22f, 25, 27, 30, 33,
36, 38–41, 44, 56, 63, 73, 75, 81f, 90,
93, 125, 138f, 141, 148, 168, 202f, 208,
214

universals
15, 27, 40
universe
1, 6f, 11, 17, 22–27, 83, 102, 130, 139f,
205, 212, 216
Upanishads
98
Uranus (planetary archetype)
36, 38, 75, 81–83, 112f, 134–138, 178,
180–182, 185–190, 205f, 208, 210, 213f
uroboros
141, 180

Vedas
98
Venus (planetary archetype)
10, 38, 144, 150f, 154, 177, 179, 181,
186, 188f, 199, 201
vertical spirituality
166
vices
16
virtues
16f, 116, 121
visions
6, 21, 23, 25, 29f, 34, 36, 60, 62, 78, 82,
110, 168, 172f, 177, 212
vocation
23, 51, 55, 59, 65f, 84, 178, 207
volition
18, 29
von Franz, Marie-Louise
147, 157f
von Hartmann, Eduard
42
voyages
49, 55, 172f

wanderer/wandering archetype
49, 105, 107, 172f, 179
warrior archetype
2, 51, 148, 179f
Washburn, Michael
138, 143
wasteland scenario
115
water (symbol)
45, 55, 76f, 98, 152, 163f, 192

Watts, Alan
10, 82
Western civilization
2f, 8, 11, 16, 21f, 25–27, 37f, 41, 84, 97,
117, 130f, 135, 170, 172f, 207
whale (symbol)
55
Whitehead, Alfred North
216
whitening
76
wholeness (of reality)
7, 60, 66, 138, 163, 170, 176, 178
wholeness (psychological)
31, 64, 68–70, 83, 102, 114, 126, 144,
153, 170, 176f, 179, 205
Wilber, Ken
78
will, the
28, 97, 138, 180
(see also Schopenhauer)
willpower
56, 57, 151
will-to-power (Nietzsche's concept)
132, 138, 141, 180
wise old man (archetype)
30, 33, 38f, 66, 75, 119–122, 149, 157,
161f, 179, 182, 205
witches
152
womb
80–82, 106f, 115, 153f, 168, 180
Wordsworth, William
68, 71
world transits
(see transits)
World War Two
68, 136
worldviews
5, 7, 8, 12, 21, 26f, 42, 58, 145, 171, 207
Wotan
39, 45, 68, 71, 136f, 173, 180
Wundt, Wilhelm
41

Yahweh
21f, 39, 57, 126
yang principle
100, 179

yin principle
  100, 107, 179
Yoda (*Star Wars*)
  120

Zarathustra (Nietzsche)
  43, 123, 159
zenith
  109
Zeus
  18, 29, 172f
Zimmer, Heinrich
  18, 20, 139, 152, 158, 172, 174
zodiac
  37, 40, 104, 177, 185–189, 214

ABOUT THE AUTHOR

Keiron Le Grice is a professor of depth psychology and co-chair in the Jungian and Archetypal Studies specialization at Pacifica Graduate Institute, California, where he also designed and co-founded the online doctoral program in Psychology, Religion, and Consciousness. He serves as an honorary lecturer in the Department of Psychosocial and Psychoanalytic Studies at the University of Essex, and was the 2023 Zürich Lecture Series speaker at the International School of Analytical Psychology.

Originally from Nottinghamshire, England, he was educated at the University of Leeds and the California Institute of Integral Studies in San Francisco where he earned his doctorate in Philosophy and Religion. He is the author of several books including *The Archetypal Cosmos, The Rebirth of the Hero,* and *The Lion Will Become Man.* He is also co-editor of *Jung on Astrology,* a compilation of Jung's writings on this topic, and co-founder and former editor of *Archai: The Journal of Archetypal Cosmology,* now serving as editorial advisor.

The author's video lecture series on archetypal astrology and depth psychology, covering much of the material included in the volumes of this book, alongside other examples of astrological correlations, are available for purchase via the links below:

Lecture Series 1: Jupiter and Saturn
https://vimeo.com/ondemand/itasjupitersaturn

Lecture Series 2: Uranus, Neptune, and Pluto
https://vimeo.com/ondemand/itasuranusneptunepluto

www.itas-psychology.com

Made in the USA
Middletown, DE
14 March 2025

72661643R00144